PIECE BY PIECE

20 modern patchwork and quilting projects to make from preloved fabrics

Lauren MacDonald

Hardie Grant

BOOKS

01 WHAT YOU NEED

02 GETTING STARTED

03 PUTTING QUILTS TOGETHER

04 PROJECTS

To my friends and family, and a special thank you to William, who has patiently put up with bits of thread everywhere in the house for many years (I suspect he's become so used to them that he would miss them if they weren't there). Thank you for the many hugs, encouraging words and cups of coffee, and for supporting me in ways I have no words for.

I first picked up a needle and thread when I was a teenager. More accurately, I picked up a decades-old overlocker (serger) and some fleece-backed sweat-shirting, and made more sweatshirts and hoodies than I can count. I made them for friends, family and myself, with soft cotton flannelette in (sometimes outlandish) prints lining the hoods and pockets.

Since then, I've made every kind of sewing project under the sun. As a prop maker for fashion sets, I've whipped up everything from shiny vinyl plinth covers to tents and silk parachutes, and in my personal life I've stitched tailored wool jackets, satin evening wear and stretchy swimsuits. But I'm perhaps best known for making quilts, and that sits just fine with me.

Of the things that I make, my quilts are the most sentimental. They're a way to wrap a big blanket of care around those I love. A metaphorical hug. They take time to make (between 40 and 100 hours, depending on the complexity and size) and somewhere stashed in all those little stitches are feelings that I am sometimes too shy or too far away to say. I love you. I'm here for you. I got you.

I'm hardly the first to feel this way about making quilts. I'm one part of a long chain of generations of (mostly) women across the globe who have made quilts to warm and care for the people they love. And I'm excited that you, dear reader, might want to join us.

I designed the projects in this book to be simple enough for the beginner and advanced enough to keep experienced makers interested. They are divided into three sections: the first for kids and babies, the second for homewares, and the third for clothing and adult accessories. Each section is laid out in a skill-building sequence, with smaller, simpler projects at the beginning of the chapter and more challenging ones towards the end.

The projects are a mix of quilting, patchwork and appliqué (if you're wondering what the difference is between those things, don't worry – all in good time), and everything is designed to be made out of second-hand fabrics. From tablecloths and pillowcases to trousers and button-down shirts, I've written this as an attempt to get myself (and you) to have a closer look at the fabrics that surround us – and perhaps to reconsider materials you might otherwise have overlooked.

In the first three chapters you'll find everything you need to make the projects in Chapter 4: information on materials and equipment, general instructions for making a patchwork or appliqué quilt top (the same process can be used for making quilted clothes, bags and other small projects), and step-by-step guides to putting your quilts together. You'll also find tips and tricks for tackling each project at the start of Chapter 4. Not every bit of information will be perfectly relevant to every single thing that you make. Instead, think of it like an all-you-can-sew buffet: take the advice you need for the project that you're working on and leave what you don't (with the full knowledge that you can always come back for round two).

By taking apart old textiles and putting them back together again, you'll soon learn the ins and outs of how different materials behave. You'll also hopefully begin looking at objects for their potential to become other things. Nothing is final. It can be remade and reformed by your skilled hands, again and again.

I can't wait to see what you make.

Lauren

CHAPTER
ONE

WHAT
YOU NEED

ILLUSTRATION KEY

To help you get your head around making patchwork and quilts, I've drawn illustrations to accompany the tutorials and projects in this book. This key will help you understand what they mean and how to use them.

....	seam allowance	⊣	notch
-----	cut line	□	right side of fabric
———	fold	■	wrong side of fabric
-------	sewn seam	▦	interfacing

PATCHWORK VS QUILTING VS APPLIQUÉ

Before we get into the nitty-gritty of fabrics and haberdashery, you need to know what those materials and tools are for. This means understanding the difference between patchwork and quilting. The words are often used interchangeably, but patchwork and quilting are different parts of the quilt-making process. A quilt is a sandwich. The slices of bread are the quilt top (which is often patchwork) and back (which is sometimes patchwork and sometimes plain). The sandwich 'filling' is a soft, squishy wadding (which is also called batting). Quilting is the process of sewing the three layers together so that they act as one.

In contrast, patchwork involves sewing pieces of fabric together into a bigger whole. You can use patchwork to create geometric patterns, abstract shapes or illustrations.

Appliqué is an English bastardisation of the French word for 'apply' – and it basically does what it says on the little Franglish tin, as it involves sewing bits of fabric cut into decorative shapes onto other, bigger pieces of fabric (or applying them, if you will). There are several different methods around, and I've outlined a few of them for you in Chapter 2.

MATERIALS

FABRIC

Fabric is what quilt making is all about, so we'll start by taking a look at different fabric types and their properties. Then we'll go down one level further to fibres, which are the base materials (cotton, silk, polyester, etc.) that fabrics are made from. From knowing the easiest materials for beginners to work with, to tips for tackling slinky silks and sumptuous wools, my goal is that you'll come out of this section feeling prepared to start sewing.

Understanding fabrics

Fibres and fabric structure might seem a little boring and technical and, if you're anything like me, you'd probably like to skip over this bit of the book and dive straight into making cute things for the nice people in your life. But I encourage you (and I'm speaking from experience) to give this section at least a skim, as understanding how fabrics work, and what, exactly, they are made of, will help you create cute things without wanting to flip your cutting board over in frustration or spend hours puzzling over why, after all that effort, you just can't get your patchwork points to line up.

The fabrics you are used to wearing, sitting on and wrapping things in are usually made in one of two ways: they are either WOVEN or KNITTED. Woven fabrics are made on a machine called a loom. The loom holds vertical threads (the WARP threads) taut and other threads (the WEFT threads) are run horizontally back and forth between them. (This process is usually fully automated, but it can be done by hand, too.) When you're thinking of woven fabrics, think crisp bedsheets, button-down shirts and tailored wool jackets.

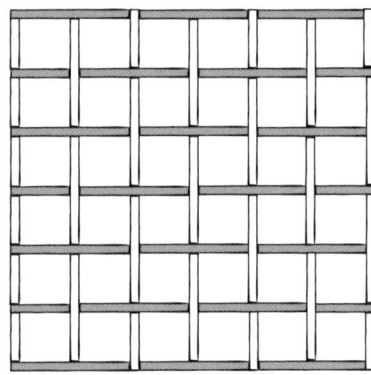

↑ *Woven fabric*

The simplest weave (and one you'll run into a lot) is called a plain weave, in which a weft thread goes over one warp thread, then under the next warp thread, then over another, then under another, forming a 1–1 grid like a chequerboard. The cotton fabrics sold as 'quilting cotton' are plain weaves. They're comparatively easy to work with, because they tend to be stable, which means that they don't stretch or pull out of shape – this is important when you're sewing tiny bits of fabric together and you want everything to line up just so.

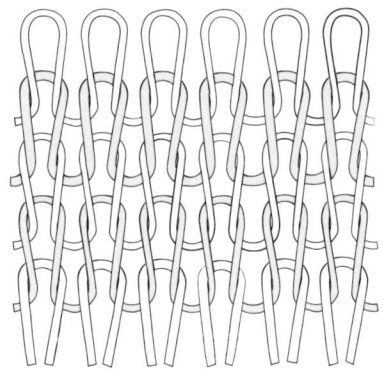

↑ *Knit fabric*

Knit fabrics have a different structure. If you've ever picked up a pair of needles to knit, you'll know that these kinds of fabric are made by creating a series of connected loops. Alongside classic handknits like cable jumpers and bobbly scarves, T-shirts, swimsuits and most exercise gear are knitted. The loop construction makes knit fabrics stretchier than woven ones – so they're perfect if you're bending about in a yoga class, but less great for making precise patchwork. As a result, knit fabrics are used less frequently for quilting.

The best fabrics for beginners

Beginners should choose woven fabrics that feel stable (not slippery, not silky). Stay away from fabrics that are heavily textured (velvets, corduroys and anything furry), as these will create an extra challenge if you're a novice. I'm not saying stay away from them forever – I'm saying one step at a time.

Likewise, think about the fabric weight. Too thick (material used to make coats and jackets, heavy denims, etc.) and you'll create bulky seams, not to mention the pain of trying to hand quilt through layers of raw denim (I've done it, so you don't have to). Too thin and you'll find the materials harder to patchwork accurately.

Fibres

If I was to climb up on a soap box for anything, it would be to say that these days it seems we're missing out on an education in what stuff is made of. Unless we work in certain disciplines, we aren't really encouraged to pay close attention to how materials feel and what they do.

Our closets are increasingly composed of plastic clothing in the form of synthetic fibres, like polyester, acrylic and nylon. One of the benefits of synthetic fibres is that they can be made to look like just about anything. You can make them into summery linen-look trousers or a cosily constructed coat that mimics wool. Plastics behave similarly in our homes. We have faux-stone Formica countertops and vinyl plank flooring aping wood.

NOTE

Fabrics that are very tightly woven can cause issues if you're hand quilting with a thicker needle and thread, like sashiko thread or perle 8 cotton. If you're using a material that you're unfamiliar with, try hand quilting a few stitches (see pages 53–5) before you cut it up and make your whole project out of it. In an attempt to make use of a pile of her husband's old clothes, a former student of mine decided to cut them all up and make them into a quilt (a great idea). But in among the soft, striped shirts there was a pair of beige chinos with a stain-proof coating. That coating, unbeknown to my poor student, rendered the fabric virtually un-puncturable. She tried quilting needles. Then leather needles. Then an enormous hooked canvas needle. In the end she gave up, and the beige bits of her quilt were left unquilted.

When these materials were invented, they were declared miraculous (they didn't need to be ironed!), but we now know they come with their own particular suite of problems. Synthetic fibres shed microplastics, which leach into waterways and bioaccumulate up through food chains. They're also made from fossil fuels, which is an issue in its own right.

Beyond understanding where materials come from and what their impact on the world is, understanding the properties of fibres can help you decide the best ones to work with for your given project. The fibres that the fabrics are made of will affect how they can be used in patchwork and quilt making. Many garments are a mix of different fibres. Wool jumpers, for example, sometimes have acrylic yarns added to them to keep their price down. Cotton jeans may have lycra (elastane) added to give them a comfy stretch.

The kind of fibre a fabric is made of will change its properties and how you work with it. Linen, for example, can be pressed at a very high temperature, while polyester fabric that has been created to look like linen will melt into a sticky goop if it's hit with the same iron. You can throw a cotton quilt in the washing machine but try that with a silk quilt and you might pull a mess out of your drum.

To help you understand how different fibres behave, I would encourage you to do two things:

1. If you don't know much about fabrics, the best way to get familiar with them is to start looking around you. Check the care labels on your favourite clothes. What are they made of? Do you have any favourite fabrics?
2. Spend some time in the shops. It's worth paying a visit to somewhere high end and feeling up some of their fabrics. Unfortunately, a high price does not necessarily indicate quality, so look, feel and always check out a garment's content label to see what it's been made from. Likewise, I recommend paying a visit to the lower end of the high-street shops and doing the same. You'll soon understand what different fabrics feel like and how they perform – and then you can begin plotting what you'll use them for!

TIP

If a material isn't the colour that you like, you can always dye it. This works best for light-coloured fabrics, and natural fibres are much easier to dye at home (either with natural dyes or shop-bought ones that are readily available at craft shops, etc.) than synthetic ones. See more on pages 14–15!

↑ *A cotton boll and flax flowers*
(linen is made from flax stalks)

To help you figure out what you're working with and how to handle it, you'll find a chart of common fibres and their properties over the page.

I tend to stick to natural fibres (cellulose and protein) where possible. I like the feel of natural fibres. I like the way they wear over time and their performance. They are easy to dye at home with natural dyes (which won't work on their synthetic counterparts). Another reason for using them is ecological. As I've mentioned, synthetic fibres are plastics and, like all plastics, they stay in the environment for an awfully long time after their initial use is over. They also shed microscopic plastic fibres, which are becoming an increasingly serious problem for marine life (and for us). Still, you might say that if we're picking things up second-hand anyway, giving a polyester top a second life in a quilt is better than it ending up in landfill, and you'd likely be right. However, the look, feel and function of natural fibres keeps me firmly in their fan camp at present.

Second-hand fabrics

Walk into any charity shop or thrift store, or type 'second-hand clothing' into your search engine, and you will be confronted with a mind-boggling number of options. I'm going to help you narrow down your choices by giving you the lowdown on my favourite second-hand fabric sources and explaining why they work well for patchwork and quilting.

SHEETS AND DUVET COVERS
Old bedsheets form a great backbone for a quilting practice that uses up old things. They contain enormous amounts of fabric, they're a great weight for quilt making, and they can be dyed different colours if a plain white sheet just isn't doing it for you. They're readily available, and even top-quality ones can be found for a few dollars/pounds each, partly because, unlike clothing, the market for old bedding understandably drives a lot less hype. Ask your friends and family if they've got worn-out sheets tucked in the back of the linen cupboard – they'll likely let you take them off their hands.

Look for: 100% cotton or cotton percale – or, if you're going luxury, why not try typing 'vintage French linen' into your search engine?

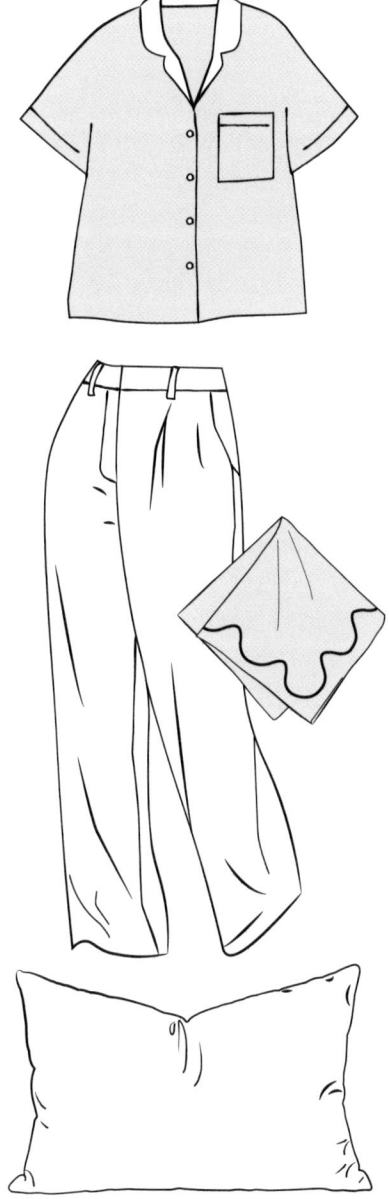

↑ *Things to cut apart*

MAIN FIBRE TYPES AND THEIR PROPERTIES

	CELLULOSE		PROTEIN	
MEANING	Cellulose fibres come from plants like cotton. They get their name from what they're made of – cellulose – which is the molecule that gives plants their rigidity and structure.		Protein fibres come from animals and have a chemical structure similar to that of human hair (this is especially true of wool and other animal hairs; silk is kind of its own thing).	

	KEY FIBRES			
	COTTON	LINEN	WOOL	SILK
USED FOR	Cotton is the most common natural fibre and is used to make jersey, sweatshirting, towelling, twill, corduroy, organdie, voile, etc.	Plain woven fabrics that are good for summer dresses and suits.	Suiting and coating fabrics.	Formal wear, like satin, chiffon and organza.
IRON	high	high	low–medium	low–medium
WASH	30°C (85°F)	30°C (85°F)	delicate/dry clean	delicate/dry clean
ABSORBENCY	medium–high	high	high	medium
TOP PATCHWORK TIP	None! Cotton is your friend when it comes to precise patchwork. Plain weaves are comparatively stable, and you can press it at high temperatures. (Cotton stays relatively smooth, unlike linen which sometimes feels like it wrinkles AS you press it!)	Use spray starch. (See my note to the left about linen wrinkling as you press it ...)	Use lots of steam! This is especially true if you're buying new wool fabric. Wool shrinks the first time you steam it, so giving it a good blast before you sew with it will help you avoid puckering and (if you're making clothes) things like too-short trousers.	Use sharp, fine sewing needles to avoid pulling threads and leaving holes in delicate fabrics. With anything that feels slippery (usually silk or viscose), consider stitching your patchwork pieces to paper before you sew them together to get crisp, neat corners.
DYE AT HOME	natural dyes	natural dyes	natural dyes	natural dyes
MICROPLASTICS	no	no	no	no

ARTIFICIAL/REGENERATED CELLULOSE	SYNTHETIC		
These are materials made of cellulose that has been chemically broken down and reformed. Historically they were mostly made of wood, but now they're made of bamboo and other plants, too.	Synthetic fibres are (mostly) plastics made from petrochemicals.		MEANING

KEY FIBRES

VISCOSE RAYON / BAMBOO	POLYESTER	ACRYLIC	
As a manufactured fibre, viscose is pretty versatile. It's made into everything from jerseys used for activewear to satins for evening wear.	Everything. Polyester is the great impersonator.	Fake wool. You'll run into acrylic in coats with blended fibre content and in jumpers.	USED FOR
medium	low	low	IRON
30°C (85°F)	30°C (85°F)	30°C (85°F)	WASH
medium–high	low	low	ABSORBENCY
Use spray starch or backing paper to help stiffen slippery fabrics and make them easier to work with.	Don't iron it at too high a temperature or it will melt.	Like polyester, this one melts!	TOP PATCHWORK TIP
natural dyes	shop-bought dyes labelled as being suitable for synthetics	shop-bought dyes labelled as being suitable for synthetics	DYE AT HOME
no	yes	yes	MICROPLASTICS

TABLECLOTHS AND NAPKINS

Vintage table linens offer an incredible array of materials for you to use. They tend to be more colourful and ornate than sheets, but also a bit smaller. If you're lucky enough to find one that has been embroidered, it's worth cutting carefully to make the best of it in your quilt.

Look for: 100% cotton, 100% linen

BUTTON-DOWN SHIRTS

Button-downs are my second most loved find for quilt making. They contain lots of fabric, are abundant, and the fabric tends to be of decent quality.

Look for: 100% cotton, 100% linen

LINEN

I love the look and feel of linen quilts, and the weight that is used across trousers, dresses, skirts, etc. is perfect for a quilt. Depending on the garment, you may get a lot or a little.

FABRIC SCRAPS AND PROJECT REMNANTS

Whether your local second-hand shop has a dedicated fabric remnant bin or you're working from a personal stash, you can, of course, use fabric leftovers from another project to make a quilt. In fact, I wholeheartedly encourage you to do so. The caveat here is the fabric's weight. While experienced quilt makers can and do mix weights of fabric (think a heavy denim and a light cotton) together, if you're relatively new to sewing this can spell disaster: broken needles, puckered seams and a frustrated sewist. So, I suggest you separate your scraps into piles, baskets or boxes based on weight.

I also suggest you pay special attention to what your scraps are made of. If you mix fibres in a project, especially delicate ones like silk and wool, your project is going to require special care. This isn't such a big deal if you're making a throw for a sofa that might need washing once or twice a year, but it's a very different situation if you're making a soft toy that is going to be loved, spilled on and dragged through the dirt by a two-year-old. So think about the fibres and what kind of care they are going to need, then sort out your scraps accordingly.

Cutting clothes apart

The key thing when you're cutting clothes apart is to pay attention to the grain of the fabric. A fabric's grain lies parallel to the warp (vertical) threads in a weave: it is the material's most stable dimension. (See pages 29–30 for more information on this.)

1. Make sure your clothes are freshly washed and pressed.
2. Use a pair of sharp fabric scissors to cut the seam allowances out of the garment (or seam rip the seams themselves if you are feeling particularly dedicated).
3. Do this for each piece so that you have plain, flat panels with no seams to work with as a starting point. Press these pieces.

WADDING (BATTING)

Wadding (batting) is the fluffy middle layer of your quilt. If you plan on hand quilting, make sure you buy suitable wadding. Some waddings have a SCRIM, which is a layer of tightly constructed film added for machine quilting, and it makes it really hard to hand quilt. There are many types and weights available. Here is a quick rundown of the most common.

COTTON WADDING is my favourite for quilts that are going to be in daily use. It tends to be low loft (or less fluffy) and is practical, as it can be easily laundered and holds up to daily wear.

I also use WOOL WADDING, which is generally loftier (fluffier), super absorbent and (I think) worth the extra effort it might take to care for it. It can be a bit trickier to use than cotton as it is more prone to bearding, which is when white wadding fibres come up through the quilt top as you stitch. Bearding earned its name because the white, fluffy tufts look like tiny Santa Claus beards.

BAMBOO WADDING looks similar to cotton but has a softer drape. Bamboo is great for warm, humid climates as it is more absorbent than cotton, so you'll be less prone to sweaty sleep.

SYNTHETIC or SYNTHETIC-BLEND WADDING is easily laundered and durable. It is also available at a low price point, though because of its environmental impact I wouldn't recommend it. If you'd like to use a synthetic wadding, I recommend sourcing one that is made from recycled materials.

SILK WADDING is lofty, luxurious and very breathable.

While these are the most common commercially available waddings, the middle bits of quilts have been made from all sorts of different materials. Wool blankets and old quilts were often used after they were worn. The middle layers of kantha quilts, which are intricately stitched blankets from Bangladesh and Bengal, are traditionally made of layers of old silk saris.

If you are going to use something like an old blanket as your quilt wadding, try stitching (see page 53) through it first, as it can be harder than you might think on your hands.

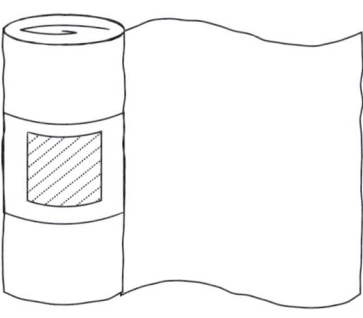

↑ *Wadding roll*

TIP

Double-check the dimensions on the pattern before you buy your wadding. Quilts vary in size and my patterns are a little bit generous.

THREADS

There are two different threads you'll need to make a patchwork quilt: one for putting the pieces of your patchwork together, stitching on your appliqué and sewing up seams, and another for hand quilting.

Sewing thread

I recommend using a good-quality cotton thread for almost all projects – it does the trick nicely. The rule of thumb is to choose the same fibre for your thread as for your project. For example, if you're sewing cotton fabric, use cotton thread. I tend to avoid polyester thread as I avoid synthetic fabrics, though a sew-all thread will work nicely with most quilt making. I like to think of my projects at the end of their lives as well as the beginning, and a biodegradable cotton quilt with a skeleton of polyester thread left behind doesn't sit well with me. Linen threads are rare, and silk threads even rarer, though both are an absolute delight to work with if you happen to manage it.

I am a big, big fan of charity shops, thrift stores, and garage or car boot sales. They are my favourite kinds of treasure troves. More than once, I have returned triumphantly from one of the above with a box (sometimes a shoe box, sometimes a cookie tin) stuffed to the brim with someone's old sewing supplies: ribbons, bobbins, needles, one of those plump, tomato-shaped pincushions and, of course, threads. If you're a fellow charity-shop connoisseur, be wary of the threads in these boxes. Thread gets more brittle over time, and so older ones have the frustrating tendency to snap, mid-seam, in sewing machines, as the tension pulls them about. For best results, I'd recommend using a thread that is less than twenty years old.

Quilting thread

Quilting threads are the threads that you'll use to stitch the layers of your quilt together. You'll use different ones depending on whether you're quilting by machine or by hand, whether you want subtle stitches or pronounced, puffy ones.

NOTE

Patchwork projects often include multiple fabrics of different colours sewn together, so which one do you match your thread to? Do you change threads throughout the project?

Quilting wisdom says that when choosing a thread for your project, you match it to the lightest colour in the patchwork. This is primarily because lighter threads are less likely to show through your quilt. For example, if you are making a black-and-white patchwork and you use black threads, your sewn seams might be visible in the white portions of the quilt top. If you use a white thread it's not going to show through a black fabric.

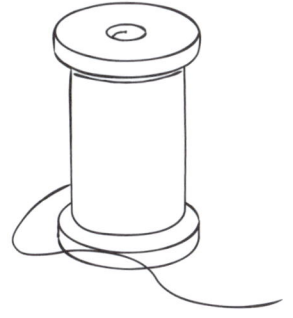

↑ *Sewing thread*

Quilting threads are categorised by 'weight'. Most quilting threads are 50 weight; these are light, strong and can be used in your sewing machine for machine quilting. Counterintuitively, as the numbers decrease, the threads become thicker. An 8- or 12-weight thread feels closer to an embroidery thread (floss) than to the one that you'd use to put a garment together.

Traditional hand-quilting thread is waxed, which makes it strong, smooth and less prone to tangling. You can wax your own thread with beeswax, which is available in little blocks or lip-gloss-like containers at most good sewing shops.

For my quilts, I often use sashiko thread or perle 8 cotton, both of which are thicker than traditional hand-quilting thread. I like the puffy, handmade look of the stitches that these threads give. I've also used silk embroidery thread (floss) to quilt, which has a beautiful sheen and feels (to me, at least) incredibly luxurious.

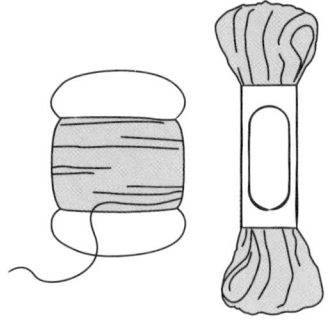

↑ *Quilting threads*

IRON-ON INTERFACING

Interfacing is used to stabilise fabric. You'll usually find it on the inside of shirt collars, waistbands and button plackets to give clothes sturdiness and structure.

You can purchase sew-in interfacing, which tends to be used in high-end tailoring, or iron-on interfacing, which is much more common. I've recommended iron-on interfacing here, as it is more readily available and very easy to use. Both come in a variety of weights, and whichever type you choose I'd recommend a mid-weight for appliqué.

Iron-on interfacing has two sides: one is smooth and fabric-like, and the other has a rougher, bubbly texture because it contains glue that will melt and stick to your fabric when heated.

When pressing, make sure the glue side is face down on your fabric (so that you don't get interfacing stuck to your iron). For this reason, I always use a press cloth when I'm interfacing – just to be safe.

EQUIPMENT

Sewing machine

You technically don't need a sewing machine – many quilts have been pieced together by hand, and some of the smaller projects in this book could be hand sewn in an afternoon or so. That said, you'll have a much quicker time making them on a machine. If you are just starting out, see if you can borrow one from a friend or family member for your first project. People who sew often love sharing their skills and knowledge, and you might even convince them to give you a little lesson in the process.

I have a small collection of vintage sewing machines I've picked up over the years, and if you're in the market for a machine, I highly recommend them. They're reliable, tough and usually great value for money, though I'd add in the cost of getting them serviced by a reliable sewing shop for your peace of mind.

You'll need needles for your sewing machine too. For more information on those, see page 33.

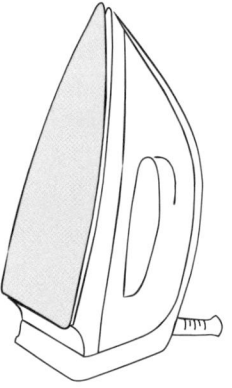

↑ *Household iron*

Iron and ironing board

A household iron will do just fine for quilt making. If you live in an area with hard water (water with a high proportion of dissolved minerals in it – if you have spots on your glasses after washing them, this is you), you might benefit from using distilled water in your iron. It will prevent mineral build-up and the subsequent (and dreaded) rusty sputter of orange water that old irons have been known to spit onto delicate fabrics. Likewise, you can keep your iron's water tank dry and use a spray bottle to moisten fabric instead.

I recommend using a PRESS CLOTH when you're ironing, too, which is a bit of cotton (I like cotton calico, which is a sturdy, undyed material) that you use as a middle layer between your iron and the fabric that you are pressing as an extra layer of protection and to help evenly distribute heat.

Quilting ruler

You can use a normal plastic or metal ruler, but, of all the tools that I'd suggest are worth buying, a quilt ruler is at the top of the

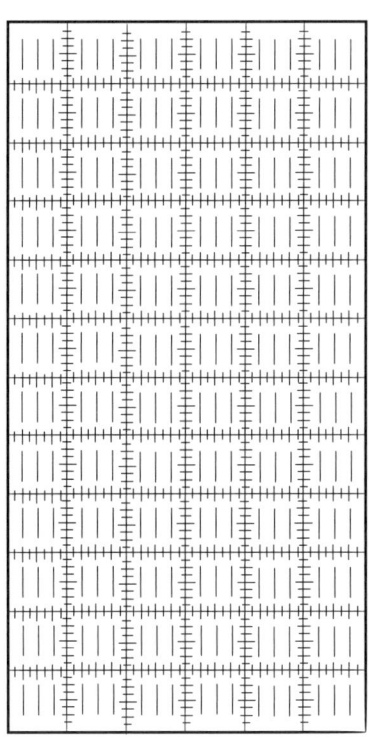

↑ *Quilting ruler*

list. It makes your measurements simple and your cutting quick. There are many sizes, but a 15 × 30 cm (6 × 12 in) ruler is a good all-rounder that will get you through most projects.

Marking tool

This is for marking out where you'll cut fabric and for marking lines out before you quilt. There are many, many different tools available, but my favourite is a hera marker. It is a slim, usually plastic tool that looks a bit like a butter knife. It creases the fabric without leaving chalk or ink on the surface.

You may also see quilting pens that iron off, quilting pencils, or the classic tailor's chalk. All will work for quilt making. If you're using a tool that you've never used before, test it out on a scrap of fabric and make sure it easily washes off or irons away before you use it on your quilt. I'd be devastated on your behalf if you were left with a bright yellow pencil that didn't wash off after the 40 or so hours of work you put into your quilt.

Scissors or rotary cutter

Until the late 1970s, all quilts were made with a humble pair of sewing shears, but the invention and widespread commercial sale of the rotary cutter in 1979 changed the game.

Rotary cutters are comparatively accurate tools that make cutting faster. Using one will help you achieve precise patchwork with less effort and skill than with scissors alone. A good, sharp rotary cutter can cut through several layers of fabric at once, too.

That said, there is something satisfying about working with the tools that you have on hand. So, if you are thinking about making your first quilt (and you may be if you've come so far as to be reading this paragraph), you might want to give it a try with what you've got in the house before running out and buying yourself some shiny new kit.

Using scissors will give you slightly more organic lines than a rotary cutter, so if you're a fan of softer lines, they'll be your friend. If you're using a rotary cutter, you'll also need a …

↑ *Dressmaker's scissors*

↑ *Marking tool (hera marker)*

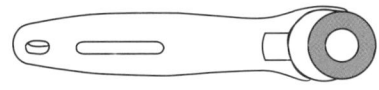

↑ *Rotary cutter*

Cutting mat

Also known as a self-healing mat. A decent sized one (at least 45 × 60 cm / 17¾ × 23½ in – the bigger the better) makes it easier to cut long strips and trim your big quilts.

Pins

Invest in some long, sharp pins for your quilting projects. I like using glass-headed pins, as the bright-coloured tops help me keep track of where I've stuck them (like the arm of my sofa, as well as my sewing projects), and the glass heads mean you can iron over them without them melting.

Hand-quilting, sashiko and embroidery needles

Hand-quilting or sashiko needles are the needles you'll use to put the layers of your quilt together. Which ones you use will depend on which thread you've chosen to quilt with. If you're stitching up your quilt with traditional hand-quilting thread, you'll want to use a small, sharp needle called a 'between'. If you decide to use sashiko thread, make sure you use a sashiko needle, so the eye of the needle is big enough for you to get the thread through. If you can't find sashiko needles but want to use a thicker thread, I'd recommend getting a pack of mixed-size cotton darning needles or golden-eye embroidery needles so you have a few options and sizes to play with.

For appliqué, you can use a specialist appliqué needle or a crewel embroidery needle. In either case, you're looking for a slim needle with a big eye and a sharp tip.

Thimble

Thimbles are wonderful tools for quilt making, even though most people are familiar with them as a souvenir-shop find or as the least-chosen piece in the board game Monopoly. They protect your hands and make it easier and faster to quilt. I like soft rubber and leather ones that fit snugly on my fingertips, though each quilt maker is different and you'll likely develop a personal preference over time.

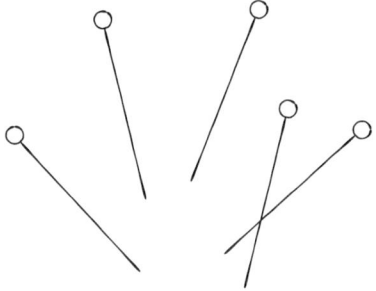

↑ *Glass-headed pins*

↑ *Quilting needles and thimble*

Paper or thin card

You'll use paper to trace or copy the templates in the back of this book. You might also use it instead of a quilting ruler. Card is great for anything you want to be a little more durable, so if you know you're cutting many of the same thing, slice up a cereal box for your template instead of using printer paper.

Quick unpick

A quick unpick (also called a seam ripper) is every sewist's best friend (and worst enemy). As the name suggests, it's designed to quickly and easily take stitches out of seams. You can use it to cut buttonholes open, too.

Spray starch (optional)

If you're working with slippery fabrics like linen, spritz them with spray starch while you're ironing them. They'll temporarily crisp up, making them easier to cut and sew accurately. You can make your own by dissolving 1 tablespoon cornflour (cornstarch) in 500 ml (17 fl oz/2 cups) cold water. Add a drop or two of your favourite essential oil (I'm fond of lavender) to make the whole thing more pleasant, then decant into a spray bottle and off you go.

Painter's tape (optional)

This low-tack masking tape is helpful for everything from marking your stitch lines to holding the quilt's layers together while you baste.

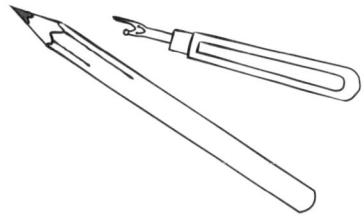

↑ *Pencil and quick unpick*

Curved safety pins (optional)

A useful tool for basting. I like to thread baste (using a medium-size hand-sewing needle and sewing machine thread), but pin basting is a fast and easy method as well.

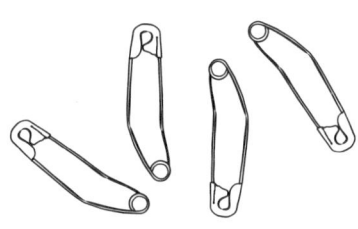

↑ *Curved safety pins*

CHAPTER TWO

GETTING STARTED

PREPARING FABRIC FOR PATCHWORK

Before you get going, wash and press your fabric. It might seem like a faff, but it'll save you time and frustration down the line.

1. Wash your fabric

You'll have already done this if you're making a quilt from old clothes, but if your fabric is new, washing it will shrink it so you don't wind up with a wildly wrinkly quilt. It will also remove factory-added finishes. If you are using brightly coloured fabrics, prewashing is extra crucial as it will remove some of the excess dye, meaning that the red-and-white quilt you might be about to make will be much less likely to come out of its first wash pink. With used fabrics there's less risk, as they have all likely been washed many times before and are unlikely to bleed in the wash.

2. Press the fabric

This will make it easier to cut precisely. Cotton and linen both press more easily when they are a little bit damp and respond well to a hot iron. Wool presses beautifully with lots of steam on a medium-heat setting. I use medium heat for silk, too, and always, always use a press cloth to prevent water marks. Polyester and other synthetics can only handle a little heat, so set your iron to a low setting.

3. Apply spray starch (optional)

If you are working with slippery or wrinkle-prone fabric, a bit of spray starch can feel like a revelation. You can use shop-bought or homemade (see page 25). If you're using a delicate fabric like silk, spray a little test first to make sure the fabric reacts well. The idea here is to stiffen the fabrics while you patchwork them together so they behave a little more like paper and a little less like slippery eels. Over the making process, and especially when you wash your project for the first time, the fabrics will soften and return to their natural form.

FINDING A FABRIC'S GRAIN

Woven fabric has a GRAIN. I mentioned this briefly under *Cutting clothes apart* (page 17), but just to get it properly stuck in your head: the grain of the fabric follows the warp (vertical) threads and is the direction in which the fabric is most stable. By this, I mean that if fabric is cut 'on the grain' or using the warp threads as a guide, it is less likely to stretch out, wiggle around and cause puckered seams than if it's not. Cutting diagonally to the grain is called cutting 'on the bias', which is the direction in which the fabric has the most stretch. When used purposefully, bias-cutting can create stunning results – think figure-hugging 1930s Hollywood gowns and draped 1970s handkerchief hems – but when used by accident, bias-cut fabrics will stretch out and cause wobbly seams and hard-to-match corners.

Sometimes, a fabric's grain is obvious. For example, a fabric might be a woven cheque or a stripe, and all you have to do is cut parallel to the stripe or cheque. Sometimes, though, it is more subtle and needs to be coaxed out by a clever sewist (you).

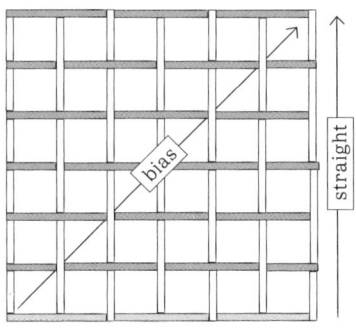

↑ *Straight and bias grain*

Here's how to find the grain

1. If you are working with fabric yardage, make a small cut (about 2 cm/¾ in long) into the selvedge edge. The selvedge edge is created by the loom to prevent the fabric from unravelling. It sometimes has a little fringe or holes running up it. It will look tidier than the cut edge of the fabric that they will have cut for you at the fabric shop. If you are working with cut-up clothes there won't be a selvedge, so take a small snip at the bottom edge instead.
2. Pull a thread. You should see the fabric bunch up around the thread and, where you have pulled, it should begin to form a line. Gently tug until the thread snaps.
3. Cut along the line that you have just made. If the thread has snapped before the end of the fabric, cut up to the end of your line and then pull another thread. (This is easier with linen than cotton. Some fabrics – like those that are tightly woven – can be a nightmare, with threads that pull just a few centimetres before snapping.)

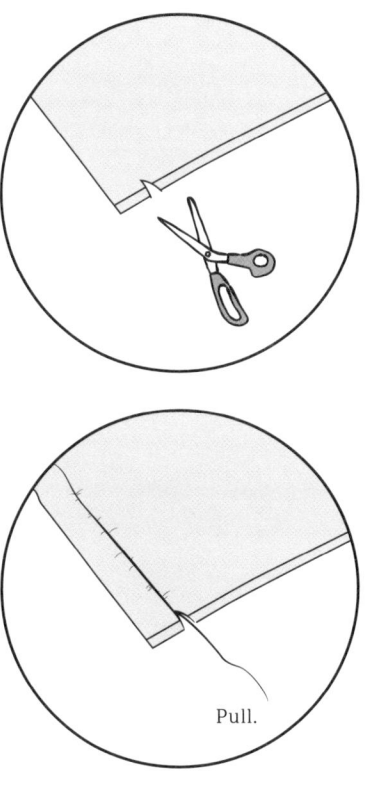

Pull.

↑ *Finding the grain*

Now the raw edge of your fabric is completely straight, so if you mark your patchwork pieces by aligning them with this straight edge before you cut them out, you'll know that they're 'on grain' and less likely to stretch out of shape.

If pulling a thread does not work (for example, if your fabric is too tightly woven) just do your best to cut a line perpendicular to the selvedge edge of the fabric. You can use your quilt rulers and marking tools to square up from the selvedge edge. Clothing can be a bit trickier, but luckily most of it is cut on the grain. It's pretty safe to assume that the centre front of a button-down shirt is straight, as is the centre of a trouser leg (think about where the pleat would be, if the trousers were pleated). If you're a little off grain, it won't matter too much and is hardly a disaster, but it will make it harder to match up your corner points and get all your blocks the same size.

CUTTING FABRIC

If you're cutting with scissors, mark your lines using your quilt ruler or template, and carefully cut using steady, even strokes.

If you're using a rotary cutter, you don't need to mark your cutting lines on the fabric. Instead place the ruler on top of the fabric where you'd like to cut, aligning it parallel to the edge of the fabric that you've just pulled a thread and snipped from.

Move rotary cutter away from you.

45° angle

↑ *Using a rotary cutter*

Using a rotary cutter

1. Use your non-dominant hand to hold the ruler in place. If you're scared you might cut yourself, you can purchase a cut-proof glove to keep your hand safe.
2. Hold the rotary cutter at a 45° angle to the cutting mat.
3. Keeping the edge of the cutter butted up to the ruler, push the cutter slowly and firmly away from you. Don't be afraid to stand up and apply a little more pressure on your rotary cutter if necessary.

TIPS

To get the best results from your rotary cutter:

Use a sharp blade. Change out the blade for a fresh one if you've borrowed the cutter from a friend or are using one at a makerspace. Spare blades are readily available online and in sewing shops.

Set up the mat, fabric and ruler so that you can comfortably cut in front of you. I find it best to cut away from my body with my arm moving perpendicular to my torso.

PATCHWORK BASICS

From seam allowances to stitch length and pressing, this section will guide you through all the tips and tricks you need for precise patchworking.

Seam allowances

The standard seam allowance for patchwork is 6 mm (¼ in). This works beautifully with tightly woven quilting cotton and is perfect for reducing bulk in seams. But when I make quilts (out of all the many materials I have made quilts from) I sometimes use a seam allowance of 1 cm (⅜ in). This is for two reasons:

1. I don't always use quilting cottons. I've used silk dresses and linen napkins and even a cotton velvet or two – and these materials fray. Giving a little extra over to seam allowance increases the longevity of my projects. I learned this the hard way: one of my first quilts, a linen baby quilt I made for a friend's new addition, frayed all around the seams.
2. My patchwork tends to be larger scale. If you're working with small scraps, shrinking down the seam allowance makes sense. It will help you make the most of the fabric you have (as less of it is used up and hidden in the seams). Think about it this way: if you have a 4-cm (1½-in) strip of fabric that is going to have a seam on either side, using a 1-cm (⅜-in) seam allowance will use up half the fabric – which is a lot! I rarely patchwork with fabric pieces this small, so my fatter seam allowances don't affect my bottom line as much as they might do otherwise.

As I tend to change the seam allowance to suit the project, I've included a specific seam allowance for each project in Chapter 4.

Setting up your sewing machine

Now we're getting to the exciting bit – actually sewing. Here are a few things to consider before you wind your bobbin and put your pedal to the metal.

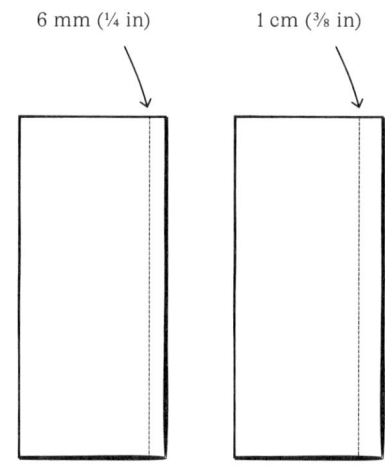

6 mm (¼ in)   1 cm (⅜ in)

↑ *Comparing seam allowances*

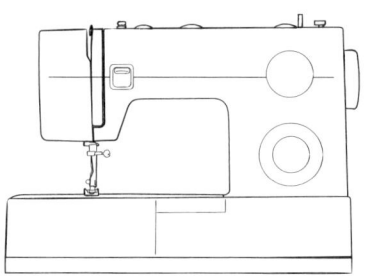

↑ *Sewing machine*

CHOOSING A NEEDLE

Sewing machine needles are marvellously engineered, beautiful things. Sewists often overlook their importance, but they make a real difference in how smoothly a project goes. Using the wrong needle or keeping one in your machine too long is like cutting a tomato with a dull knife. You may get where you want to go, but the effort (and mess) to get there takes away a bit of the fun.

For mid-weight woven fabrics (which I hope I've convinced you is what you should use for your first patchwork projects), try universal needles, sized between 90/14 and 80/12. The bigger the needle number, the thicker the needle is. So if you're making yourself a canvas quilt (god help you) use something like a denim needle at 120/19. If you're making yourself some patchwork chiffon curtains (please) use a dainty microtex sharp at 70/10.

SELECTING STITCH LENGTH

When you're sewing clothes it's common to use a stitch length of 2.5 mm, but for patchwork we usually shrink this down to 1.8–2 mm. This is because you usually don't backstitch when you're sewing patchwork, as you'll sometimes cut into patchwork seams after you've sewn them. Reducing the stitch length helps make the seams more secure even without a backstitch.

Starting to sew

SEWING IN A STRAIGHT LINE

The little lines etched into the metal plate of a sewing machine are there to guide your fabrics through the machine straight, but I've never quite mastered it. If you've got a high-spec machine, it might come with a built-in seam gauge, which creates a physical barrier to help you go straight. If not, I've had great success with a piece of painter's tape (low-tack tape that won't stick to the bed of the machine). I stick it all the way down the bed of the machine and line up my fabric to it. It is much easier to see than the little etched 'tick' and it works a treat.

SEWING YOUR FIRST SEAM

If you're new to sewing, I recommend you grab a scrap of fabric and play around, going back and forth and turning corners on your sewing machine without the pressure of making anything or getting it right the first time.

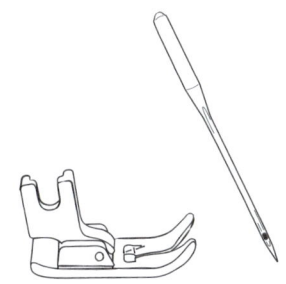

↑ *Presser foot and needle*

TIP

You can speed up the patchwork process by chain piecing, which means feeding two pieces through the machine, then two more, then two more, without cutting your thread or taking the fabrics off the machine. It's called chain piecing because you'll end up with a long chain of patchwork pieces. It's quick! But beware: double-check your units are in the correct positions. Otherwise, your speedy, time-saving trick will mean you have to do a lot of slow unpicking.

NOTE

Backstitching is when you reverse the direction of your stitches to secure your seam. It can be done by hand or on your sewing machine.

Pressing seams

Pressing is arguably the most important bit of sewing. It will transform your projects from amateur to professional standard, so it's worth doing frequently and properly.

1. First, 'set the seam'. Place your iron firmly over the seam you've just sewn. This flattens the stitches and sets you up for step 2.
2. Press the seam allowances to one side. This is the traditional method in patchwork for a few reasons:

    a. It creates a slightly stronger seam than pressing open.
    b. It creates one side of the seam with no seam allowance in it, which makes that side easier to hand quilt (thicker layers = sore fingers).
    c. Seam allowances pressed to one side can be used to create a small ridge that helps hold your corners in place. This is called 'nesting your seams'.

The general rule is to press towards the darker-coloured fabric, as the seam allowance is less likely to show up through the quilt top this way. As many blocks have seam allowances that go over each other, you may not always be able to do this.

3. Press the seam, holding the iron down firmly.

Nesting seams

This is a technique for getting precise corners on your patchwork. It also helps reduce bulk. I find it very useful, though some people find it easier to match seams by pressing the seam allowance open.

1. Press each seam towards the darker-coloured fabric.
2. Sidle up the pieces or rows that you'd like to sew together. Lay one on top of the other (right sides together) matching up the seam allowances. You should be able to feel a little ridge with your fingers where these seams fit snugly together. Pin.
3. Sew your seam. Press (this is one of the occasions where your seams are going to go over both dark and light fabrics, so just choose which direction to press the seam allowance and be consistent with it). Enjoy your tidy, nicely matched corner!

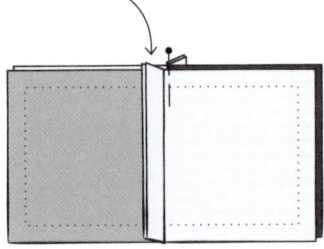

Press to darker side.

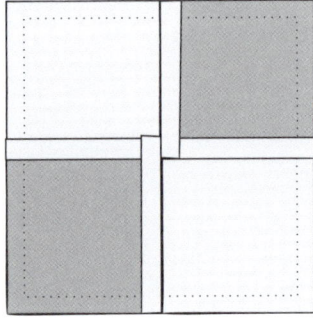

↑ *Nesting seams (steps 1–3)*

UNDERSTANDING QUILT GEOMETRY

Many quilts are made up of blocks. A quilt block can either be a single piece of fabric or a patchworked unit of smaller pieces. In this section, we'll go over some common units and how to put them together.

With time and practice, you'll be able to identify the units and elements in traditional quilt patterns. Then, it's great fun to try to make those for yourself, mix and match them, or update them to fit your preferences. Sometimes it is comforting to have the guidance of a pattern, and sometimes it's a fun challenge to work without one (it can also help you build confidence in your creativity and skills).

One of my favourite ways to get inspired is to look at old quilts. The International Quilt Museum has an enormous online collection that is a delight to scroll through. If you're more of a book person, online marketplaces and charity shops often offer a choice of old craft and quilt reference books. It is also worth paying your local quilt guild a visit, as you'll doubtless meet some kind, talented and inspiring people there, too.

Without further ado, here are a few common techniques and units to get you started.

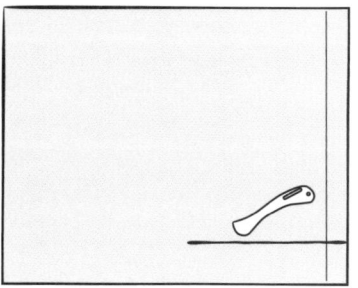

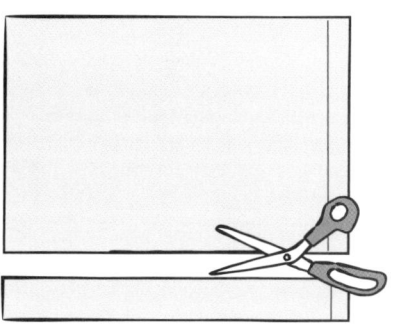

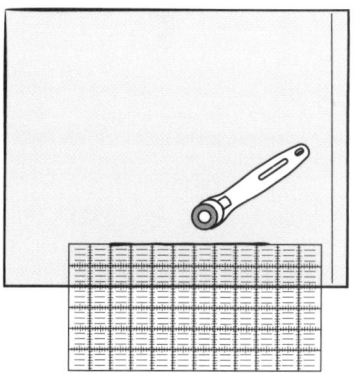

↑ *Marking and cutting strips (overleaf)*

STRIPS AND SQUARES

These are the building blocks for the simplest quilt patterns.

If you are using fabric yardage or something like bedsheets, you'll be able to speed along the patchwork process by cutting and sewing long strips instead of individual pieces.

The first thing to do is determine the width of strips you'll need. If you're making a project from this book, the width is specified on the project page. If you've designed your own, you can calculate the strip width by adding twice your seam allowance to the finished measurement that you want. For example, if you want 5-cm (2-in) strips and your seam allowance is 6 mm (¼ in), then you'll cut strips 6.2 cm (2½ in) wide.

If you're working with a large piece of fabric and finding it difficult to handle, carefully fold the fabric in half lengthwise to make it more manageable.

STRIP PATCHWORK

1. If you're using fabric yardage, mark and cut out strips of the required width, going from selvedge to selvedge. If you're using a bedsheet, go from one side to the other.
2. If you need individual squares for your pattern, subdivide the strips into squares.
3. Sew the strips together with your desired seam allowance. Then cut them into the units you require.

You can create a vast range of secondary patterns by playing around with how you place your units and stitch them together.

CUTTING PIECES INDIVIDUALLY

If you are working with smaller fabric scraps, where you don't have the length to do strip patchwork, cut the pieces one by one.

You can use your quilt ruler or make a template out of paper or thin card. Remember to add your seam allowances! Pin the paper to your fabric (or draw around the card) and cut out. You can also buy acrylic templates in a range of shapes and sizes for the same purpose.

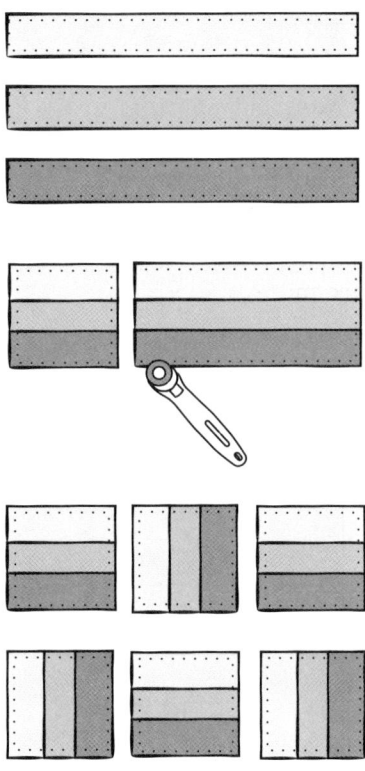

↑ *Strip patchwork (steps 1–3)*

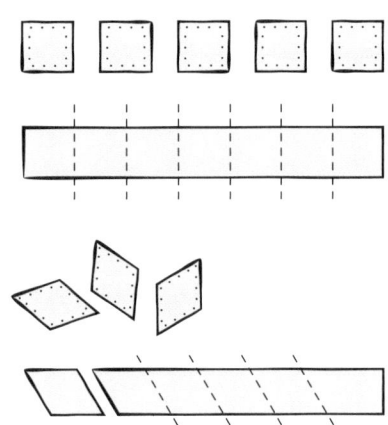

↑ *Cutting pieces individually*

TRIANGLES

Sewing triangles is generally considered to be a little harder than strips and squares. This is because triangles are cut on the bias (that stretchy, diagonal fabric direction I spoke about on page 29). But, dear reader, don't worry. There are ways to cut triangle blocks quickly, easily and accurately, without fiddling around with bias cuts. And the results are well worth the effort.

Half-square triangles (HSTs)

Half-square triangles are the simplest triangle units to make and can be sewn into many patterns on their own or mixed and matched with other units to create a countless variety of blocks.

HSTs are two 90° triangles stitched together to make a square.

To avoid cutting and sewing on the bias, HSTs are usually made by working with two squares that are sewn together on the diagonal and then sliced apart. I've outlined two methods for making HSTs: a simple one to make two HSTs at a time and a (only slightly) more complicated way of making eight at a time.

TWO-AT-A-TIME METHOD

This method is great if you're working with smaller scraps of fabric and is very simple. First, decide on the finished size of your HST. Then, take that measurement and add 2.5 cm (1 in). For example, if you want your finished HST units to be 10 cm (4 in), make a note of 12.5 cm (5 in).

If you're worried about getting the final dimensions right (because you find maths challenging or you find your seam allowance zigzagging more than it should), make your initial squares a little bigger, then cut your HSTs down to size.

You'll need: marking tool, ruler, rotary cutter and mat (or scissors), sewing machine, iron and ironing board

1. Cut two contrasting squares of fabric to your chosen size.
2. Lay your squares neatly on top of each other with the right sides together.
3. Pin the squares together so that they won't shift about when you're sewing them. Mark a line diagonally across the squares, from corner to corner.
4. Put your 6-mm (¼-in) presser foot onto your machine. If you don't have one, mark lines 6 mm (¼ in) from each side of the diagonal line you drew in step 3 and sew along them. Press the sewn squares to set the seams.
5. Cut along the line that you marked in step 3.
6. Open out your HSTs and press them, turning the seams towards the darker fabric.
7. Trim your HST units.

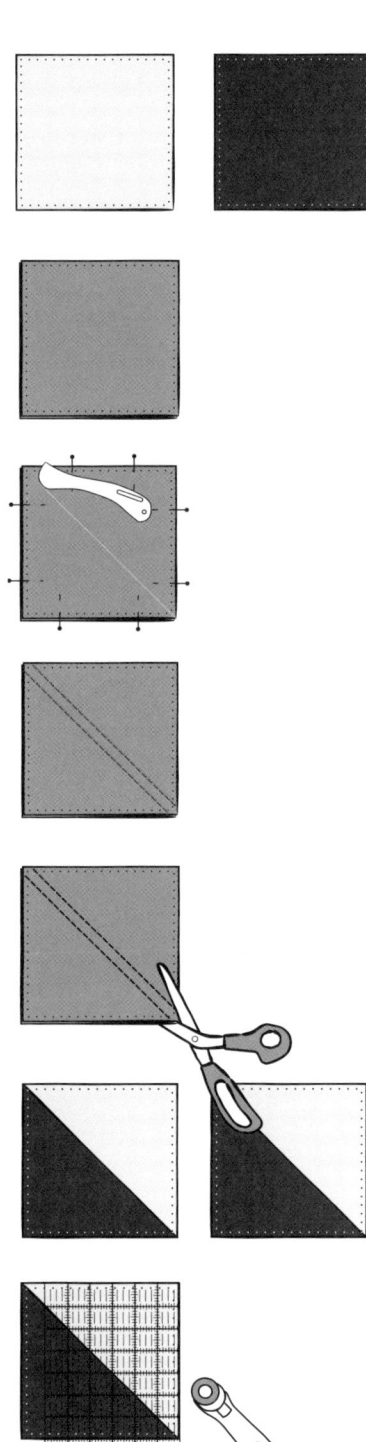

↑ HSTs two-at-a-time (steps 1–7)

MAGIC 8 METHOD

The magic 8 method allows you to make eight HSTs at a time. Like the two-at-a-time method, you sew a pair of squares together and cut them into HST units afterwards. It's quick and accurate – and was an absolute game changer for me!

You'll need at least two fabrics, and there is a bit of maths involved in figuring out the dimensions. Whatever the HST size you want, there is a rule: multiply the finished size by 2, then add 4.5 cm (1¾ in). Cut two squares this size.

Remember, you can always make your squares a little bigger and cut the units down to size afterwards.

You'll need: marking tool, ruler, rotary cutter and mat (or scissors), sewing machine, iron and ironing board

1. Cut your two squares to the size required.
2. Place the squares neatly on top of each other, right sides together.
3. Pin the squares together so that they don't shift about when you're sewing them. Use your marking tool and ruler to draw two diagonal lines on the top square, each running from corner to corner.
4. Put your 6-mm (¼-in) presser foot on your machine. If you don't have one, mark lines 6 mm (¼ in) from each side of the diagonal lines you drew in step 3 and sew along them. Press the sewn squares to set the seams.
5. Mark vertical and horizontal lines going straight through the centre of your square.
6. Cut along your marked lines (both diagonal lines, the vertical line and the horizontal line) to separate the square into eight HSTs.
7. Open out your HSTs and press the seams.
8. Trim your HST units.

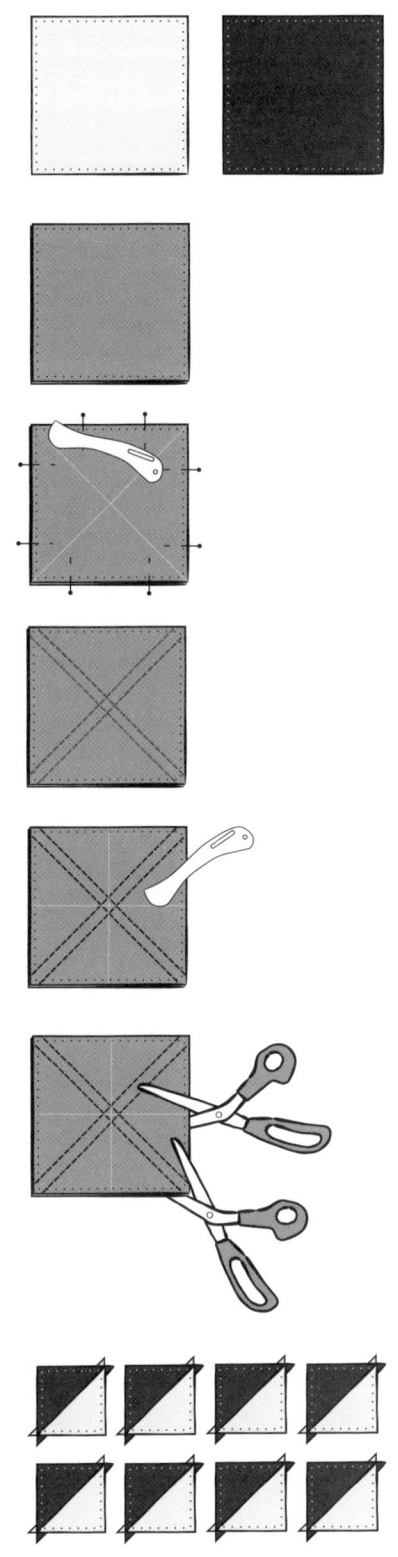

↑ *HSTs magic 8 (steps 1–7)*

Quarter-square triangles (QSTs)

Quarter-square triangles are simpler than they look: follow the HST process (although the measurements change a little) and then do just a few more steps.

TWO-AT-A-TIME METHOD
To make two at a time, choose the finished size that you'd like and add 4 cm (1½ in).

1. Cut two contrasting squares to the required size, then follow the instructions to make two HST units (see page 38).
2. Place your two HST units right sides together, lined up so that the contrasting triangles are on top of each other. The seam allowances should nest up together. Pin your squares together so that they don't shift when you sew them.
3. Draw a diagonal line running from corner to corner, crossing over the seam line.
4. Put your 6-mm (¼-in) presser foot on your machine. If you don't have one, mark lines 6 mm (¼ in) from each side of the diagonal line you drew in step 3 and sew along them. Press the sewn squares to set the seams.
5. Cut along the line that you marked in step 3.
6. Press your QST units.
7. Trim your QST units.

MAGIC 8 METHOD
1. Multiply the finished size by 2, then add 6 cm (2½ in).
2. Follow the magic 8 method to make eight HSTs (see page 39), and then pick up from step 1 of the two-at-a-time method for QSTs (above).

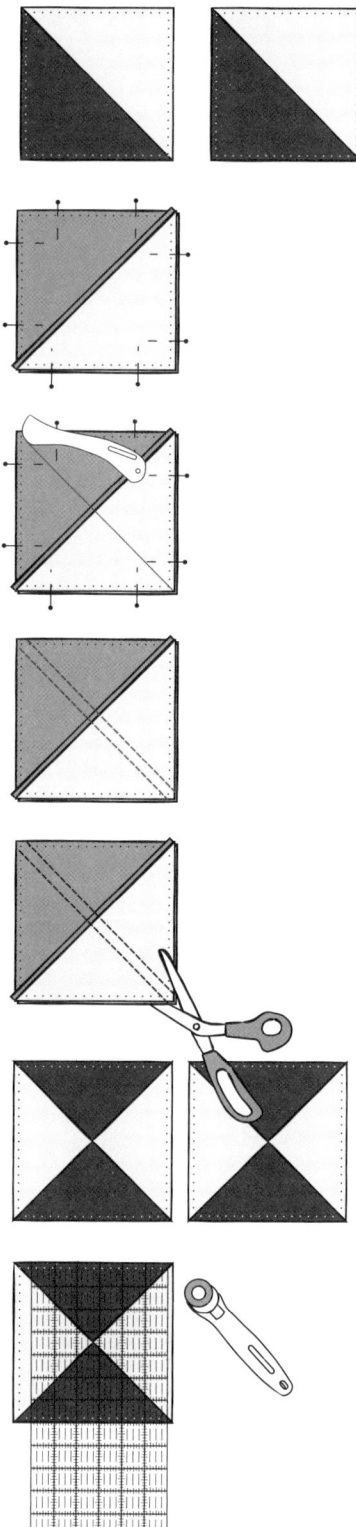

↑ *QSTs two-at-a-time (steps 1–7)*

CURVES

Curved patchwork might look a bit intimidating, but with a little patience it's not too tricky. My main piece of advice when it comes to curves is to go slow. I like to pin my curves carefully, too, though not all quilt makers recommend it.

Here are a few other tips and tricks for sewing curved patchwork.

1. Fold each of your curved pieces in half and press in a crease.
2. Use this crease to line up the curves you'd like to sew together, and pin outwards in either direction from there, taking care not to stretch the fabrics.
3. Sew along the curve, taking care not to stretch the fabrics as you stitch. Stop sewing every few inches (make sure that the needle is in the down position when you do) to readjust your material.
4. Clip small, V-shaped snips out of the seam allowance along the curve, being very careful not to clip through your stitches. This will help the seam relax and lie flat in your quilt.
5. Press the seam allowances towards the darker fabric. Trim the block as needed.

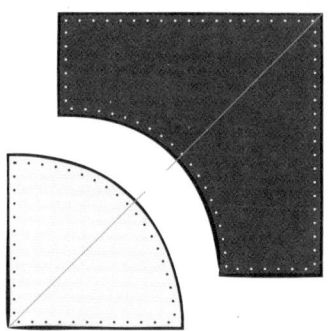

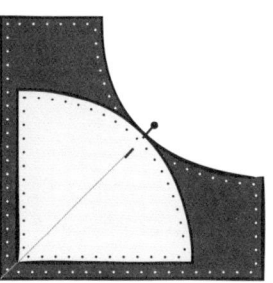

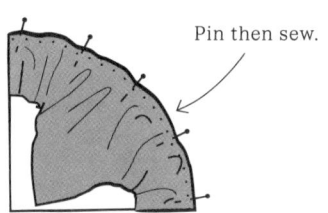

Pin then sew.

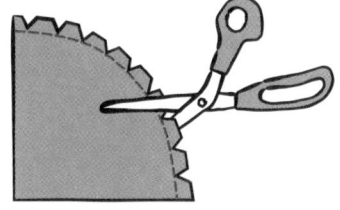

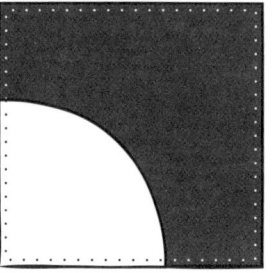

↑ *Sewing curves (steps 1–5)*

IMPROVISATIONAL PATCHWORK (ODD ANGLES)

Improvisational patchwork is one of my absolute favourite techniques. It's more fluid and flexible than following a pattern and has gained popularity over the previous few decades. This is due, in large part, to the quilt makers of Gee's Bend, Alabama. Made by an intergenerational collective of women artists, the patchwork quilts of Gee's Bend have become some of the most influential textile art of the twentieth and twenty-first centuries. Some are abstractions, some playful and intricate iterations of traditional patterns. You can learn more and support their ongoing artwork through the Souls Grown Deep Foundation.

Here is a basic process for improvisational patchwork:

1. Decide on a rough size for each block. This will depend on the size of the scraps that you're working with. If you've got small pieces, something around 40 × 40 cm (15¾ × 15¾ in) is a good start. If you've got big scraps, you might even make up a whole quilt top in one go!
2. Trim your pieces into rough rectangles and squares. They don't have to be perfect, but this will help keep things simple (at least for your first few improv patchwork projects).
3. Start by sewing two of your pieces together. To keep it simple, always work with straight seams and trim off excess length. For example, if you have two fabrics that you'd like to sew together and one is longer than the other, sew them, then cut the longer one to the same length as the shorter one.
4. Following on from your first seam, whenever you add another panel to your patchwork, cut the whole shape back to a rectangle.

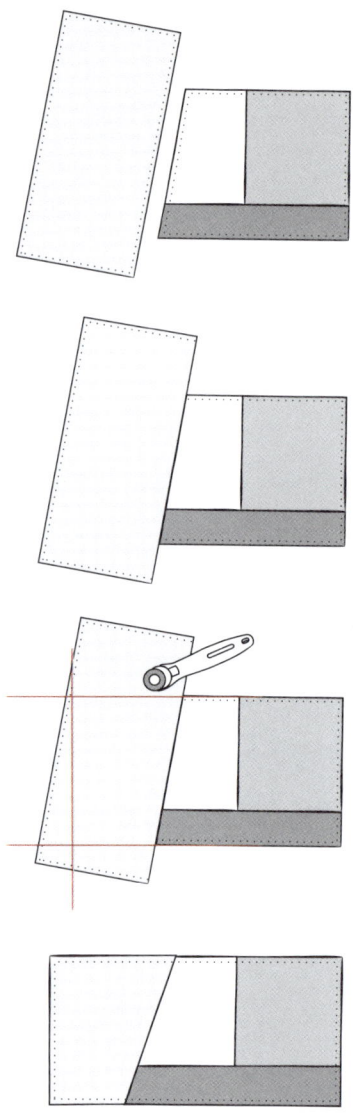

↑ *Building an improvised block (steps 1–4)*

APPLIQUÉ

Machine appli-kway

My friend Bryn is one of the best self-taught quilt makers I know. He does a lot of machine appliqué and, like the work that he makes, his pronunciation of 'appliqué' has a signature style. Bryn makes appli-kway. And since hearing him say that, I can't help but call it appli-kway too. So here is a machine appli-kway tutorial, in honour of my friend Bryn.

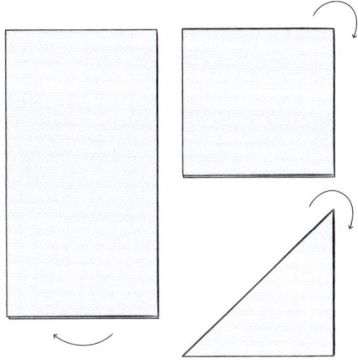

You'll need: iron-on interfacing (see page 20), thread that matches your appliqué fabric, pins, scissors, pencil, iron and ironing board

1. Mark your backing fabric so that your appliqué is easy to position. The easiest way to do this is by pressing creases into the fabric to use as guidelines. So, fold your fabric in half lengthwise (right sides together) and press. Fold it in half again, widthwise this time, and press. Finally, fold it diagonally into a triangle and press. Open out your fabric.

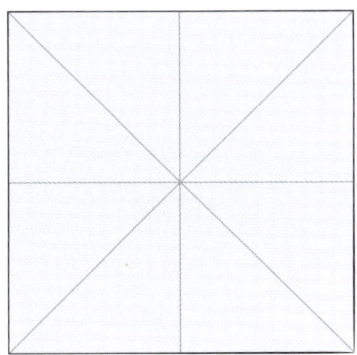

2. Use your creases as a guide to lay out your paper appliqué templates on the backing fabric. Once you're happy with the positioning, draw around your templates.

3. Interface your appliqué fabric. I like to do this before I cut out my specific pieces (which is a technique called 'block interfacing'). Pay close attention when cutting your interfacing to make sure that the glue side is the one that will stick to your fabric pieces. Use an iron on medium heat to fuse your interfacing to the wrong side of your fabric.

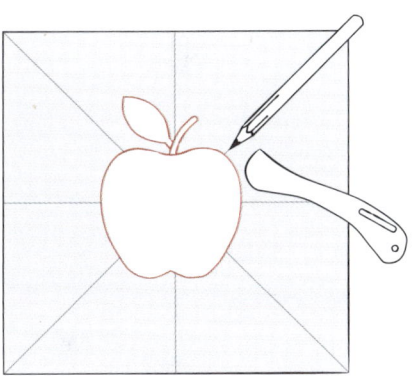

4. Cut out the appliqué templates in your interfaced fabric.

5. Pin or baste (see page 50) your appliqué pieces to the backing fabric, following the tracing you made in step 2. You can use a water-based glue stick to tack the pieces on, though sometimes this can get a little messy.

6. Set up your sewing machine. Use a thread that matches the colour of the fabric you're appliquéing. I like to use a zigzag stitch with a 3 mm stitch width and 0.1–0.2 mm stitch length. You want the stitch to be wide enough to encompass the edge of your appliqué and reach the backing fabric, so that it hides the raw edge. Your machine might vary a little, and I'd encourage you to play around with fabric scraps first

↑ Machine appliqué (steps 1–2)

to make sure that you are happy with the stitch size. Once you're happy with the stitch length and width, make a note of it so that you remember for next time.

7. To begin, set your stitch width and length to 0.1 mm and 0.1 mm. Starting on an edge, take two stitches to secure the seam (any more and you might start to clog up your machine with thread). It's easiest to start on a smooth edge, away from any corners or sharp turns.

8. With the needle in the raised position, change your stitch length to your desired width and length and slowly work your way around your appliqué.

9. To pivot or go around curves, stop the machine with the needle in the down position. Raise the presser foot and turn the fabric as needed. Lower the presser foot and begin stitching again.

10. Finish by setting your stitch width and length to 0.1 mm and 0.1 mm once again, and take two or three more stitches to secure your sewing.

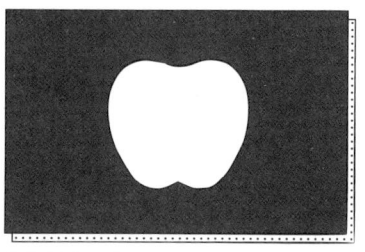
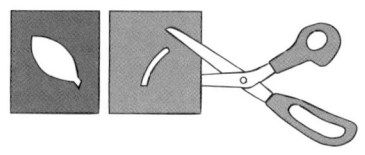
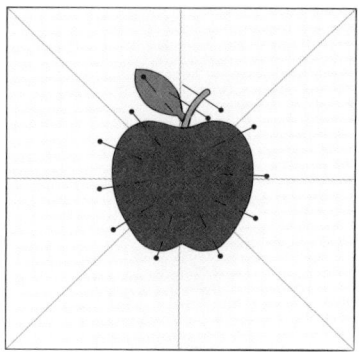

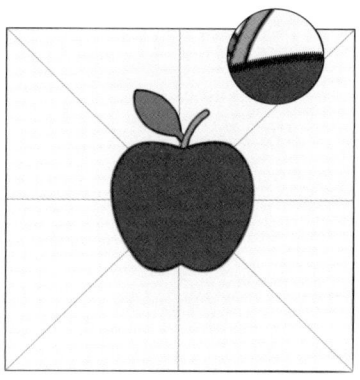

↑ *Machine appliqué (steps 3–7)*

Needle-turned appliqué

Needle-turned appliqué is a simple, traditional technique.

You'll need: a needle (appliqué or crewel embroidery needle), thread that matches the colour of your appliqué fabric, pins, scissors, pencil, iron and ironing board

Optional: freezer paper (a thick paper that has a plastic or wax coating on one side – note it is not the same thing as wax or greaseproof paper. Cut into shapes and ironed on to fabric, it provides an edge to fold your seam allowance into when doing appliqué.)

1. Mark your backing fabric so that your appliqué is easy to position. The simplest way to do this is by pressing creases into the fabric to use as guidelines, in the same way as for machine appliqué (see page 43).
2. Use your creases as a guide to lay out and draw around your paper appliqué templates.
3. Cut out the appliqué templates in fabric, adding a 3-mm (⅛-in) seam allowance all around each piece.
4. Snip any points that will make folding the fabric easier.
5. Pin or baste (see page 50) your appliqué pieces to the backing fabric, following the tracing you made in step 2. Leave a 3-mm (⅛-in) clear space around the edge of your appliqué, so that you can turn it under.
6. Fold the 3-mm (⅛-in) seam allowance along your pencil line for 2.5–5 cm (1–2 in) ahead and crease with your fingernail. Stitch this section down using blind stitch (page 68). As you work, use the needle tip to continue rolling the seam allowance under the appliqué.

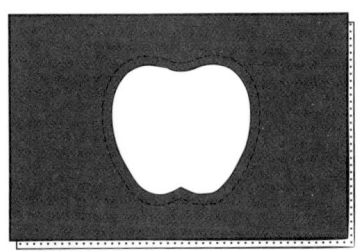

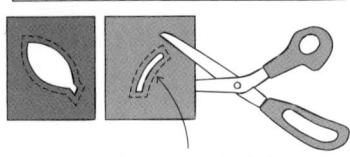

Add 3 mm (⅛ in).

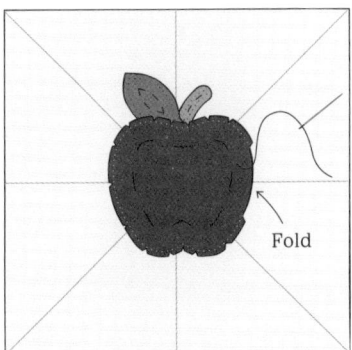

Fold

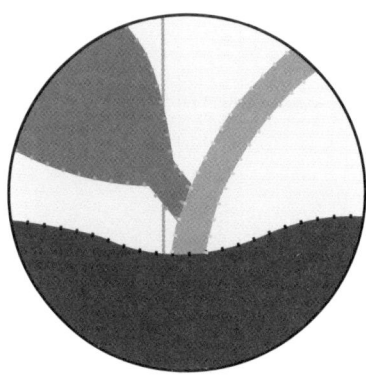

↑ *Needle-turned appliqué (steps 2–5)*

ASSEMBLING
YOUR QUILT TOP

Now that you've got a handle on how to make up different blocks and some appliqué techniques, it's time to put your quilt tops together. This can feel bewildering or incredibly satisfying. To set yourself up for the latter, think logically and make a plan before you begin.

If you're working with a pattern made from blocks, the general process is:

1. Cut and sew the block's different elements – for example, half-square triangles, squares or quarter-square triangles.
2. Sew these elements together into their blocks.
3. Lay out the individual blocks in rows, and then stitch each row together. Press the seam allowance on each row in the opposite direction to the last. For example, press the seam allowances in the first row that you make to the left, and in the second row press them to the right. This will allow you to nest your seams together and get accurate corners more easily.
4. When you've sewn each row, pin the rows carefully together, ensuring that the corner junctions of the blocks meet up neatly. I find it useful to start pinning from the centre and work my way out evenly on each side, as I'm able to get my corners to line up more reliably this way. Stitch the rows together.
5. Once you've sewn your quilt top, give it one final press. Then pat yourself on the back for a job well done, make yourself a cup of tea and have a read through the next chapter!

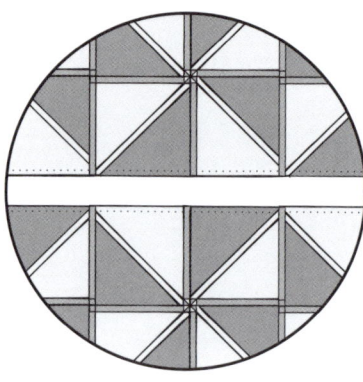

↑ *Remember to press all your seam allowances in opposing directions so you can nest your seams.*

TIP

If you're working with a double-sized quilt or larger, sew half the rows together to make the first half of the quilt, then sew the other half of the rows together to make the second half. Then join the two halves. Big quilts can be tricky to manoeuvre around your sewing machine, and this method means that you only have to put your enormous quilt top through the sewing machine once!

↑ *Step 1*

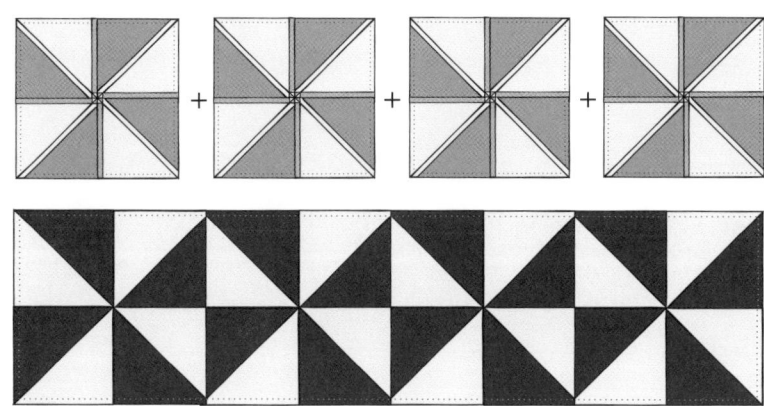

↑ *Step 3*

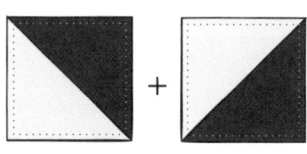

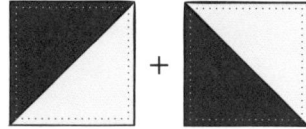

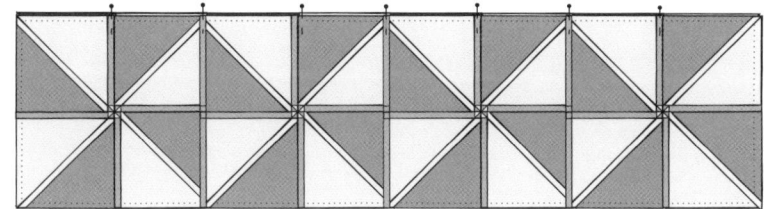

↑ *Step 4*

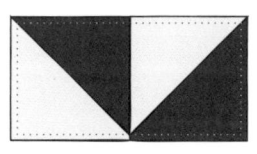

↑ *Step 2*

↑ *Step 5*

CHAPTER THREE

PUTTING QUILTS TOGETHER

BASTING

Basting is the process of securing the layers of the quilt together so that they don't shift or wobble while you're quilting them. This is a crucial step; if you do it carefully, you will have a much easier time with the quilting process.

1. Press your quilt back to get rid of any creases. Then lay out the quilt back right side down on a large table or on the floor. Whatever surface you use, make sure it is flat and hard (no carpet, mattress, rug, etc.). Smooth it out with your hands. Use painter's tape to secure the corners and edges down. If you don't have painter's tape, you can use weights or heavy books instead.
2. Once the quilt back is secure, lay out the wadding (batting) on top. Aim to centre it right in the middle of the quilt back. You may have a small border of quilt back around all the edges. Take some time to smooth it out. Pin the wadding to the quilt back using quilting pins (if you do this, just pin the edges and not the centre, so that you can remove the pins once you've added the quilt top) or you can tape the edges down, just as you did for the quilt back.
3. Lay out the quilt top right side up to complete the quilt 'sandwich'. Place it right in the middle so you have an equal border of wadding around all sides. Smooth it with your hands to get rid of any wrinkles or puckers. Pin the edges of the quilt top to the other layers – it's a bad idea to use tape at this point, just in case it sticks a little too well later on.
4. Now you're ready to start temporarily fixing the layers of the quilt together. This is done in one of two ways.

   a. STITCH BASTING: basting stitches, sometimes called tailor's tacks, are worked diagonally and are about 3–5 cm (1¼–2 in) in length. Start in the middle of the quilt and work outwards, or on one side and work across to the other, so you minimise the risk of trapping a bulge of fabric as you go.

   b. PIN BASTING: as with stitch basting, start in the middle and work your way out. But, instead of sewing, pierce through all three layers of the quilt with your pin, then close it. Place your safety pins about 8 cm (3¼ in) apart.

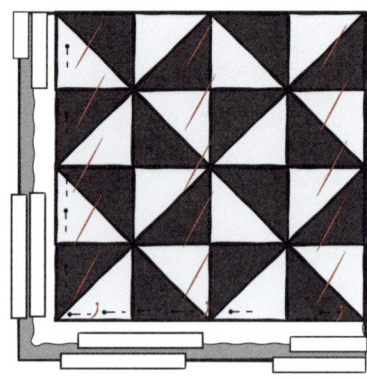

↑ *Stitch basting*

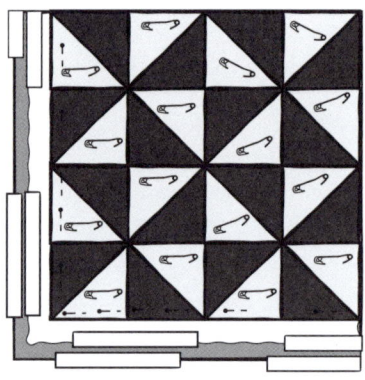

↑ *Pin basting*

NOTE

Quilting wisdom has it that the larger the project that you are working on, the closer together your basting stitches should be. Spacing them 15–25 cm (6–10 in) apart suits most projects.

MARKING

Once you've basted your quilt, you're ready to mark out your quilt top with lines to guide your quilting. Marking these lines can be done in a number of different ways: using templates or rulers, or simply by following the seams on your quilt top.

If you want to do the latter (a technique called 'STITCHING IN THE DITCH') you don't need to mark anything – in fact, I'd avoid it. Instead, use the seams as guides for your quilted lines and stitch a needle's width to one side of them. Even the most accurate sewist may find themselves a millimetre or two off at some point, and following your seam instead of a marked line will mean that those small errors are much less obvious.

TIP

If you're planning to quilt a grid, first mark and stitch all your lines going in one direction, then mark and stitch in the other direction. This will save you time. (And if you, like me, sometimes bite off more than you can chew, it also means that a half-done project still looks finished!)

Marking straight lines

The simplest way to mark your quilt is with a fabric pencil, hera marker or another marking tool and a ruler. If you are working in straight lines, you don't need to mark your whole quilt top at once. Instead, you can do it in smaller sections to keep the marked lines from fading as you work.

1. Place your quilt ruler parallel to the quilt's edge along the line that you'd like to start stitching at. Nestle your marking tool up to the ruler and draw a line. For your first quilt, I recommend marking lines 5–10 cm (2–4 in) apart. It's a good starting point for making a quilt that feels handmade and 'quilty' without taking 10,000 hours to complete. Most commercial quilt waddings (battings) have information on their packets about how densely they should be quilted. For example, many cotton waddings will say something like 'quilt or tie up to 20 cm (8 in) apart'. Why, you ask? Rows of stitching at or smaller than this distance will mean that the wadding stays relatively stable over its lifetime.

2. For your next row of stitching, align your ruler with the line you've just drawn, using the numbered gridlines to guide you. Mark your next row, then repeat until you have marked the whole quilt.

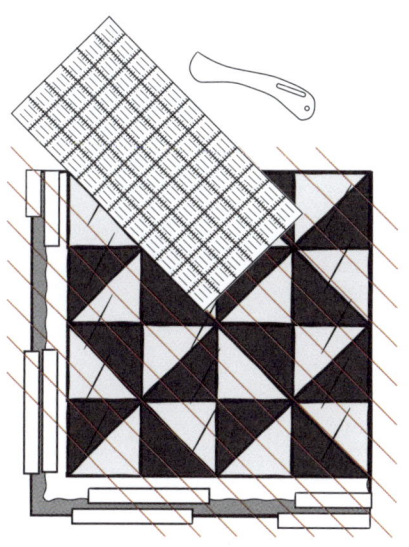

↑ *Marking straight lines*

Marking curved lines

The process for marking curved lines is a little more varied. You can use:

RULERS
Try drawing your lines with a curved ruler (there are many different kinds available).

HOUSEHOLD OBJECTS
Have a hunt around your home for round things with interesting, repetitive curves that you can trace. You'll generally find good stuff in the kitchen, like bowls, mugs and plates. Once I used a bundt pan. Go ahead, get creative.

TEMPLATES
Shop-bought or homemade templates work great for intricate quilting patterns. These thin pieces of acrylic come carved with any number of floral and abstract designs for you to place on your quilt and draw around.

Don't feel limited to shop-bought templates either, which tend to stick to fairly traditional designs. You can make your own template by printing or drawing a design onto a thick card or acrylic sheet and then cutting it out with a scalpel or utility knife. I had a student once who was an architect. She used computer-aided design (CAD) to create templates, then laser-cut them (to the envy of everyone else in the class). Not everyone has access to that kind of kit, but it's worth asking yourself what you do have access to, and how you can get creative with it.

DESIGN TRANSFERS
Iron-on design transfers are used for embroidery and quilting. There is a huge range out there. Vintage options can be found on online marketplaces – think lots of doe-eyed animals, cherubic babies and elaborate florals. Most either wash out or can be peeled off afterwards, but it's worth carefully following the instructions that come with the packet.

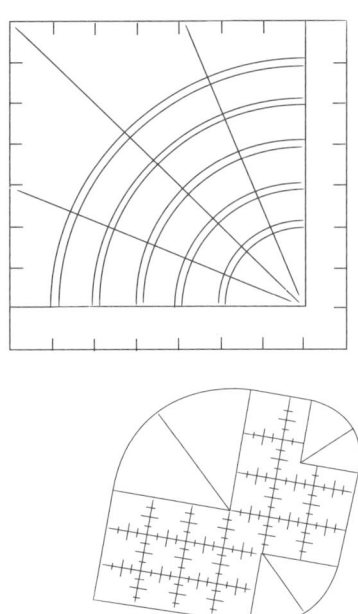

↑ *Curved rulers*

TIP

If you don't have a quilt ruler, cut out a template from thick card (a cereal box or similar will work nicely). The dimensions of the template are:

DESIRED WIDTH BETWEEN QUILTED LINES

×

A LENGTH THAT FEELS EASY TO MOVE AND WORK WITH

For example, I like mine to be around 5 × 45 cm (2 × 17¾ in).

HAND QUILTING

Now that you've marked out how you'd like to quilt, you're ready to begin! Hand quilting can be done on a quilting frame, with a quilting hoop or in your lap. Your choice will depend on what style of stitching you'd like to end up with. (Flip back to Chapter 1 for more detail on needles and threads to use.)

When you begin quilting, always work from the middle of your quilt outwards or from one side of the quilt to the other. Just like when you're basting, this reduces the risk of trapping a wrinkly fabric bulge in your quilt.

Rocking stitch

You typically hand quilt using a special technique called a rocking stitch. Using the rocking stitch helps you get small, even stitches quickly and efficiently. It can feel awkward, especially if you are used to other types of hand work, but I'd encourage you to keep trying. The results are worth it.

1. Thread your needle with a thread 45–50 cm (18–19¾ in) long. You don't have to be precise – having thread lengths that vary slightly is a good thing (I'll explain why in a moment). Tie a knot at the end of the thread.
2. For your first line of quilting stitches, you want to snuggle this knot in the wadding (batting) and then bring your needle back up through the quilt top, about 1 cm (⅜ in) away from the edge of the fabric. Doing this means that you won't have any stitches showing up on the back of your quilt yet.
3. Put your thimble on your middle or ring finger of your dominant hand. With the same hand, grip the needle between your thumb and index finger. Place your other hand under the quilt where you'll be sewing. Then insert the tip of the needle back into the quilt top at a 90° angle, so that it goes through all the layers of the quilt (remember, quilts are sandwiches: you want to secure all three layers together).
4. Using your thimble fingertip, gently rock the top of the needle back towards the edge of the quilt, so that it's almost parallel to the surface of the quilt top.
5. Bring the tip of the needle back through the layers of the quilt so that it comes up through the quilt top.

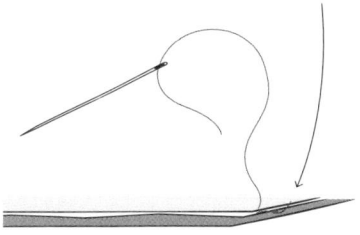

Secure your knot between the quilt's layers and come up through the quilt top.

↑ *Rocking stitch (steps 1–2)*

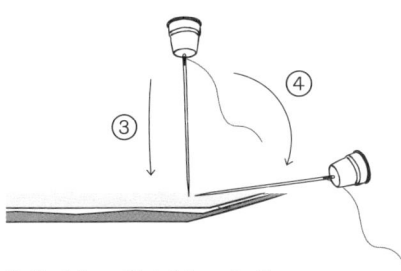

↑ *Rocking stitch (steps 3–4)*

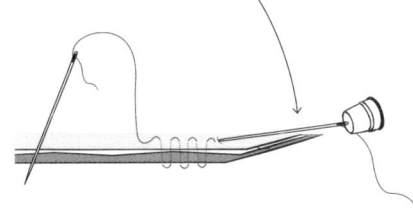

Rock the needle up and down while pushing forward to pick up stitches.

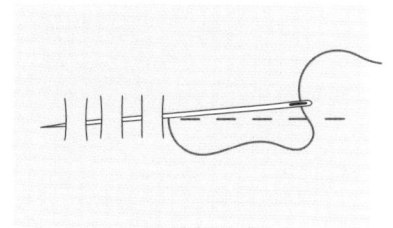

↑ *Rocking stitch (steps 5–6)*

6. Use your thimble fingertip to rock the needle back and forth between the quilt top and back, so you pick up stitches. Beginners should aim for two to three stitches on their needle. More advanced hand quilters may take on between five and ten stitches before pulling the thread through the quilt. The number depends on the size of the stitches, length of the needle, weave of the fabrics and preference of the quilt maker.

7. Before you pull your needle through all the layers of the fabric, have a look at the stitches on your needle. How big are they? Are they even? If you're happy, pull through. If you want to try again, slip the stitches off your needle tip and take them again. Be aware that there will be thousands and thousands of stitches in every quilt you make, and getting stuck on perfecting three of them will make the quilting process slower than snail's pace.

8. Continue quilting until you have about 7–10 cm (2¾–4 in) of your thread left. Now you're ready to 'tie off' the thread.

A NOTE ON THREAD LENGTH

Popping the knot creates a slightly bigger gap between the stitches on the back of the quilt than a normal stitch. Over the whole of the quilt, this is pretty subtle. However, if you have threads that are all the same length and pop the knot at the same point over your whole quilt, those slightly larger gaps will line up. The negative space caused by these gaps-in-a-row will read as a line and be more noticeable. To counter this, vary your thread lengths slightly (it doesn't have to be by much).

Tying off in the middle of your quilt

1. Make a small loop knot about 1 cm (⅜ in) from the quilt top.
2. Take a 'fake' stitch. This is a stitch that doesn't go through all the layers of the quilt. Instead, just go through the top layer and into the wadding (batting).
3. Bring the tip of your needle back up through your quilt top about 2–3 cm (¾–1¼ in) away from your line of stitching.
4. Pull the needle through, popping the little knot you made underneath the surface of the quilt so that it is nestled in the wadding (batting). If your fabric is woven quite tightly, this might be a little tricky.
5. Pull your needle so your thread is taut, then trim your thread so that it sinks back into the quilt top and becomes invisible.

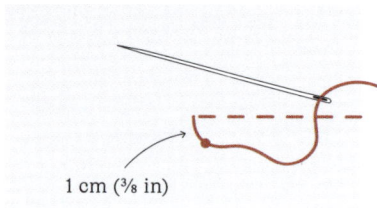

1 cm (⅜ in)

↑ Tying off in the middle (step 1)

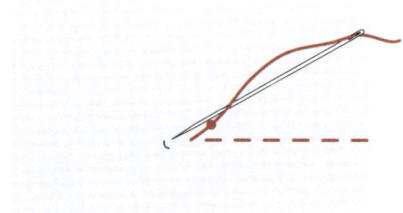

↑ Tying off in the middle (step 2)

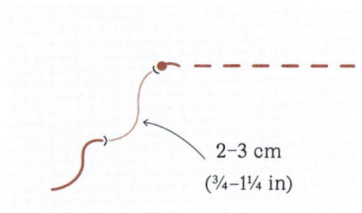

2–3 cm (¾–1¼ in)

↑ Tying off in the middle (step 3)

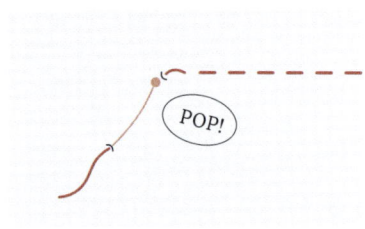

POP!

↑ Tying off in the middle (step 4)

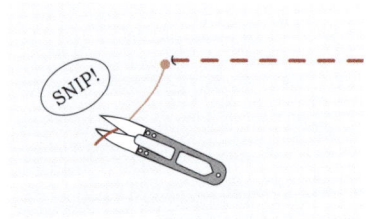

SNIP!

↑ Tying off in the middle (step 5)

Start stitching with a new thread

1. Thread your needle with about 45 cm (17¾ in) of thread. (If you don't feel like measuring, cut a piece roughly the length of your arm.) Tie a small knot in the end.
2. Look at where you ended your last stitch. About 2–3 cm (¾–1¼ in) away from that point, push your needle tip into the quilt top and wadding (batting), without going through the quilt back.
3. Bring your needle up through the quilt top in your line of stitching as if you were continuing from your final stitch on your previous thread.
4. Pull the needle through, gently popping the knot under the surface of the quilt top so it is hidden in the wadding (batting).
5. Use the rocking stitch technique to continue quilting.

When you get to the end of the quilt top

Take your last stitch about 1.5 cm (⅝ in) before the edge of your quilt top, going through just the quilt top into the wadding (batting) – *not* the quilt back.

You're going to tie a knot in this thread, but before you do check the tension of your stitches. Is your quilt top looking a little crimped? If it is, tie your knot 1.5 cm (⅝ in) away from the end of your stitching so that the thread has some slack to it. Tie off in the same way you would in the middle of the quilt top (see page 54), then trim off the excess thread.

(see page 54)

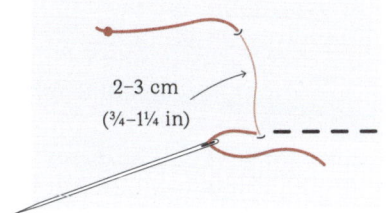

2–3 cm
(¾–1¼ in)

↑ *Start stitching with a new thread (steps 1–3)*

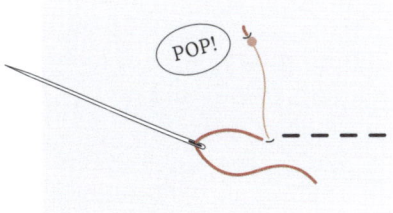

POP!

↑ *Start stitching with a new thread (step 4)*

TIE QUILTING

Tying a quilt is a traditional technique that is both speedy and simple. Like the name suggests, tie quilting secures the quilt layers by tying them together. It adds a different texture to the quilt. Tying is fantastic for quilts constructed from thicker layers, so if you want to sandwich your patchwork around an old wool blanket, pay close attention to this section.

Tie quilting really lends itself to a quilting bee. I've created tie quilts for baby showers and bachelorette parties, making the quilt top, basting and marking it beforehand, then having guests stitch the blanket together. It's a fun way to make a warm, cosy communal gift.

Materials for tie quilting

For tie quilting, choose similar threads to those that you might use for hand quilting: hand-quilting thread, sashiko thread, perle 8 cotton or embroidery thread (floss). You can also go thicker and stitch with wool or cotton yarns or even ribbon. Depending on the look you want, you can mix and match colours and threads on the same quilt for added texture.

Whatever you choose, it needs to be strong enough to hold the layers of your quilt together.

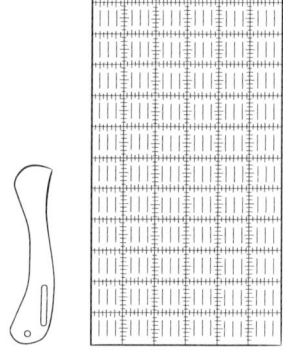

Marking for tie quilting

Think about where you'd like the ties to be on your quilt top. Many quilt makers use the seam joins as a natural place to add in their ties. An offset grid pattern is another common choice.

As with hand quilting, check your wadding (batting) package to see how far apart you can place your ties without compromising the wadding's integrity. A good starting point is 7.5–12.5 cm (3–5 in) between ties.

Instead of drawing lines, just use your quilt ruler and marking tool to draw 1 cm (⅜ in) crosses where you want to place your ties.

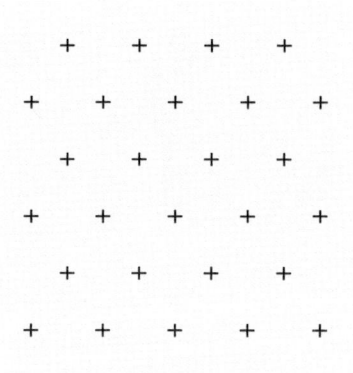

↑ *Marking for tie quilting*

Tying a quilt with reef knots

Thread a sharp needle with two 18–25 cm (7–10 in) strands of your chosen thread. This is a good length for tying and long enough for you to add a decorative bow if you wish.

1. Starting in the centre of your quilt, stitch through all the layers of the quilt around the horizontal line of one cross, leaving a 15-cm (6-in) tail at the start of your stitch.
2. Bring your needle up at the other side of your cross.
3. Bring the needle down again, this time stitching around the vertical line of the cross.
4. Bring your needle up through the quilt layers and underneath the stitch on your quilt top, pulling the thread into an X shape.
5. Make a reef knot by passing the right thread over the left and then the left over the right.
6. Tie the knot tight and trim the ends to your desired length. (Keep it longer than 1 cm/⅜ in for a stronger tie.)

If you're making a quilt that will be washed frequently, tie the knot twice so it's extra secure. You can also tie in buttons or beads to add visual interest and texture.

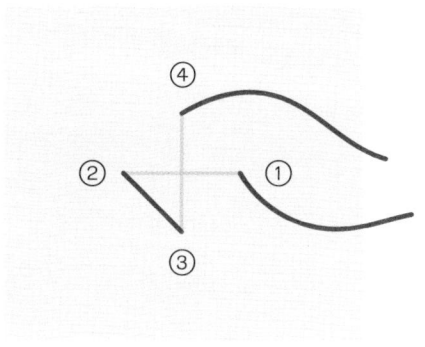

↑ Tying a quilt with reef knots (steps 1–4)

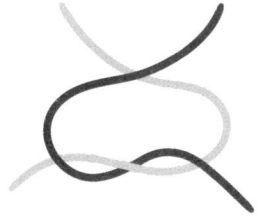

↑ Tying a quilt with reef knots (step 5)

TRIMMING YOUR QUILT

Once you've finished your quilting (well done, you), it's time to trim the excess wadding (batting) and backing.

If you are using a rotary cutter, now is a really, really good time to change out the old blade for a fresh one so that you can slice through those layers like gently warmed butter.

1. Line up your quilt ruler (if you don't have a quilt ruler, use another object with a 90° corner) with the edge of your quilt top and make sure your corner is square.
2. If you are using a rotary cutter, trim the quilt alongside your ruler. If you are using scissors, use your marking tool to trace around the edge and then follow the line.
3. Once you have trimmed and squared all the sides, fold the quilt in half and then again into quarters to see how well your edges match up.

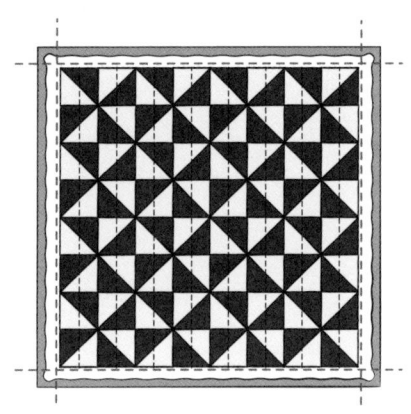

↑ *Excess wadding and backing*

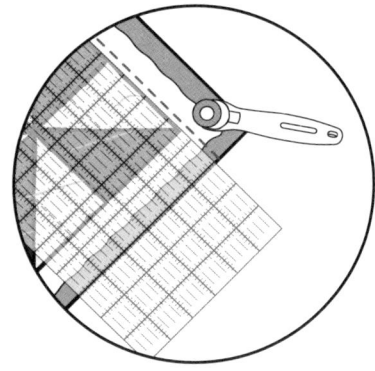

↑ *Trimming with a rotary cutter*

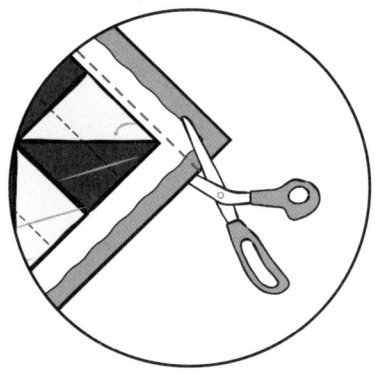

↑ *Trimming with a pair of scissors*

BINDING

There are a few different methods for finishing the edge of a quilt. My personal favourite is a classic double-fold quilt binding. It's sturdy and beginner-friendly (it helps to tidy up any dodgy edges).

Standard quilt binding is cut 5–6.5 cm (2–2½ in) wide and is about 1.2–1.5 cm (½–⅝ in) when finished, though you can adjust this to suit your own taste. The instructions below outline how to make 5-cm (2-in) binding.

↑ *A mitred corner is a neat and tidy diagonal corner finish.*

Calculating how much binding you'll need

Measure the perimeter of the quilt (the length of all four sides added together), then add 30 cm (12 in).

Choosing your binding fabrics

While you can buy ready-made quilt binding, I'm a big advocate for making your own. The process is simple and you have complete control over how it looks. For example, you may have a simple monochrome quilt that you want to make bolder with a contrast binding.

I often make mine from scraps left over from the patchwork process. If you want to do this, I'd recommend using scraps that are at least 30 × 10 cm (12 × 4 in).

Straight-grain binding vs bias binding

Straight-grain binding is cut parallel to a fabric's grain. It's stable, strong and uses a lot less material than cutting on the bias.

The only time you need to use bias binding is if you're finishing a curved edge (for example, if you're making a round play mat like the Pierrot on page 93). Bias binding has more stretch, so it can hug those curved edges without puckering. It requires a little extra effort, but the continuous method outlined on page 61 really isn't too tricky!

STRAIGHT-GRAIN BINDING

You can buy binding makers that help with this process, but I find them a bit finicky.

1. Cut strips of fabric 5 cm (2 in) wide until you have roughly the length needed for your quilt.
2. Press the strips. I always do this before I sew them together, as otherwise I end up sewing them wrong sides together at some point and have to unpick them. The process is as follows:

   a. Press the first 15 cm (6 in) of the binding in half lengthwise, wrong sides together.
   b. Open the binding out again, then fold the raw edges in towards the centre crease, so that the raw edges are either side of the centre. Press them in place.
   c. Once you've pressed the first 15 cm (6 in), make a guide with pins on your ironing board so that you don't have to manually fold the whole length.
   d. Stick two long pins through the ironing board cover and over the binding, one at the very end of the strip and the second about 10 cm (4 in) into it. Be careful not to pin the binding to the ironing board. Instead, create a little pocket for it.
   e. Pull the unfolded binding through the guides and watch them pull it into shape. Press the binding as you go.

3. Once you've pressed the strips, open them up so that they lie flat. Pin two strips right sides together at a 90° angle, so that the ends look like a cross or a plus sign.
4. Sew the strips together at a 45° angle across the diagonal. This helps to distribute the bulk across the seam and avoids lumpy binding.
5. Trim the seam allowances to 6 mm (¼ in) and press the seam allowances open.
6. Repeat this process until you have a continuous length that is long enough to wrap around the whole quilt top with 30 cm (12 in) spare.

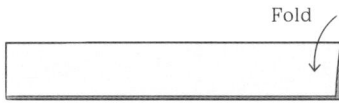

↑ *Straight-grain binding (step 2a)*

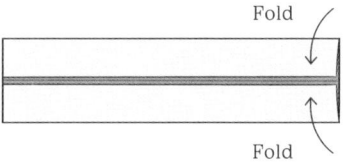

↑ *Straight-grain binding (step 2b)*

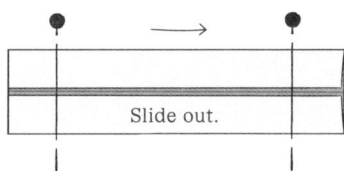

↑ *Straight-grain binding (steps 2c–e)*

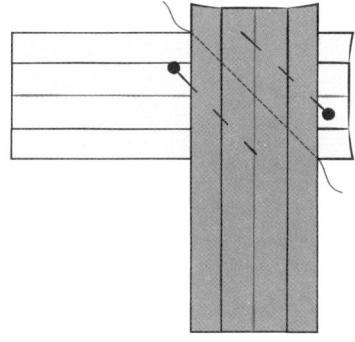

↑ *Straight-grain binding (steps 3–4)*

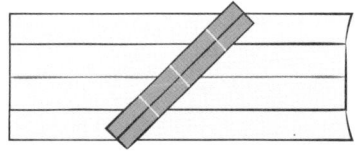

↑ *Straight-grain binding (step 5)*

CONTINUOUS BIAS BINDING

1. Cut a 45 cm (17¾ in) square. You can use any size square to make bias binding, but I find this a good size to work with.
2. Use your marking tool to draw a diagonal line from corner to corner.
3. Cut along this line so that you have two triangles.
4. Place the two triangles right sides together along one of the short straight sides. Pin. Stitch together with a 6-mm (¼-in) seam allowance.
5. Open the fabric out. It should now be a parallelogram shape. Press the seam open.
6. Rotate your fabric so that the seam runs diagonally. Starting at the bottom corner of the fabric's edge, mark lines 5 cm (2 in) apart, running parallel to the long edge on the wrong side of the fabric. Continue all the way up.
7. With right sides together, fold the narrow tips of your parallelogram lengthwise to make a small tube.
8. Match the marked lines together, but offset your square by one set of lines. This is VERY important: it will give you a long, continuous piece of binding instead of a series of small loops.
9. Once it's offset, pin the row in place so that you have a tube. Sew these pieces together with a 6-mm (¼-in) seam allowance. Press the seam open.
10. Starting at the first offset row of lines, use scissors to cut along the line until you reach the end.
11. Pick up at step 2 for making straight-grain binding.

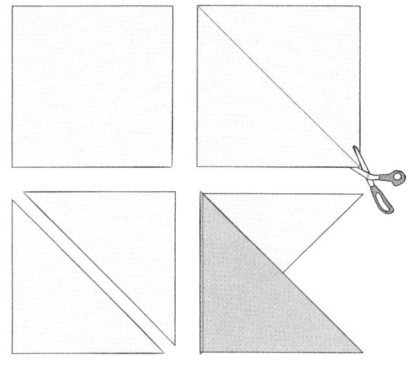

↑ *Continuous bias binding (steps 1–4)*

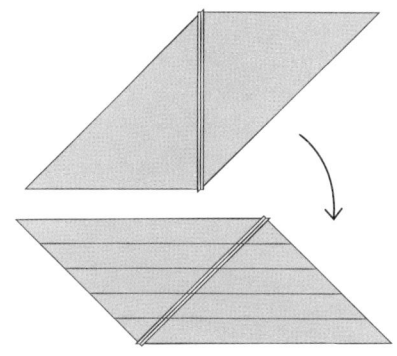

↑ *Continuous bias binding (steps 5–6)*

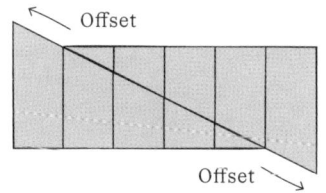

↑ *Continuous bias binding (steps 7–8)*

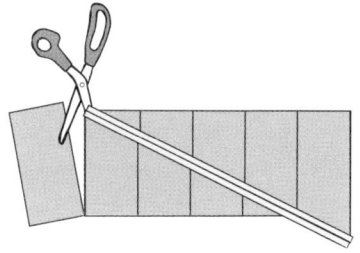

↑ *Continuous bias binding (step 10)*

Attaching binding

1. Get your sewing machine set up and ready to go.

   a. Consider changing to a stronger needle if you've used a lightweight one for your patchwork.
   b. If you have a walking foot, put it on your machine now.
   c. Adjust the stitch length to 2.5 mm (make sure that you backstitch at the beginning and end of your seams).
   d. Do a sewing test on scraps of extra material if possible – especially if this is your first time attaching binding.
   e. Adjust the tension on your sewing machine if necessary.

2. Lay out your quilt right side up. Unfold your binding and lay it flat so that a raw edge of the binding is lined up flush with the edge of your trimmed quilt.
3. Start at least 30 cm (12 in) away from any of the corners. (It's much easier to join the ends of your binding if you're not worrying about going around a corner while you're doing it.)
4. Leave yourself a 15-cm (6-in) tail of binding unattached to the quilt top.
5. Pin the binding along one edge of the quilt, putting your last pin in 6 mm (¼ in) from the end of the quilt.
6. Stitch the binding onto the quilt top along the crease that you pressed into your binding, stopping at the last pin 6 mm (¼ in) away from the end of your quilt. Backstitch.
7. Take your quilt off your sewing machine.
8. Fold the binding so that the long tail lines with up flush with the next quilt edge you're about to sew. This should leave a small triangular flap of fabric at your quilt corner.
9. Fold this flap neatly towards the edge of the quilt that you've just sewn, so that it lies flush with the edge of your quilt. Pin.
10. Pin your binding to the next edge of your quilt top so that the edges are flush. Place your last pin 6 mm (¼ in) from the corner of your quilt, where you will stop sewing.
11. Sew down your binding, beginning at the very top of the crease you've pressed into your quilt, until you're 6 mm (¼ in) away from the corner.
12. Repeat steps 7–11 until you are about 15 cm (6 in) away from the point you began stitching your binding to the quilt.

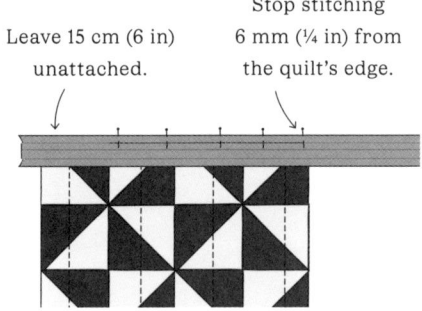

Leave 15 cm (6 in) unattached.

Stop stitching 6 mm (¼ in) from the quilt's edge.

↑ *Attaching binding (steps 2–6)*

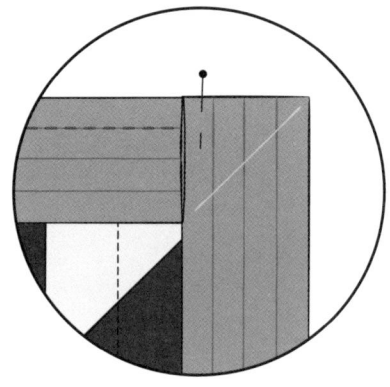

↑ *Attaching binding (steps 8–9)*

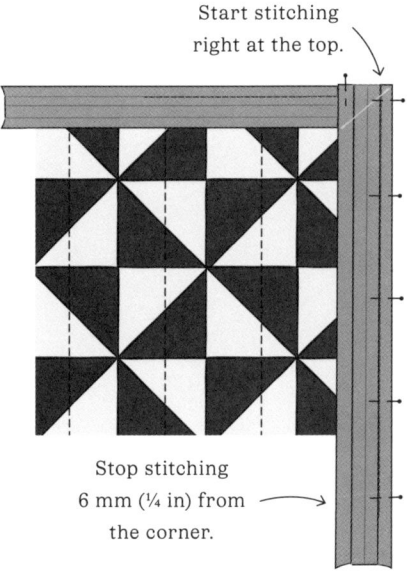

Start stitching right at the top.

Stop stitching 6 mm (¼ in) from the corner.

↑ *Attaching binding (steps 10–11)*

Joining the ends of your binding

1. Take your quilt off your sewing machine and lay it right side up. You should have two 'tails' of binding – one from where you began sewing your binding, the other from where you finished.
2. Bring the tails of the binding together so that they nearly meet, leave about 6 mm (¼ in) between them and fold the excess away. Finger press your folds so that you have creases to use as guides.
3. Position the creases so they make a cross (right sides together). Be careful not to twist them.
4. Use your ruler to mark a diagonal line (on the wrong side of your binding) where the two pieces meet.
5. Pin the line you've marked.
6. Stitch along the drawn line.
7. Take out the pins and lay the binding on the quilt to check that you've got the right length and that it will lie flat.
8. Trim the excess so that you have a 6-mm (¼-in) seam allowance on your diagonal binding seam. Finger press or press with your iron.
9. Lay the binding on your quilt and stitch over the gap.

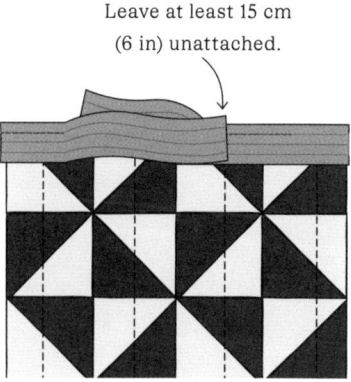

Leave at least 15 cm (6 in) unattached.

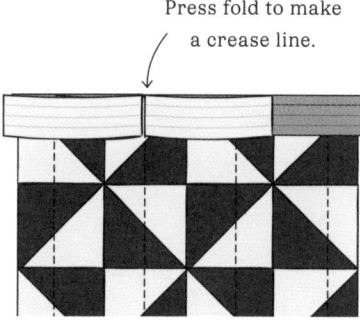

Press fold to make a crease line.

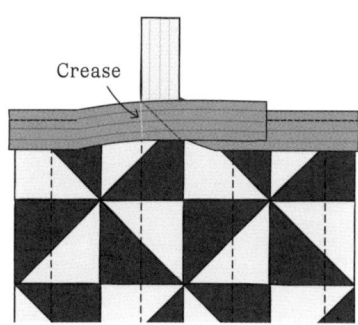

Crease

↑ *Joining the ends of your binding (steps 1–4)*

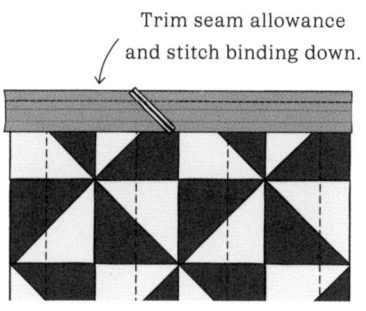

Trim seam allowance and stitch binding down.

↑ *Joining the ends of your binding (steps 6–8)*

Hand finishing binding

After you've attached your binding by machine, it's time to do a final bit of handwork. You can, of course, stitch your binding down by machine, but I love the invisible finish of a hand stitch and find it gives me more control.

1. Pin about 30 cm (12 in) of the edge of your binding over the seam allowance on the back of your quilt.
2. Thread your needle. I like to double up my thread when I sew on binding so that my stitches are very strong. Tie a knot in the end of the thread.
3. Take your first stitch into the seam allowance of your quilt (6 mm/¼ in away from the edge). Backstitch to secure.
4. Slipstitch or ladder stitch (see page 68) the binding to the quilt back, making sure that your binding covers the line of machine stitches. As you stitch, make sure you aren't going through all the layers of the quilt (otherwise your stitches will show up on the quilt top).
5. At each corner, fold the binding into a mitre (see illustration page 59), as on the front of your quilt. Slipstitch down and secure with a backstitch.
6. Just like when you're hand stitching binding, double up your thread for a strong stitch and tie a knot in the end of your thread. Take your first stitch between the layers of your quilt so you can bury your knot in the seam allowance.
7. Continue this until you have around 10 cm (4 in) of thread left. Then, take a stitch into the seam allowance of your quilt and tie off.
8. Rethread your needle. Pop your knot into the binding (as you did when connecting lines of hand quilting in the middle of your quilt, see page 54). I like to begin stitching an inch or so before my previous thread runs out, so that there are no weak points in the binding seam.
9. Continue until you have bound your entire quilt.

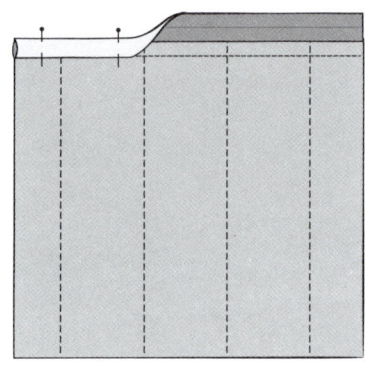

↑ *Hand finishing binding (step 1)*

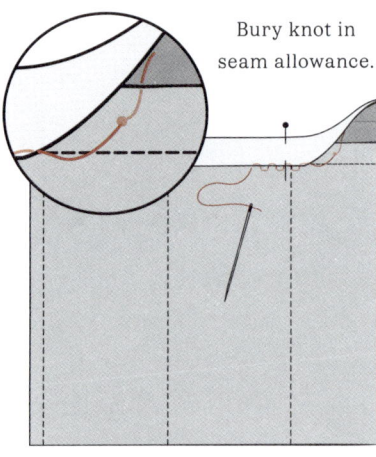

Bury knot in seam allowance.

↑ *Hand finishing binding (steps 3–4)*

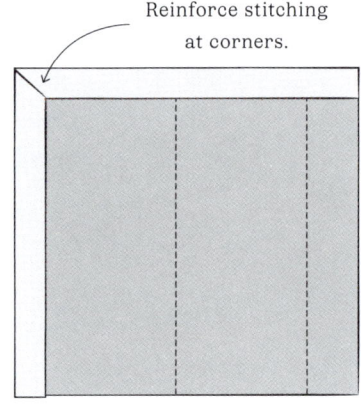

Reinforce stitching at corners.

↑ *Hand finishing binding (step 5)*

KNIFE-EDGE FINISH

A knife-edge (or 'butted') finish is another way to finish quilts. Unlike binding, no extra fabric is used.

1. Trim the wadding (batting) and backing to the same size as the patchwork. Hand or machine quilt all around the perimeter of the quilt, 2.5 cm (1 in) from the edge.
2. Next, trim 6 mm (¼ in) off the wadding around the whole perimeter of the quilt. Be very careful not to trim your patchwork or backing fabric during this process.
3. Turn in the edge of the backing so that it overlaps the wadding. Pin. Turn in the edge of the patchwork so that it lines up with the edge of the backing. Pin. Keep your edge as straight as you can.
4. At each corner, fold the seam allowances in opposite directions, overlapping them and then tucking them into your quilt.
5. Use a ladder stitch or slipstitch (see page 68) to close the edge.
6. Optional: quilt another line all the way around the edge of your quilt 6 mm (¼ in) from the edge. This helps to give you a flat, secure edge.

Wadding trimmed
6 mm (¼ in) smaller

Backing trimmed to
match patchwork

↑ *Knife-edge finish (steps 1–2)*

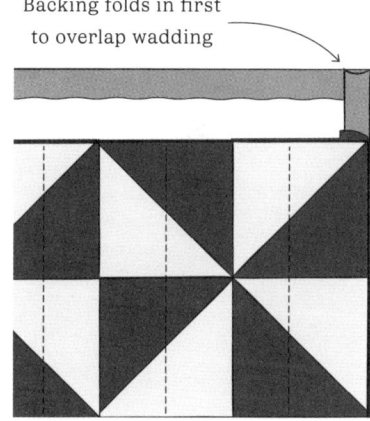

Backing folds in first
to overlap wadding

↑ *Knife-edge finish (step 3)*

↑ *Knife-edge finish (step 6)*

LABELLING YOUR QUILT

I'm a big advocate for signing your work. There are a couple of reasons I feel strongly about it. The first is feminist. Over the centuries, women (who are often the ones making quilts) have been limited in the kinds of art they've been allowed to make. As a result, we've made a lot of 'domestic' art: needlework and quilts and knitted socks. Many of these objects lack the social cachet of an oil painting or bronze statue, and their stories (like women's generally) are told far less frequently. Signing a quilt puts your name into the historical narrative.

The second reason is more sentimental. Think of your quilt in 30 years' time, in the cupboard of your friend or grandchild, or sitting on a shelf in a charity shop. The owner or buyer might pause when they see your name. It might remind them of a fond memory of you, or make a stranger wonder for a moment who you were, where you lived and how this quilt came to be. A little signature can create a big moment of connection.

I'd include your name and the year the quilt was made. You could add a message for the quilt's recipient, and practical information like what the quilt is made of and how to look after it. Sometimes quilts are made collectively, so signing a quilt individually doesn't make sense, but I know you'll think of something to honour the process and the object you've made together.

NOTE

There are many ways to label a quilt.

Most quilt shops have some form of READY-MADE LABEL available, with sections to write your name and the quilt's composition. Use a permanent marker designed for fabrics for extra longevity when filling these in. Online craft marketplaces offer the production of personalised quilt labels that can be sewn in your binding.

You can EMBROIDER into your quilt. If you're new to embroidery, I recommend you do this on a separate patch and then appliqué the patch onto your quilt. This way you have a few chances to practise and make sure you're happy with the result (and that you haven't spelled something incorrectly, which has, unfortunately, happened to me before).

You can purchase a QUILT STAMP or have one made. Paired with permanent textile ink and permanent markers, these can provide a simple and effective way of labelling your quilt.

CUTTING QUILTS APART

There has been a trend in recent years to cut apart vintage quilts and turn them into garments and accessories, and it's caused some debate. Some quilt historians argue that it takes important artefacts and histories out of the narrative. Personally, I'm conflicted. We have too many textiles in the world, we're overproducing more all the time, and some of them are precious works of craft that should be preserved.

My advice is this: think hard about what you're about to cut up before you begin cutting, and make sure you do your best possible work putting it back together again.

What to look for

I recommend looking for quilts that are damaged in some way (stained or torn), have probably lived the best quilty lives possible and are ready for something new.

If you know what you'd like to make, I recommend searching for a quilt to fit that purpose. For example, a couple of Christmas stockings could be made from a smaller quilt than an oversized jacket. Otherwise, feel free to collect like a vintage-quilt magpie. If you have the means and the space, pick up a few that you love and let them dictate what you make.

Fussy cutting

Fussy cutting involves choosing an aspect of a printed or embroidered fabric and positioning it strategically in your block. For example, you might choose to centre a particular flower or bird.

Take the same thoughtful approach as cutting quilts apart. The quilt might have a central appliqué that you want to repurpose for the back of a jacket, or you might want to use the corner edges of the quilt to make the front panels of a jacket (and save yourself some serious time binding in the process). Make a plan and play around with pattern placement until you're happy.

↑ *Fussy cutting*

STITCH AND SEAM GLOSSARY

Here is a quick visual guide to some of the techniques that appear frequently throughout the projects in this book, from useful hand-sewing and embroidery stitches to neat machine finishes.

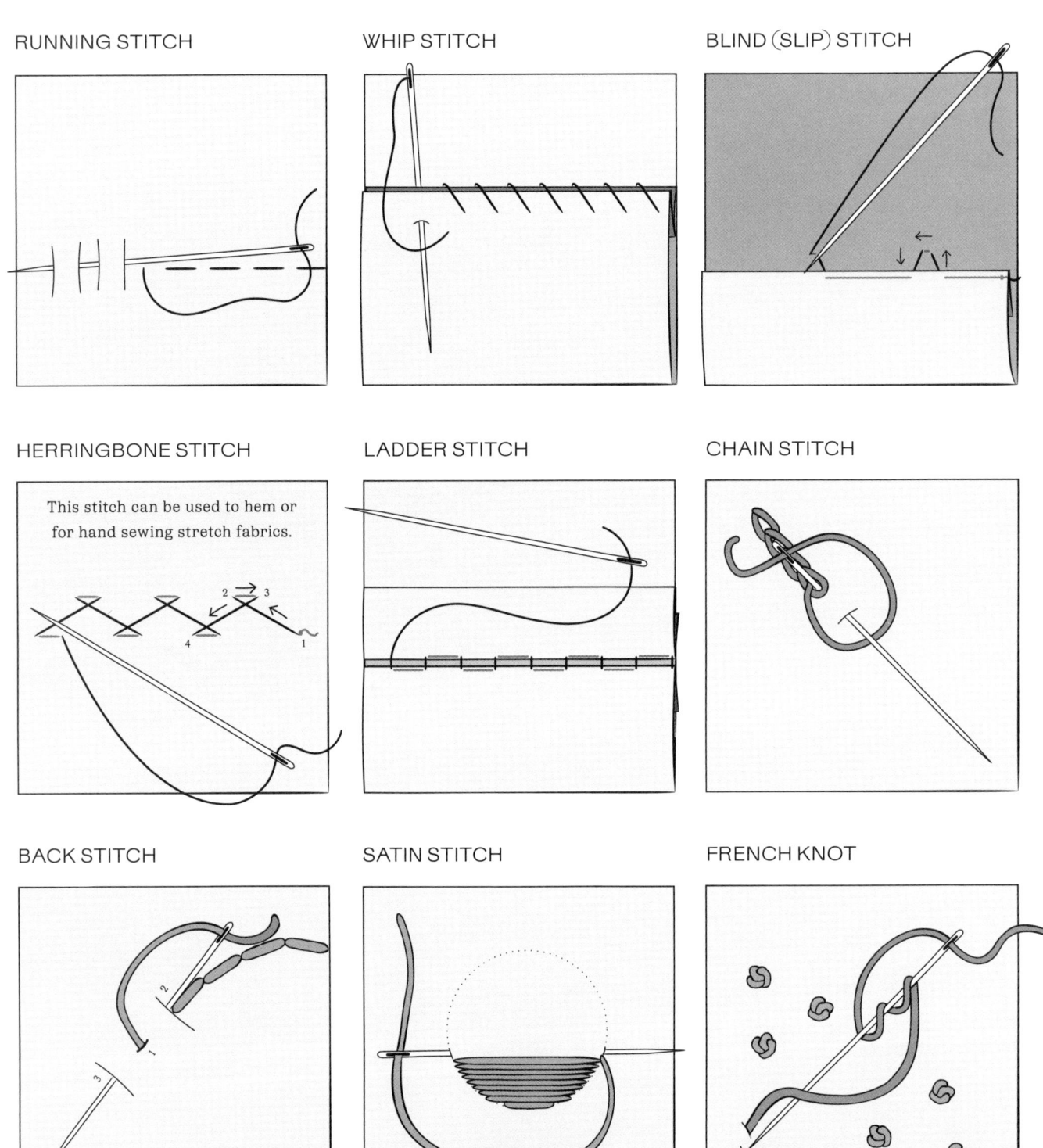

RUNNING STITCH

WHIP STITCH

BLIND (SLIP) STITCH

HERRINGBONE STITCH

This stitch can be used to hem or for hand sewing stretch fabrics.

LADDER STITCH

CHAIN STITCH

BACK STITCH

SATIN STITCH

FRENCH KNOT

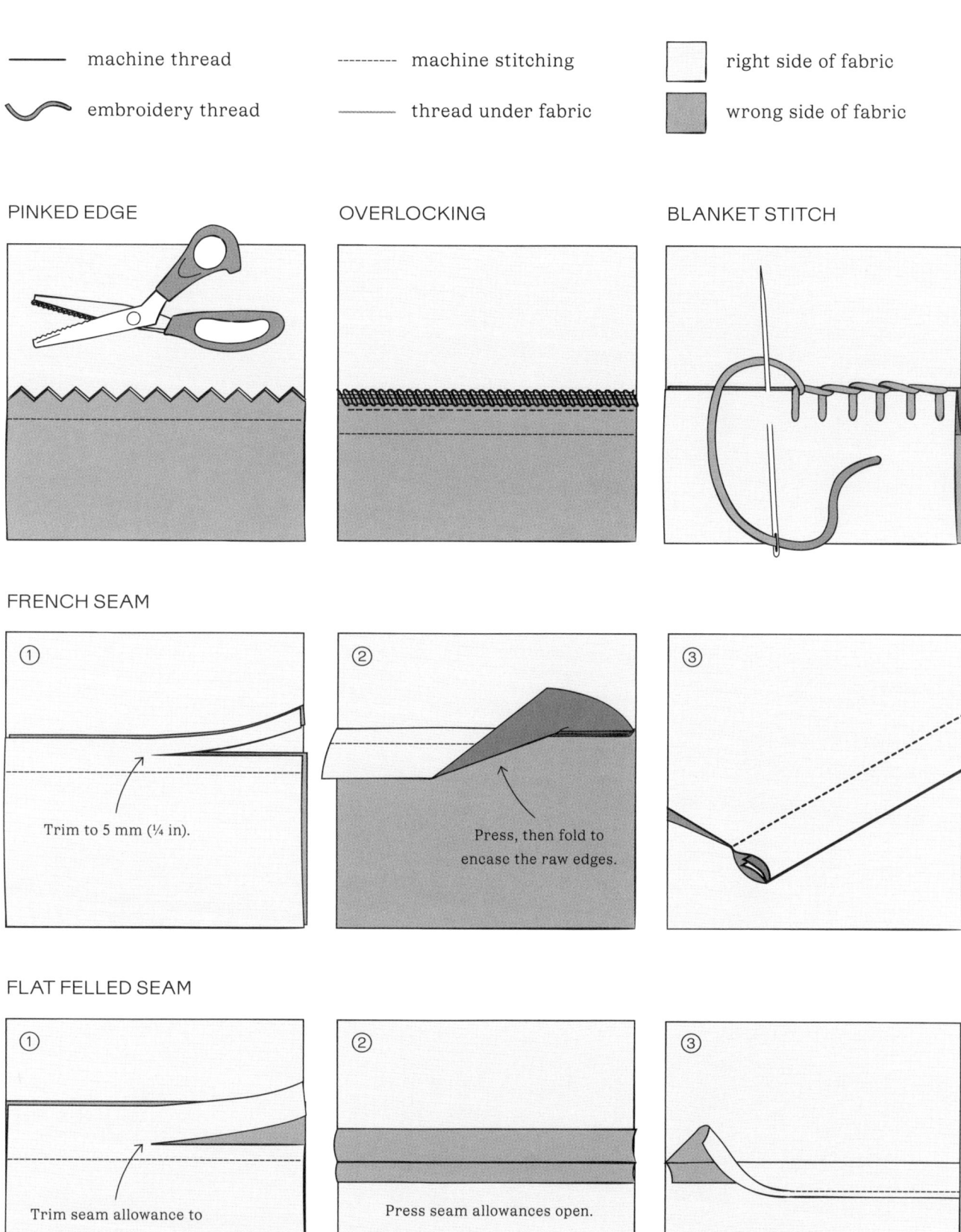

machine thread

embroidery thread

machine stitching

thread under fabric

right side of fabric

wrong side of fabric

PINKED EDGE

OVERLOCKING

BLANKET STITCH

FRENCH SEAM

① Trim to 5 mm (¼ in).

② Press, then fold to encase the raw edges.

③

FLAT FELLED SEAM

① Trim seam allowance to 5 mm (¼ in) on one side.

② Press seam allowances open.

③ Wrap the bigger seam allowance around the smaller. Stitch down.

CHAPTER
FOUR

PROJECTS

BEFORE YOU GET SEWING

There are a few (final) things to mention before you get to it. I've rated each project on a scale of 1 to 5, based on how easy or challenging it is to make, and how long it might take you make it. The Marion drawstring bag (page 161) is simple to put together and takes about an hour from start to finish. It's a 1 on both scales. The toadstool jacket (page 107), by contrast, is a combination of appliqué, embroidery and quilting. The amount of work required means that it scores much higher on both scales. If you're new to sewing, I suggest you make a few of the quick-and-easy projects before attempting something more complicated.

Whichever project you choose, read through all the written instructions for what you're about to make. It's good to know where you are going before you get there.

Finally, gather your equipment. You'll need a BASIC QUILT-MAKING KIT for all the projects in this book, listed on the next page.

HOW TO USE THE PATTERNS IN THIS BOOK

To keep this book to a manageable size, I've scaled down the sewing patterns that have curved pattern pieces. Unless you're keen on making clothes and quilts for Thumbelina, you're going to want to scale them up again. The good news is that you don't have to do this for rectangular pieces (of which there are many in this book). Instead, simply transfer the measurements onto pattern paper or directly onto fabric.

NOTE

The projects in this book are named in a way that's a little haphazard, quite sentimental and more than a little personal. The Ellie quilt, for example, is named for my favourite childhood stuffed toy, while the projects with women's names (Alice, Ellen, Rose, etc.) get their monikers from good friends of mine who have inspired me in one way or the other. Some of the projects felt a little strange with names, so a few (like the patchwork bear and ABC soft blocks) are just called exactly what they are.

Low-tech scaling

The most direct, low-tech way to scale a pattern is by getting some gridded pattern paper. If it's tricky to get a hold of where you are, you can buy an A2 grid paper pad and tape pieces together, or draw your own grid on butcher paper.

You'll need: a ruler, a curved ruler (a Pattern Master is ideal), a pencil, a flat surface and concentration

1. Check the scale! This sounds basic, but it's crucial. Is it 1:4? 1:10? Check! Then check again! And make sure you're working with either centimetres or inches (never both)!
2. Start by marking your corner points first. These are called anchor points, and once you have them in, it becomes easier to work out where everything else goes. It's like doing the edges of a jigsaw puzzle before you fill in the middle.

Higher-tech scaling

You'll need: Adobe Photoshop or another image software, a scanner and a printer (or access to one – you can get big patterns printed in A0 format at copy shops and some fabric shops and libraries)

1. Scan in the gridded pattern. Make sure your page is flat in the scanning bed and there is no distortion, as it can wreak havoc on the pattern's dimensions. Make sure you scan it at 100% original size.
2. Open the scan in image software.
3. Scale it up. The formula I use is: take the size you want the pattern to be (e.g. 25 cm/10 in) and divide it by the actual size of the template (e.g. 12.5 cm/5 in), then multiply that figure by 100. In this example, you end up with the figure 200 – so you enlarge the template by 200 per cent. Check the dimensions after you've completed this step if you're a bit dodgy at maths (like I am).
4. Print it out. You can either do this at home in tiled format and tape them together, or get it printed in A0 format at a copy shop, fabric shop or library.

BASIC QUILT-MAKING KIT

You'll need the following equipment for all the projects in this book.

ESSENTIAL
- > sewing machine
- > sewing machine needles
- > sewing machine thread
- > iron and ironing board
- > quilting ruler
- > marking tool
- > scissors
- > hand-quilting, sashiko or embroidery needles (depending on the quilting thread you choose)
- > quilting thread
- > thimble
- > paper or thin card
- > quick unpick (seam ripper)

VERY USEFUL
- > overlocker (serger)
- > rotary cutter
- > cutting mat (if using a rotary cutter)
- > pinking shears
- > painter's tape
- > curved safety pins
- > spray starch
- > freezer paper (appliqué only)

KIDS AND BABY

ELLEN CRIB QUILT

This is the sort of project that suits beginners perfectly. It's a variation on one of the oldest and most popular quilt patterns and it is, as they say, a classic for a reason.

The Ellen crib quilt is simple and quick to put together. Mine is made of three colours. The pinks are from a madder root–dyed bedsheet, the blue from the hem of a linen skirt, and the yellows were gifted to me by my friend Ellen, a fellow lover of all things craft. Ellen agreed to be my partner in crime when sourcing the materials for this book, ferrying me around charity shops in her little orange car and dunking fabrics into dye pots with me in her back garden.

My 'Ellen' also includes some plain whites (more bedsheets) and the real stars of the show: snipped-up bits of old embroidered tablecloths, napkins and runners, carefully cut to highlight the existing embroidery work (and avoid stains). Using other people's embroidery makes this quilt look much more complicated than it is. You could use a vibrant printed fabric instead, or add in bold colours and textures by stealing from your scrap bag and your fabric stash. For the minimalists out there, simply use two contrasting fabrics to create a classic chequerboard look.

ξ METHOD ξ

Cutting

1. If you are using scraps or fabric samples, cut individual squares. If you're using embroidered fabrics, as I have, take time and care fussy cutting them (see page 67).

2. If you are using shop-bought fabric, cut it into strips and then subdivide the strips into squares afterwards to speed the process along (see page 36). On the row plan, you'll see each coloured or embroidered square is next to a white one. You can speed up your sewing by stitching a coloured or embroidered strip to a white one, pressing, and then cutting two squares at once.

3. You will need the following pieces:

fabric	piece	qty
◯ fabric 1 (white)	11.2 cm (4½ in) square	58
◉ fabric 2 (embroidered/contrast)	11.2 cm (4½ in) square	30
◔ fabric 3	11.2 cm (4½ in) square	13
◯ fabric 4	11.2 cm (4½ in) square	8
● fabric 5	11.2 cm (4½ in) square	8

Sewing

1. Lay out the squares in rows according to the row plan.

2. Stitch the squares in the first row together, then press the seam allowances to the left. Lay the row back down.

3. Stitch the second row together, then press the seam allowances to the right. Lay it below the first row.

4. Continue until you have sewn all 13 rows, alternating the direction you press the seam allowances.

5. Starting with rows 1 and 2, pin and sew the rows together, nesting your seams (see page 34). Double-check your layout before you sew, so if you make a mistake you catch it early.

6. Press the quilt top one final time.

7. Following your preferred method (see Chapter 3), baste your layers together, quilt them up, then trim and bind your quilt. For my hand quilting, I stitched in the ditch (see page 51) as I felt the embroidery was bold enough on its own. I bound my Ellen quilt in creamy white cotton.

FINISHED SIZE

91.5 × 132 cm (36 × 52 in)

9 × 13 blocks, each 10 × 10 cm (4 × 4 in)

FABRICS

Note yardages are estimated for fabric 115 cm (45 in) wide.

> fabric 1 (white): 1 m (1 yd)
> fabric 2 (embroidered/contrast): 1 m (1 yd)
> fabric 3: 0.25 m (¼ yd)
> fabric 4: 0.25 m (¼ yd)
> fabric 5: 0.25 m (¼ yd)
> backing fabric: 1 × 1.4 m (1 × 1½ yd; can be patchworked together)

HABERDASHERY

> wadding: 1 × 1.4 m (1 × 1½ yd)
> binding: 4.8 m (5¼ yd) of straight-grain binding 5 cm (2 in) wide
> thread for piecing
> 2 × 40-m skeins of sashiko thread or 1 × 80-m spool of perle 8 cotton thread for quilting

EQUIPMENT

> basic quilt-making kit (page 73)

NOTES

> A 6-mm (¼-in) seam allowance is included in the pattern.

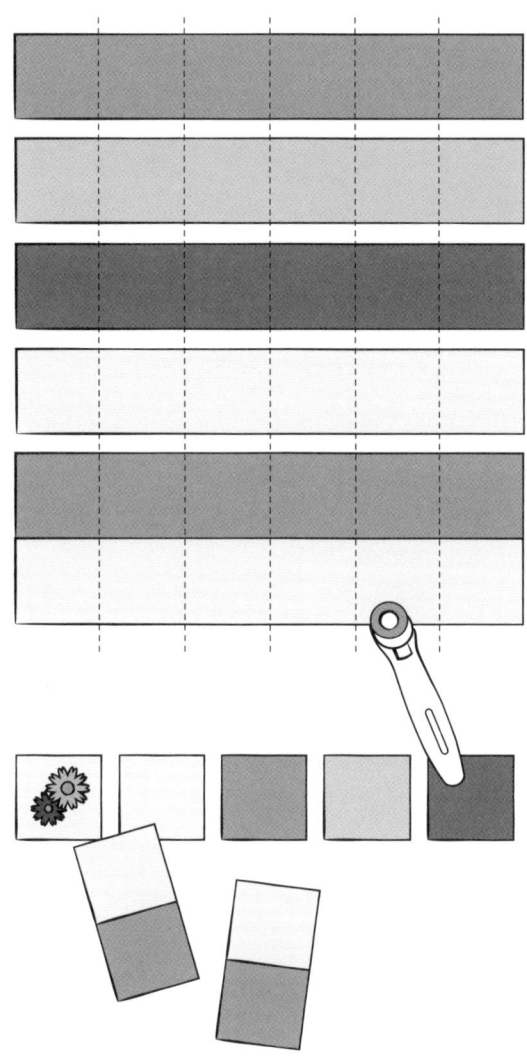

↑ *Cutting (strips and squares)*

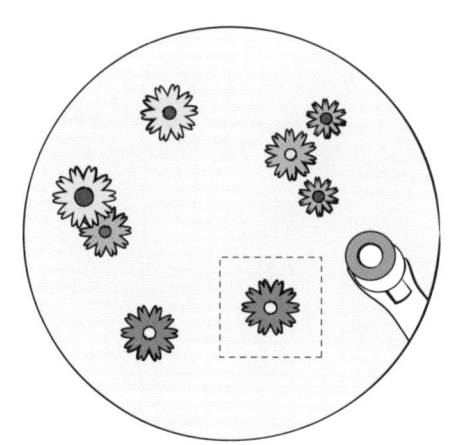

↑ *Cutting (fussy cutting)*

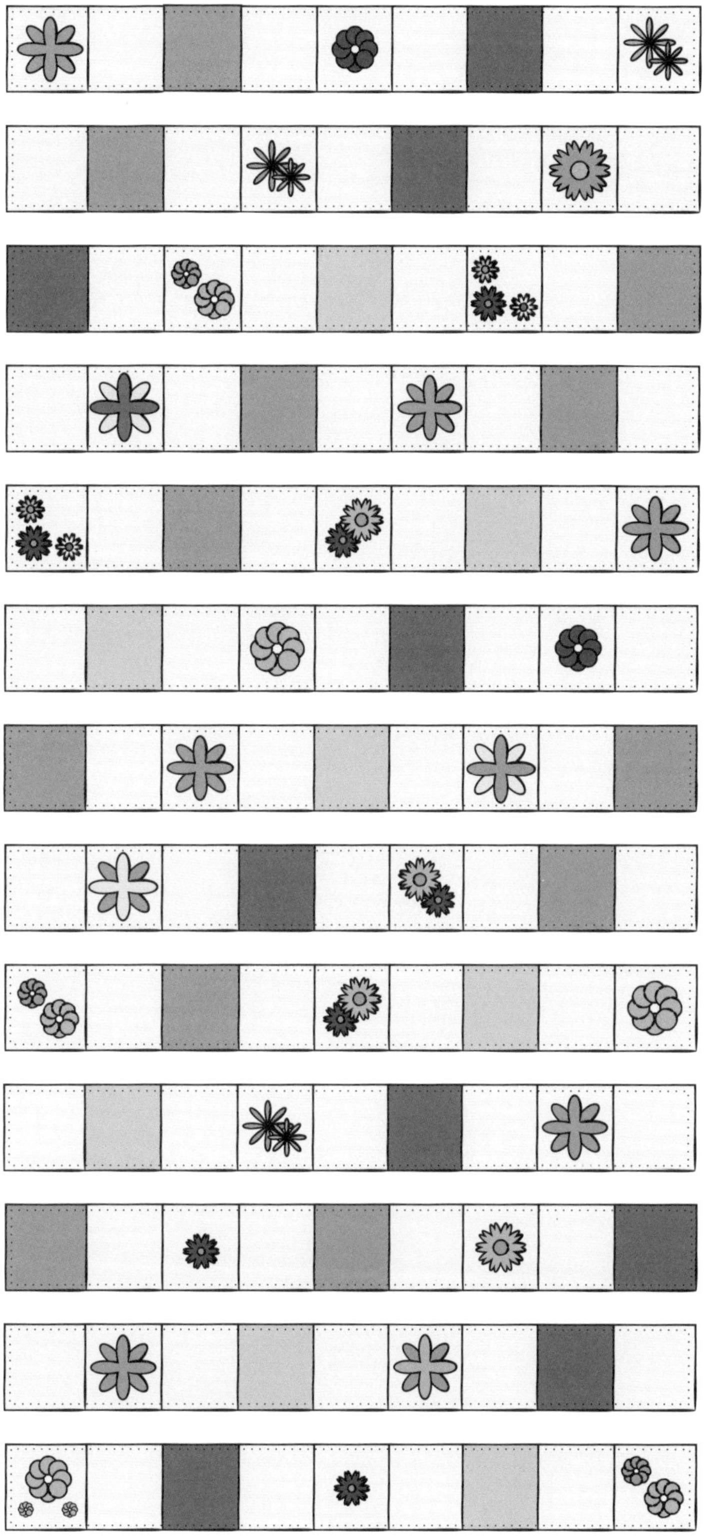

↑ *Row plan (Sewing, step 1; note solid fabrics are in diagonal lines)*

PATCHWORK PARTY HAT

This delightful party hat is inspired by the work of Abbie Shaw, a designer I had the privilege of working with when I first moved to London many years ago. Abbie taught me much of what I know about quilt making and was something of a design mentor. In later years we briefly shared a studio, where I saw some of the brilliant things she was making for her young son (among them an excellent snail costume). This hat is inspired by a rainbow-striped one that she had made, which sat jauntily on our studio shelf.

As well as being very cute, this hat has the added benefit of not requiring much fabric – so little, in fact, that it almost feels like making something from nothing. Each slim triangle measures about 5 × 13 cm (2 × 5 in). You can use just two fabrics, as I've done here, or make up a rainbow hat from colourful scraps.

᎓ METHOD ᴣ

Cutting

1. Scale up (see pages 72–3) the triangle and lining templates on page 207 onto thick paper or card and cut them out.
2. Place the templates on your fabric, pin them down or draw around them, and cut out the pattern pieces. Repeat for the interfacing. You will need the following pieces:

fabric	piece	qty
⬤ fabric 1	triangle template	4
○ fabric 2	triangle template	4
	lining template	1
⊙ interfacing	triangle template	8
	lining template	1

Sewing

1. Using an iron on medium heat, press the interfacing onto the wrong side of the fabric pieces.
2. Trim off the top tips of the triangles to reduce the fabric's bulk as you sew, making sure you've still got enough seam allowance to stitch your pieces together at the top.
3. With right sides together, stitch the long sides of the triangles, alternating colours. Stop before you sew the last edge so that you have a flat piece instead of a cone (this is because it's much easier to iron a flat shape than a conical one). Press the seams open.
4. Sew up the final edge so that you now have a cone shape. Trim the seams at the top of the cone so you get a nice, sharp point. Give the whole thing a good press.
5. Stitch the long edges of the lining, right sides together, so that it is now a cone, too.
6. Cut a chin strap from your elastic (approx. 26 cm/10¼ in, though if you have a little one around, test it out on them to get a perfect fit).
7. With the patchwork cone right side out, line up one end of the elastic with a seam in the patchwork, then line up the other end with the seam on the opposite side of the hat. Pin and sew the elastic in place with a 3-mm (⅛-in) seam allowance.

height 12–13 cm (4¾–5 in)
circumference 37 cm (14½ in)

FABRICS

Note yardages are estimated for fabric 115 cm (45 in) wide.

> fabric 1: 0.25 m (¼ yd)
> fabric 2: 0.5 m (½ yd)

HABERDASHERY

> firm iron-on interfacing: 0.5 m (½ yd)
> thread for piecing
> elastic (or ribbon or string): 0.5 m (½ yd) with a width of 5 mm (¼ in)

EQUIPMENT

> basic quilt-making kit (page 73)

POMPOM (OPTIONAL)

> a piece of cardboard at least 20 × 20 cm (8 × 8 in)
> 2 circular items to trace that are different sizes (a bottle cap and a small jar lid work well, for example). The larger size will be the diameter of your pompom.
> pen or pencil
> paper scissors
> fabric scissors
> yarn (Aran wool makes nice, fluffy pompoms)

Continued overleaf →

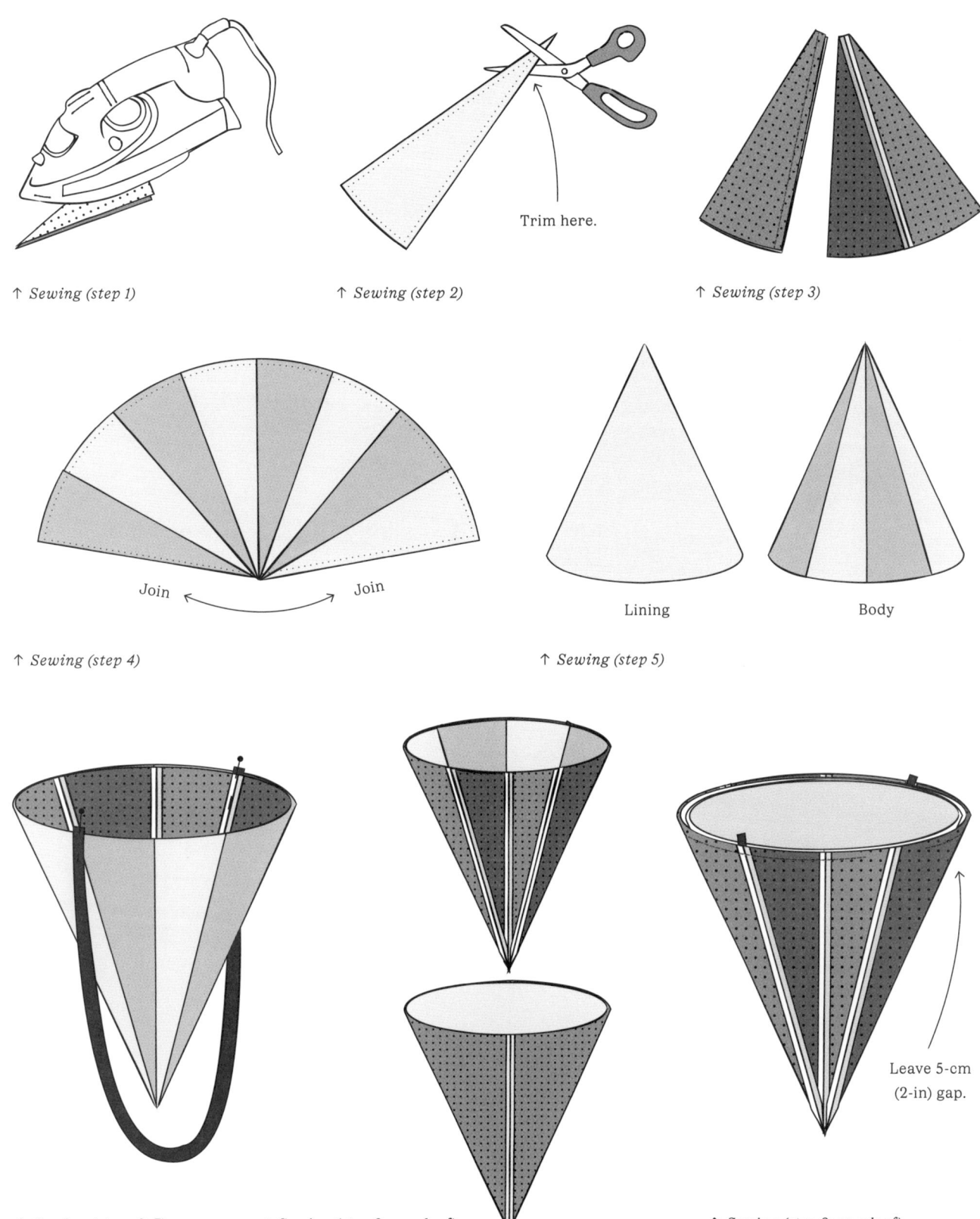

↑ *Sewing (step 1)*

↑ *Sewing (step 2)*

Trim here.

↑ *Sewing (step 3)*

Join ← → Join

↑ *Sewing (step 4)*

Lining

Body

↑ *Sewing (step 5)*

↑ *Sewing (steps 6–7)*

→ *Sewing (step 8; overleaf)*

Leave 5-cm (2-in) gap.

↑ *Sewing (step 9; overleaf)*

8. Place the lining cone inside the patchwork cone, right sides together, lining up the seam in the lining with one of the seams in the patchwork.

9. Stitch the lining and the patchwork layers together around the circumference of the hat, reinforcing the sections where the elastic is secured by stitching over the elastic two or three times. Leave a 5-cm (2-in) gap unstitched.

10. Flip the hat right side out through the gap. Push the lining to the inside. Press.

11. Slipstitch or ladder stitch (see page 68) the gap closed.

FOR THE POMPOM (OPTIONAL)

Setting up

1. Trace around the larger of your two circular items on cardboard.

2. Centre the smaller item inside the circle that you've just drawn and trace around it.

3. Cut out the larger circle. Then cut a slit through to the smaller circle and cut the centre away so you are left with a cardboard ring.

Making and attaching

1. Starting close-ish to the slit (but not so close that the yarn slips off the end), wrap the yarn around the cardboard ring until it is plump and squishy.

2. Use sharp scissors to cut the yarn all the way around the outside edge of the cardboard ring, making sure that you slice through every strand.

3. Cut a 30-cm (12-in) length of yarn. Tie it around the middle of the pompom, close to where the cardboard ring is sitting. Wrap it around 2–3 times and tie off with a double knot. Leave the yarn ends long so that you can use them to attach the pompom to your hat later.

4. Remove the cardboard template.

5. Your pompom might be looking a little wonky. Trim the scraggly ends with your sharp fabric scissors, then gently roll it between your hands to fluff it up.

6. Stitch the pompom to the top of your hat.

NOTES

> A 6-mm (¼-in) seam allowance is included in the pattern.

> Full-size templates are available to download at workingcloth.com

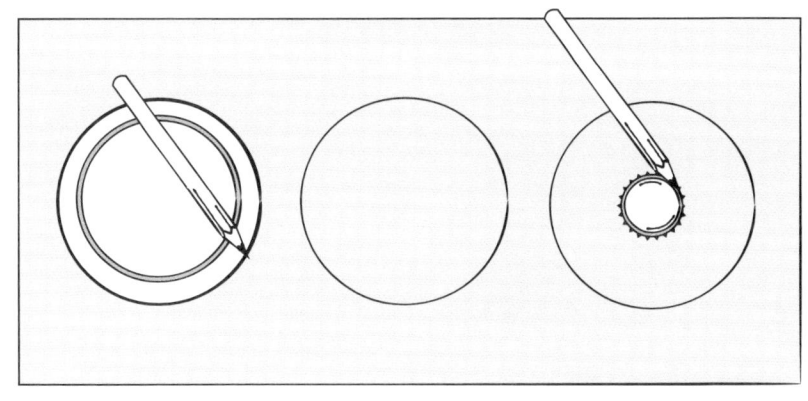

↑ Setting up (steps 1–2)

↑ Setting up (step 3)

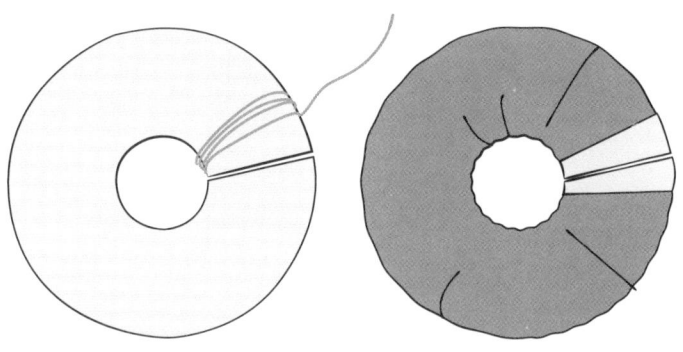

↑ Making and attaching (step 1)

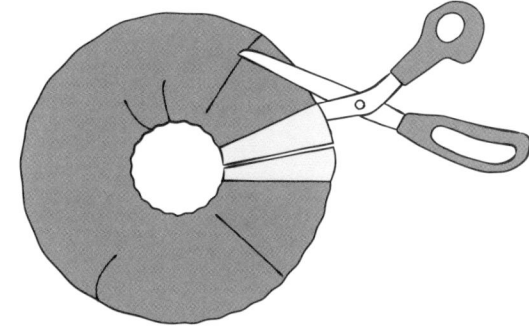

↑ Making and attaching (step 2)

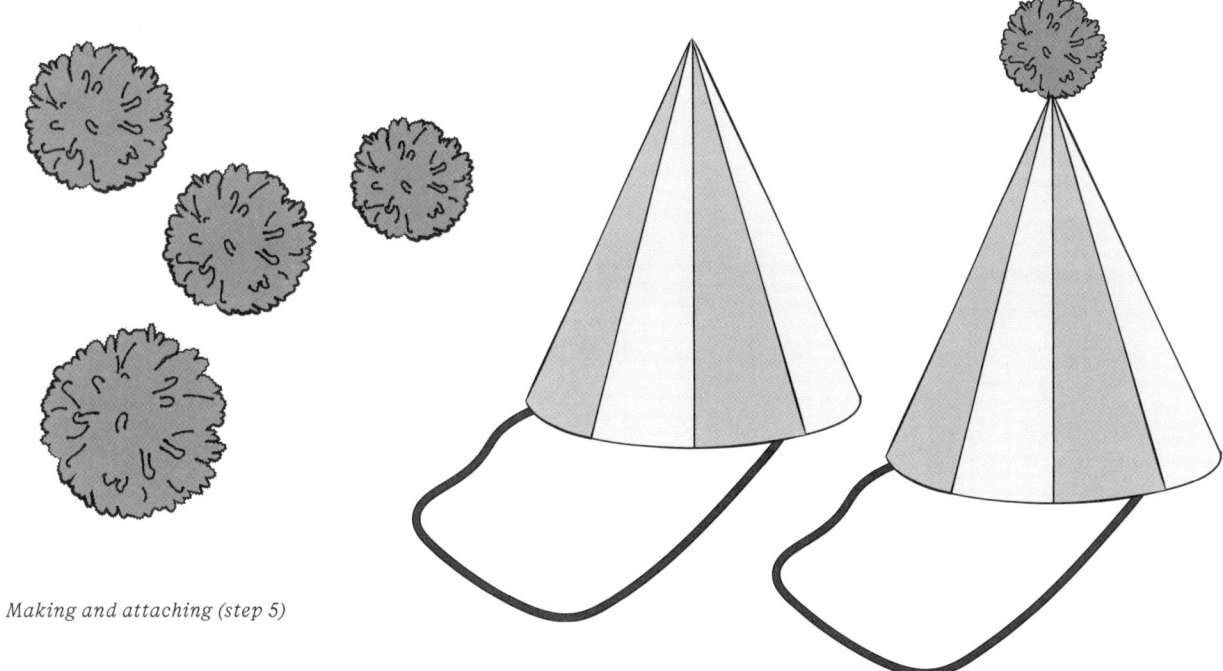

↑ Making and attaching (step 5)

PATCHWORK BEAR

This bear was born from a roll of blue-and-white striped cotton that haunts the back of my closet. I purchased it three Christmases ago, intending to make crisp, striped pyjamas for each of the six people I was celebrating with. I managed one and a half sets before the big day, and the remaining roll has lurked in my fabric stash since. Admittedly, sewing this bear hardly made a dent, but it did make me feel better about my fabric-hoarding tendencies.

I first came across this method for making teddies in Doris King's excellent book, *Make Your Own Teddy Bears*. This pattern has been adapted from King's to be made with finer fabrics instead of faux fur.

I designed this bear, like the party hat, to use your smallest fabric leftovers. You can use thick woven cottons, linen or blends. If you're experienced with a sewing machine, try a napped fabric like faux fur, velvet or corduroy. Mix and match for a colourful teddy or keep the colour palette monochrome. While the bear's small size means that the sewing can feel fiddly, it's also quick and satisfying to put together.

₹ METHOD ₹

Cutting

1. Using your chosen method (see pages 72–3), scale up the templates on pages 204–5 onto thick paper or card, making sure you copy all notes and notches, and then cut them out.
2. Cut out your pattern pieces in your chosen fabric(s), making sure you transfer all the notches onto the fabric.

fabric	*piece*
○ fabric 1	templates A–I
● fabric 2 (contrast)	templates J and K

Prep work and sewing

The easiest way to make the bear is to make all the separate parts first, then stitch them together. Start with the smaller, simpler bits and work your way up.

Making the ears and tail
1. Press the bottom edges of the ears (C) and tail (I) to the wrong side by 6 mm (¼ in). You'll hand sew this edge closed later, and pressing now will make the job easier.
2. With right sides together, pin two of the ear pieces around the outside edge. Stitch along the pinned edges.
3. Repeat for the other ear and the tail.
4. Using sharp scissors, clip little Vs into the curved seam allowances, being careful not to clip into the seams themselves. Turn the ears and tail right side out.
5. Stuff the ears and tail with toy stuffing. I like them stuffed enough to hold a pert, upright shape.
6. Whip stitch or ladder stitch (see page 68) the ear and tail openings closed. Set aside.

Making the face
1. Pin the bear's lower face pieces (A) right sides together, carefully lining up the notches. Stitch together from point *a* to point *b*. Clip Vs into the seam around the curve. Press.

FINISHED SIZE

height from ear to paw: 45 cm (17¾ in)
sitting down: 22.5 cm (9 in)

FABRIC

Note yardages are estimated for fabric 115 cm (45 in) wide.

> fabric 1: 0.5 m (½ yd)
> fabric 2 (contrast) or scraps: 10 × 25 cm (4 × 10 in)

HABERDASHERY

> thread for piecing
> embroidery thread (floss) for the eyes, nose and mouth
> about 200 g (7 oz) toy stuffing (see Tip, overleaf)

EQUIPMENT

> basic quilt-making kit (page 73)

NOTES

> A 6-mm (¼-in) seam allowance is included in the pattern.
> All seam allowances are pressed open unless otherwise noted.
> There are lots of different pieces for this project, so I have specified the number of pattern pieces to cut on each template.
> Full-size templates are available to download at workingcloth.com

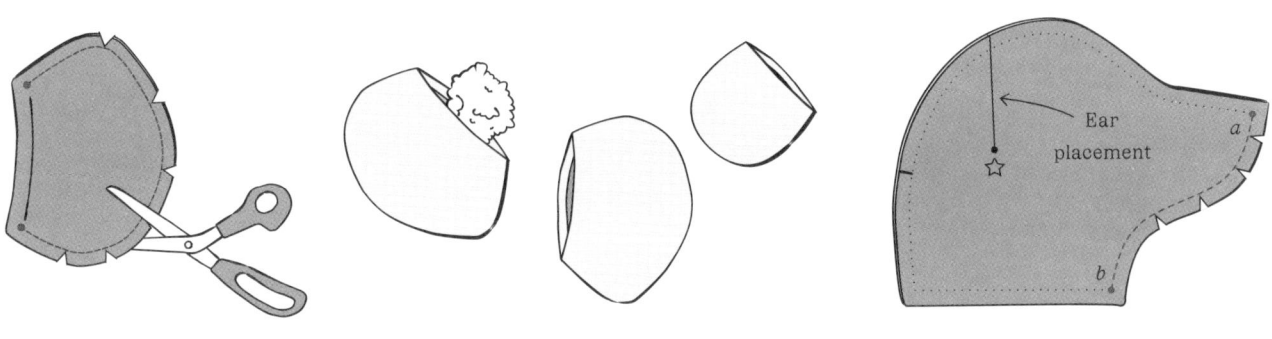

↑ *Making the ears and tail (steps 2–4)*   ↑ *Making the ears and tail (step 5)*   ↑ *Making the face (step 1)*

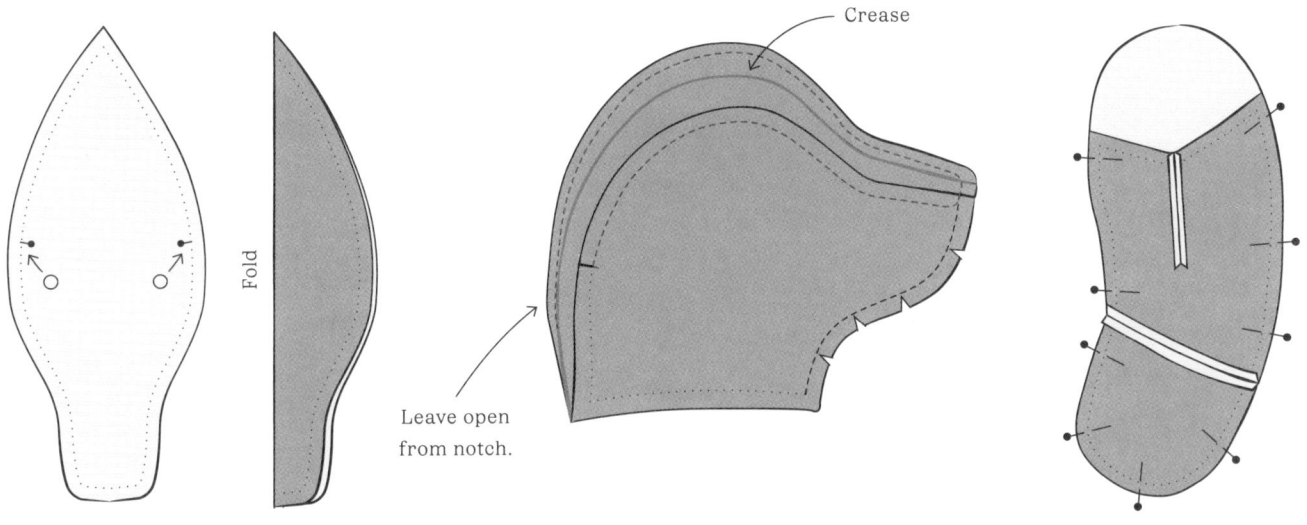

↑ *Making the face (step 2; overleaf)*   ↑ *Making the face (step 3; overleaf)*   ↑ *Making the arms (step 3; overleaf)*

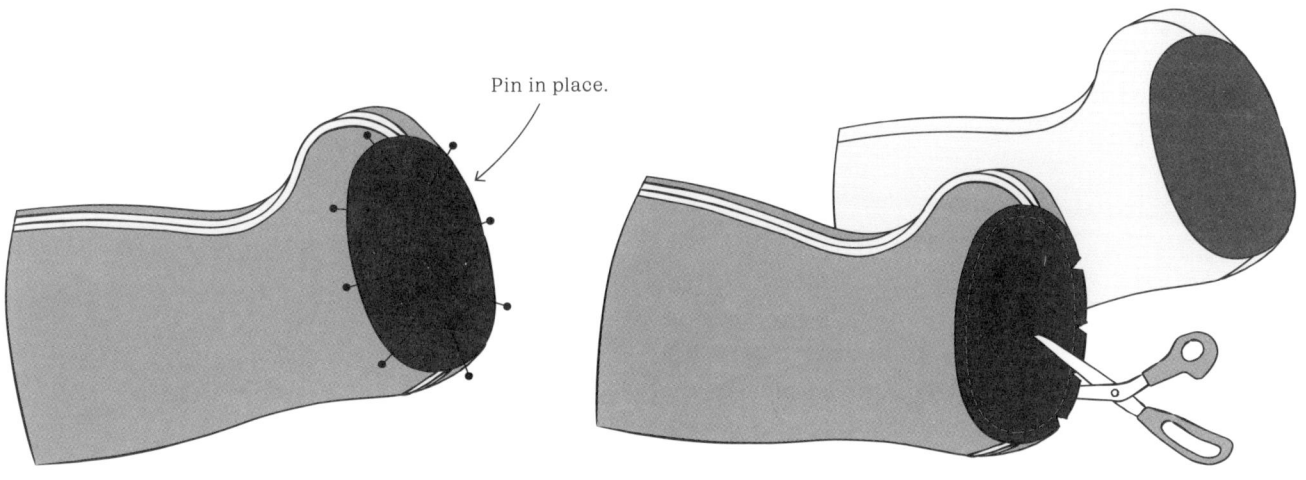

↑ *Making the legs (steps 1–2; overleaf)*   ↑ *Making the legs (steps 2–3; overleaf)*

2. Fold the top face piece (B) in half lengthwise, right sides together. Press the fold so that you have a reference line for the centre of the bear's head.

3. With right sides together, line up the fold with the seam in the lower face piece (this will be the bear's nose). Pin in place, working around either side of the nose and matching the notches as you go. Sew the top face piece on, leaving 5 cm (2 in) open at one of the back seams to make it easier to stuff the bear's head later. Press. Set aside.

Making the arms

1. Sew the inner arm (F) darts, stitching from the outer edges to the dart tips. Press the darts open.

2. With right sides together, sew the straight edge of the hand paw pads (J) to the straight lower edge of the inner arm pieces. Press.

3. Pin the inner and outer arm (G) pieces right sides together around the outside edges, lining up the notches. Stitch.

4. Turn each arm right side out. Set aside.

Making the legs

1. With right sides together, pin and sew together two leg pieces (H) for each leg. Press.

2. Open out the bottom of the leg, so that you have an oval opening. Pin the foot paw pad (K) to this opening, right sides together. Stitch. Clip little Vs into the seam allowances. Repeat for the second leg.

3. Turn the legs right side out. Set aside.

Making the body

1. Sew the darts on the back body pieces (D), stitching from the outer edges to the dart tips. Trim the seam allowances and press the darts open.

2. Pin the two back body pieces right sides together and stitch up to the notch. Leave the upper section of the back open for stuffing – you'll close it by hand later. Press.

3. Pin and sew the front body pieces (E) right sides together.

4. Place the front and back body pieces right sides together, matching the shoulders and side seams. Pin and sew the shoulder seams. Repeat for the side seams.

5. Stitch the back and front crotch seams. Reinforce by backstitching.

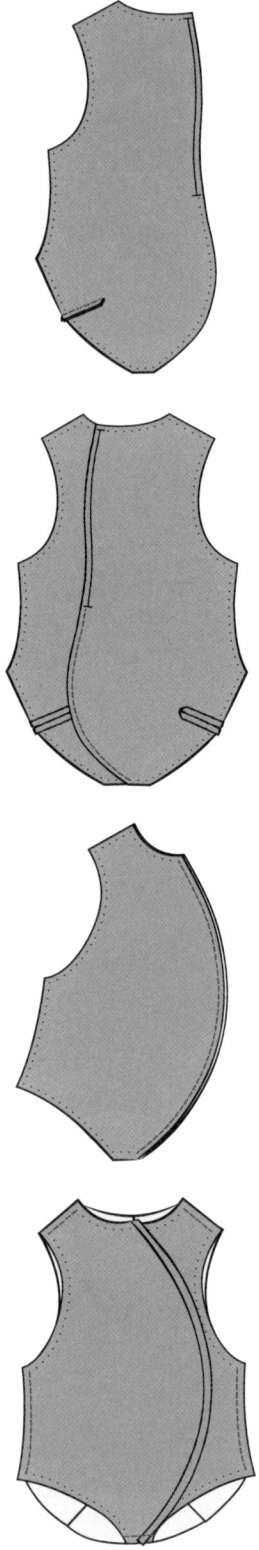

↑ *Making the body (steps 1–5)*

Putting it all together

1. Join the head to the body. The easiest way to do this is flip the body inside out, and put the head (right side out) inside it. Match the centre front seams (the right sides should be together) and pin. Ease to fit around the neck seam, stitch, then push the head out when you've finished.

2. The technique for joining the legs to the body is similar to the head. Start with the body wrong side out, and insert the legs (right side out) into their openings. Pin the legs into the body (right sides together), aligning the side and centre seams. When you do this, make sure the toes are pointing towards the front of the body! Ease to fit while you sew. Push the legs out.

3. Attach the arms in the same way as the head and legs, making sure the paw pads are facing the body and pointing in the right direction. (See illustrations for *Putting the jacket together*, page 113.)

4. Turn your bear right side out and stuff firmly. Ladder stitch or whip stitch (see page 68) the back opening closed.

5. Where each eye is marked, work a French knot (see page 68), using the embroidery thread (floss) of your choice. You could give your bear button eyes or purchase a pair of special teddy-bear eyes instead.

6. Satin stitch (see page 68) the nose.

7. Ladder stitch (see page 68) the ears and tail to the body.

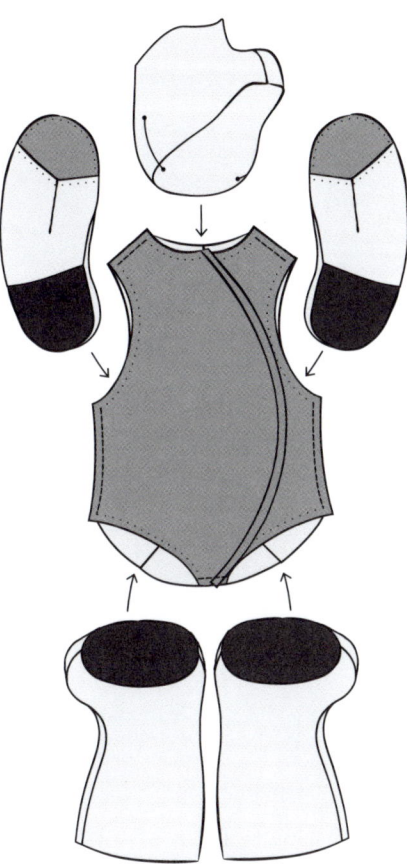

↑ *Putting it all together (steps 1–3)*

TIP

I used wool stuffing, but you can try recycled polyester for an easily washable option. During the course of experimenting for this book, I shredded smaller scraps of fabric and stuffed a few bears with them. While this works, it leads to a slightly lumpier bear. If you're using scrap fabric for stuffing, I recommend using a thicker outer fabric like felt, as it will help cover some of this texture.

PIERROT PLAY MAT

For no particular reason, I think of this as a summer project. My own sewing practice is seasonal. In spring and summer, I make clothes. Come autumn I am more likely to be quilting, like a sleepy bear making a patchwork den for her impending winter hibernation. This play mat feels somewhere in between. It's a comforting addition to any place that children play, whether a summertime garden picnic or a bedroom floor.

I made this out of a white tablecloth (fabric 1). You could also use about half of a single white bedsheet. The pink is from a single bedsheet (fabric 2), though a button-up shirt would also have about the right amount of material, as would about two pillowcases. The candy-coloured stripes I cut from a men's XL striped button-up shirt (fabric 3). The blue (fabric 4) is the fabric that you need the least of; I cut mine from a scrap left over from another sewing project.

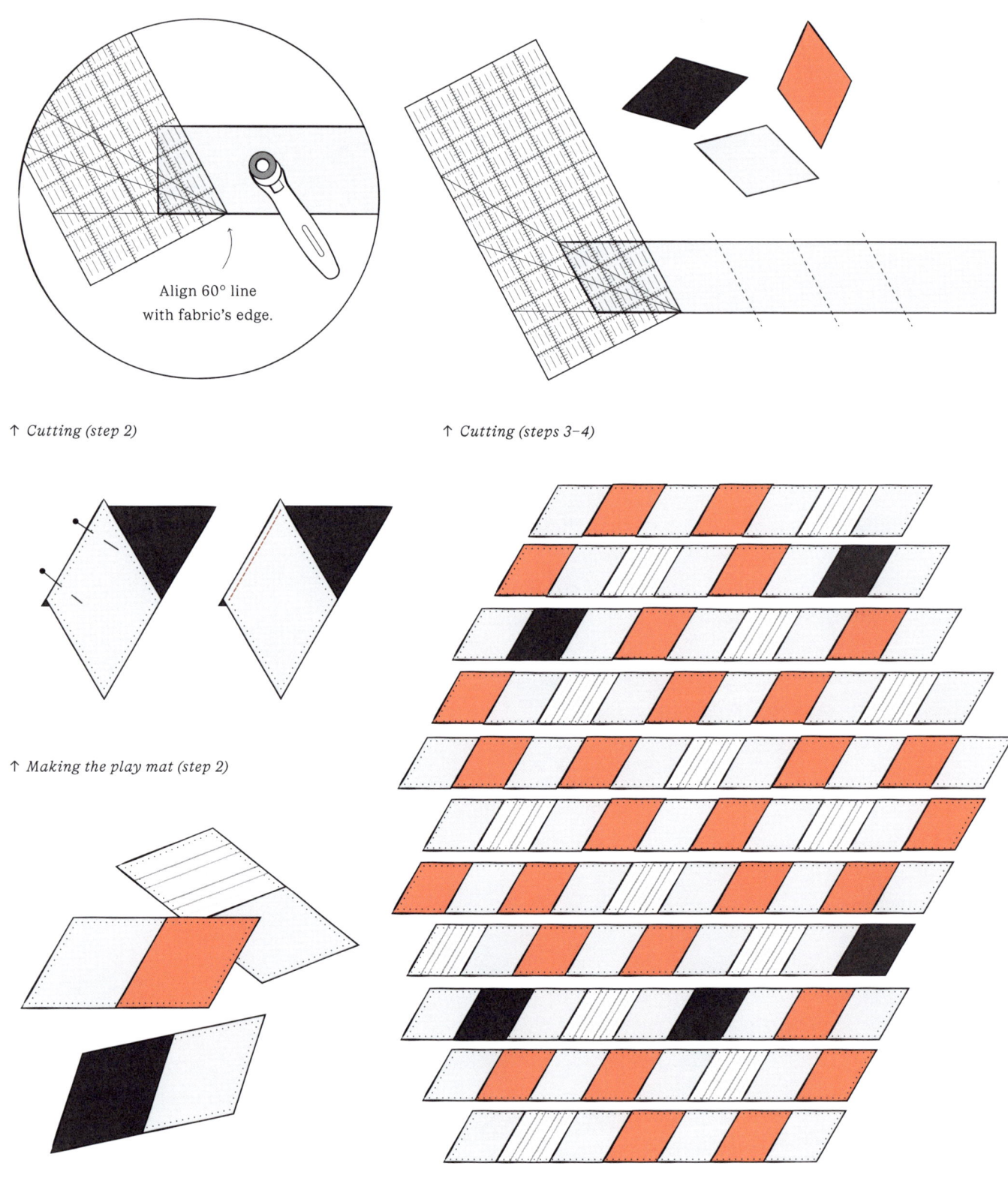

↑ *Cutting (step 2)*

Align 60° line with fabric's edge.

↑ *Cutting (steps 3–4)*

↑ *Making the play mat (step 2)*

↑ *Making the play mat (step 2)*

↑ *Row plan*

⧾ METHOD ⧿

Cutting

1. If you are using fabric that is wider than 30 cm (12 in), cut it into strips 11.2 cm (4½ in) wide.
2. Rotate your quilt ruler so that the 60° lines up with one of the edges of your strip. Trim off the excess fabric in the corner (the little triangle).
3. Shift your ruler along, but don't twist it – keep the 60° mark aligned along the bottom so that the 11.2 cm (4½ in) line of the ruler aligns with the short edge you've just cut. Slice along the other side of your ruler to make a diamond.
4. Continue cutting along the strip (see page 36) until you've made all your diamonds (see table below).

fabric	piece	qty
○ fabric 1	diamond with 11.2 cm (4½ in) edges	51
● fabric 2	diamond with 11.2 cm (4½ in) edges	28
◐ fabric 3	diamond with 11.2 cm (4½ in) edges	14
● fabric 4	diamond with 11.2 cm (4½ in) edges	5

Making the play mat

1. Lay out the diamonds in rows, following the row plan.
2. Pin and stitch the diamonds in the first row together, working methodically. Press the seam allowances to the left, then lay the row back down.
3. Pin and stitch the diamonds in the second row together. Press the seam allowances to the right, then lay it below the first row.
4. Continue in this way, alternating the direction in which you press the seams, until you have sewn all 11 rows.
5. Double-check your layout before you sew, so that if you make a mistake you catch it early. Starting with rows 1 and 2, pin and sew the rows together, nesting your seams (see page 34).
6. Press the quilt top.

FINISHED SIZE

105 cm (41½ in) in diameter

FABRIC

Note yardages are estimated for fabric 115 cm (45 in) wide.

> fabric 1: 0.75 m (¾ yd)
> fabric 2: 0.5 m (½ yd)
> fabric 3: 0.25 m (¼ yd)
> fabric 4: 0.25 m (¼ yd)
> backing fabric: 110 × 110 cm (43 × 43 in; can be patchworked together)

HABERDASHERY

> wadding: 110 × 110 cm (43 × 43 in)
> binding: 3.4 m (3¾ yd) of bias binding 10 cm (4 in) wide
> thread for piecing
> 2 × 40-m skeins of sashiko thread or 1 × 80-m spool of perle 8 cotton thread for quilting

EQUIPMENT

> basic quilt-making kit (page 73)

NOTES

> A 6-mm (¼-in) seam allowance is included in the pattern.
> If you are using small scraps, make yourself an 11.2 × 11.2 cm (4½ × 4½ in) diamond template out of card first and cut each diamond individually.

Making the circle template

1. Making your circle template is almost exactly like making the paper snowflakes every Canadian child whips up at school each winter. Only less complicated. If they can do it, so can you. Fold your paper or fabric in half, and then in half again. If you're using fabric, press it after you've folded it to set the creases.
2. Using your quilting ruler and a pencil, mark 24.7 cm (9¾ in) from the centre point of the folded square along the folded side and bottom edges, then make four more marks in between, measuring from the centre point each time.
3. Use your pencil (and a curved ruler if you have one) to smooth out this curve. If you don't have a curved ruler, regress to your early school days: tie a pencil to a piece of string, pin one end of the string to the centre point of your template and swing the pencil over the marks to draw the quarter circle.
4. Cut out the paper or fabric and unfold it. Congratulations, you've made your play mat template!
5. On a flat surface, lay your template on your play mat top. Pin or weigh it down (you can use whatever you've got around the house: dinner plates, books, etc. – no need to get fancy here) to keep it from shifting around.
6. Draw around the template, then cut the patchwork into a circle.
7. Repeat the process above for your backing fabric and wadding (batting). Remember to add 2 cm (¾ in) or so along the edge of each so that they are bigger than your play mat top.

Quilting and finishing up

Following your preferred method (see Chapter 3), baste your layers together, quilt them up, and then trim and bind your play mat. I stitched in the ditch (see page 51) along the patchwork, tracing out the diamonds. The quilt's curved edge means that you'll have to use bias binding to get a smooth finish. I made my own extra-wide bias binding as I wanted a more dramatic edge. To do the same, cut strips 7.5 cm (3 in) wide on the bias and follow the instructions for making and applying bias binding on pages 61–4.

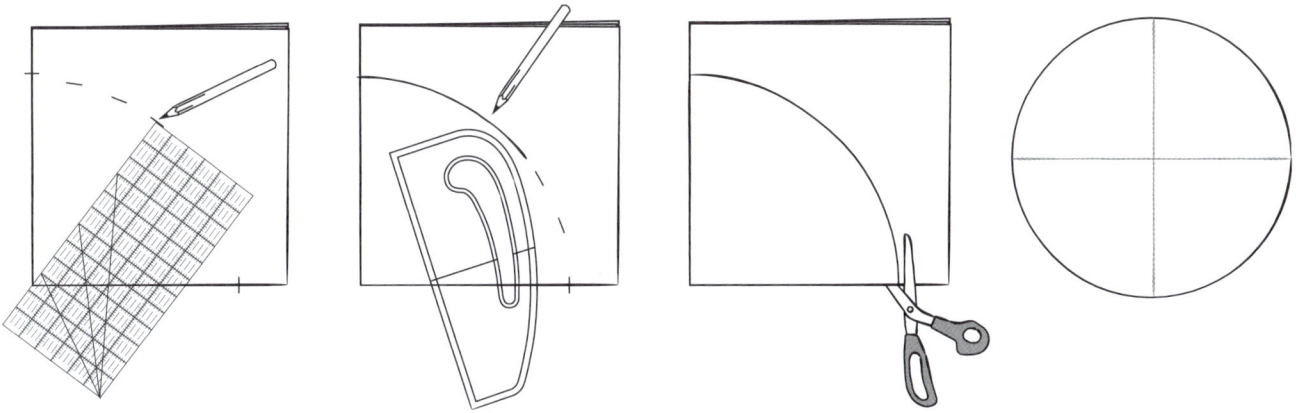

↑ *Making the circle template (steps 2–4)*

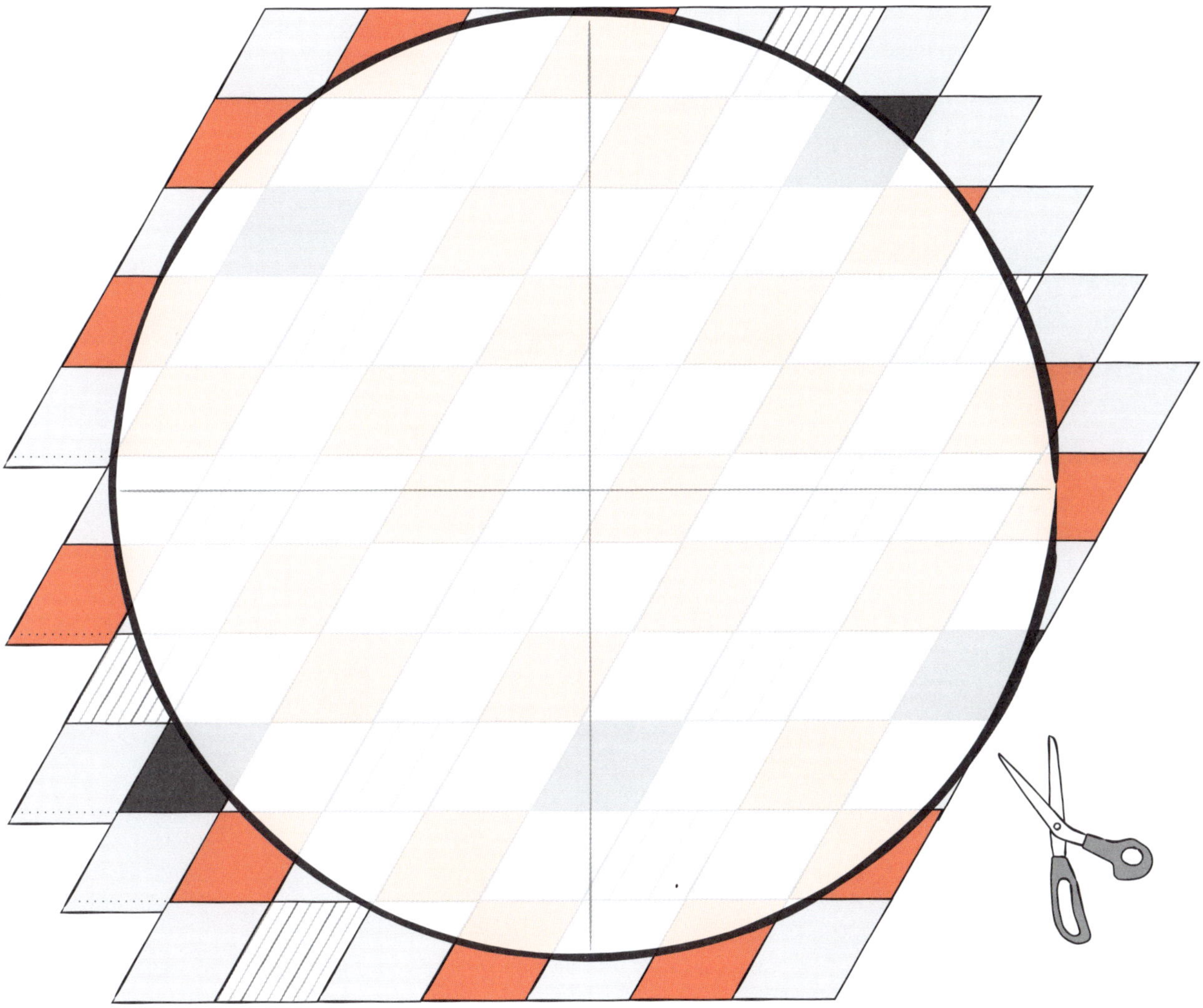

↑ *Making the circle template (steps 5–6)*

ABC SOFT BLOCKS

In my experience, blocks are one of those rare things that satisfy children and adults alike. To the young and old, blocks seem like an invitation to play. These ones are oversized. They have a good squish to them and (unlike their wooden counterparts) are unlikely to do any lasting damage in the event that a toddler decides they are better used as projectiles than building blocks.

I made mine from an old book of linen fabric samples, split into their colour groups (a red one, a green one, etc.). They'd be fun made out of craft felt, which is thick enough for you to be able to skip the interfacing step. You could make rainbow blocks or stick to a single colour.

I've named these blocks after the ABCs I've sewn onto them, but don't feel you have to stick to alphabet appliqué. You could try simple shapes, animals or plants instead. Draw or trace outlines onto paper and use them as templates instead of the ones provided in this book. Or forgo the appliqué altogether and use textured fabrics to make satisfying, sensory blocks.

ϛ METHOD ϡ

Cutting

For each block, trace a letter or number template (page 203) onto thick paper or card and then cut it out. Place each template on your fabric of choice and cut it out.

Making each block

1. Apply interfacing to the wrong side of each fabric square.
2. Appliqué (see pages 43–5) the letters or numbers onto your chosen squares.
3. Once you are happy with how your appliqué looks, arrange the squares in a T shape. Pin and stitch the squares right sides together to complete the T. Press the seams open.
4. Stitch the remaining seams, leaving a 4-cm (1½-in) hole in one seam so that you can flip the block right side out.
5. Press the seams open and snip off the corner points to reduce bulk.
6. Flip the block right side out. Using a point turner (if you don't have one, a chopstick or a mechanical pencil with no lead makes a pretty good substitute), make your corner points sharp and neat.
7. Generously stuff the block with toy stuffing.
8. Slipstitch or ladder stitch (see page 68) the hole closed. Press the outside of the block to give it a crisp final shape.

FINISHED SIZE

10 × 10 × 10 cm (4 × 4 × 4 in)

FABRIC

Note yardages are estimated for fabric 115 cm (45 in) wide.

> fabric for blocks: six 12 cm (4¾ in) squares for each block
> fabric for lettering or numbering (one of the letters A, B or C, or numbers 1, 2 or 3): 12 cm (4¾ in) square for each letter or number

HABERDASHERY

> firm iron-on interfacing: six 12 cm (4¾ in) squares for each block, plus enough for the letters or numbers (total 0.25 m/¼ yd)
> thread for piecing and appliqué
> approx. 100 g (3½ oz) toy stuffing per block

EQUIPMENT

> basic quilt-making kit (page 73)
> point turner (optional)

NOTES

> A 1-cm (⅜-in) seam allowance is included in the pattern.
> If you're making the blocks out of six different colours, you'll need 12 × 12 cm (4¾ × 4¾ in) of each. You could also make them out of 0.25 m (¼ yd) of a single colour.

↑ *Making each block (step 1)*

↑ *Making each block (step 2)*

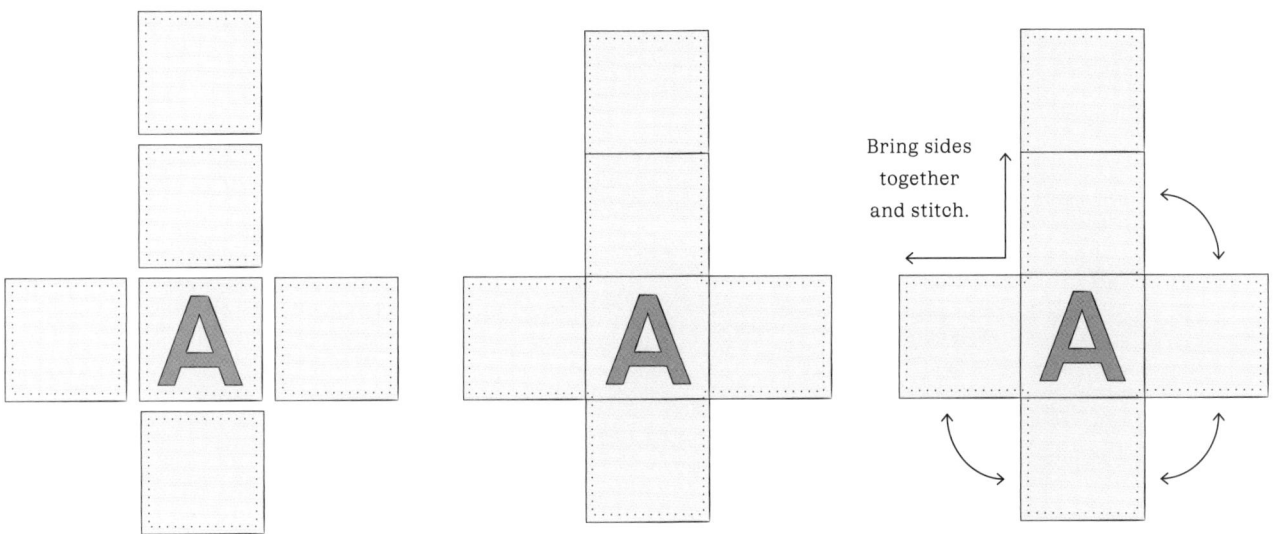

↑ *Making each block (step 3)*

Bring sides together and stitch.

↑ *Making each block (step 4)*

Trim corner.

↑ *Making each block (step 5)*

↑ *Making each block (steps 7–8)*

ELLIE QUILT

This quilt is an homage to the purple nylon elephant that sat loyally on the end of my bed from the age of two to the age of seventeen. The simple, round shapes make it suitable for beginners who'd like to take a crack at appliqué. It's fairly quick (for a hand-sewn quilt), and you could take the idea and swap out the elephant for any animal that you'd like. I made the elephant from one of my friend Ellen's bedsheets that we indigo-dyed on a cloudy Saturday. To make the background, I cut up two XL button-up shirts and stitched them together into a flat panel.

⁊ METHOD ⁊

Making the pattern

Scale up the appliqué templates on page 204 onto paper or card using your chosen method (see pages 72–3).

Cutting

Follow the table below to cut out all the pieces you will need. For the elephant, place the templates on the appropriate colour of fabric and carefully cut out your appliqué pieces.

fabric	piece	qty
○ fabric 1 (background)	120 × 120 cm (47¼ × 47¼ in)	1
◔ fabric 2	elephant body template	1
◕ fabric 3	elephant ear template	1
● fabric 4	elephant eye template	1

Sewing

1. If your background fabric (fabric 1) is one piece, press it. If you are making up the background piece from multiple pieces of fabric, then do that patchwork now and press the quilt top smooth.
2. Position the appliqué pieces on your background fabric and stitch in place, following the instructions for machine appliqué (pages 43–4) or needle-turned appliqué (page 45).
3. Press the quilt top.
4. Following your preferred method (see Chapter 3), baste your layers together, quilt them up, and then trim and bind your quilt. I quilted this one with lines spaced 5 cm (2 in) apart.

FINISHED SIZE

120 × 120 cm (47¼ × 47¼ in)

FABRIC

Note yardages are estimated for fabric 115 cm (45 in) wide.

> fabric 1 (background): 1.5 m (1¾ yd; can be patchworked together)
> fabric 2: 0.75 m (¾ yd)
> fabric 3: 0.25 m (¼ yd)
> fabric 4: 10 × 10 cm (4 × 4 in)
> backing fabric: 130 × 130 cm (51 × 51 in; can be patchworked together)

HABERDASHERY

> wadding: 130 × 130 cm (51 × 51 in)
> binding: 5.1 m (5⅝ yd) straight-grain binding 5 cm (2 in) wide
> thread for piecing
> 2 × 40-m skeins of sashiko thread or 1 × 80-m spool of perle 8 cotton thread for quilting

EQUIPMENT

> basic quilt-making kit (page 73)

NOTES

> A 6-mm (¼-in) seam allowance is included in the pattern. Remember to add 3 mm (⅛ in) to each of the appliqué pieces if you're going to do needle-turned appliqué.
> Full-size templates are available to download at workingcloth.com

Elephant eye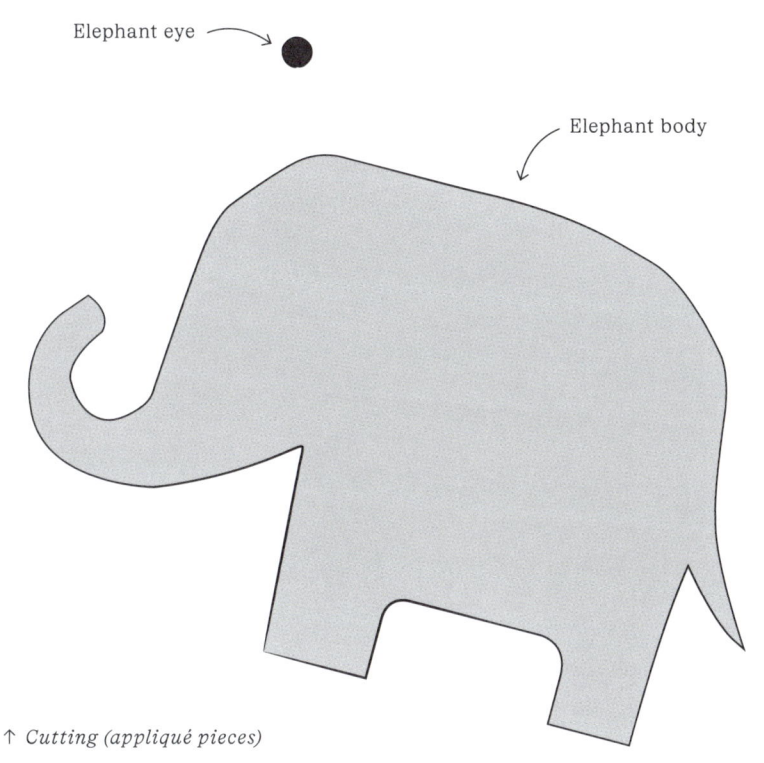

Elephant body

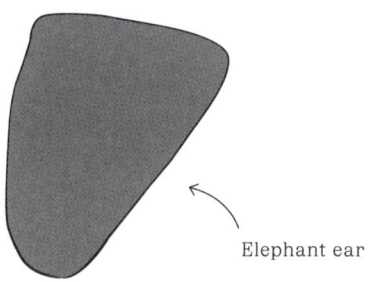

Elephant ear

↑ *Cutting (appliqué pieces)*

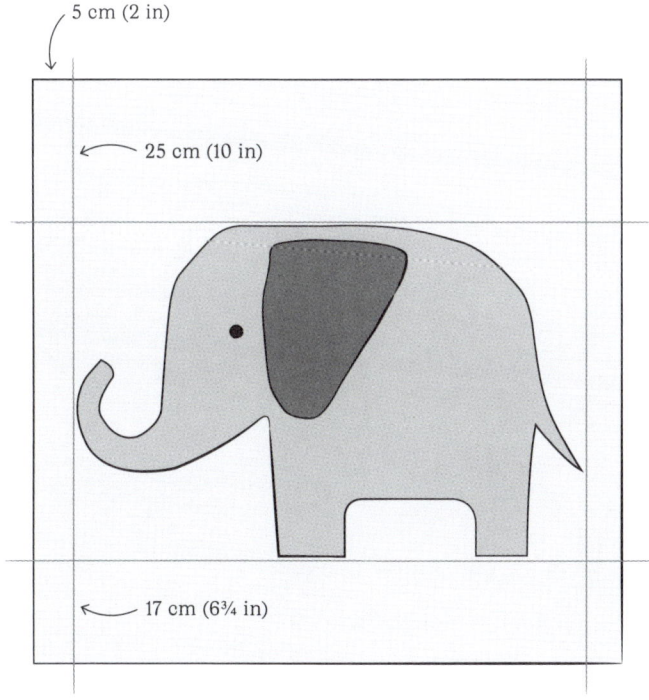

5 cm (2 in)

25 cm (10 in)

17 cm (6¾ in)

↑ *Sewing (step 2)*

↑ *Sewing (step 4)*

TOADSTOOL JACKET

The mushrooms decorating this jacket are fly agaric, a species with a rich folkloric history that often makes its home in shady corners of birch forests. Its bright-red cap with little white spots is both beautiful and instantly recognisable, factors that mean it pops up everywhere from Super Mario Kart to *Alice's Adventures in Wonderland*. I thought I would join the fray of fungi celebration, too.

This jacket is the most complex project in the children's section of the book, though I think it's well worth the effort. If you disagree, simplify the process by appliquéing the toadstools onto an existing quilted jacket, a pillowcase or a quilt. Likewise, if toadstools aren't your thing, you could make the jacket plain or create your own appliqué design.

The beige-y background is cut from a gored linen skirt from a charity shop and a linen towel that had seen better days. Somehow, despite their different origins, the fabrics were exactly the same colour. The cherry red came from the hem of a too-short dress that I cut up for the Holly quilt (page 123). The white spots came from my scrap basket. For the lining I used a men's size L chequered shirt, salvaged from a charity shop.

⧙ METHOD ⧘

Before you begin

When I make quilted clothes, I cut, baste and quilt rectangles that are bigger than I need for the pattern because it gives me a little breathing room if I don't align my layers perfectly. After I've quilted everything up, I position the pattern pieces then cut everything out accurately. So, to begin with, set aside your pattern pieces except the collar and pockets.

Getting started

1. Scale up (see pages 72–3) the appliqué templates on page 206 onto paper or thin card. Remember to add a 3-mm (⅛-in) seam allowance all around each piece if you're doing needle-turned appliqué (see page 45). Set aside.
2. Scale up the jacket pattern templates on page 206 onto paper or card, making sure you copy all notes and notches.
3. Cut out the collar (fabric 2) and pocket pieces (fabric 1), as well as the wadding (batting) for the collar piece. Cut the collar wadding piece 1 cm (⅜ in) smaller all around than the fabric pieces.
4. Cut out the remaining rectangles in your fabric 1, lining fabric and wadding, as outlined in the chart below.

fabric	piece	qty
○ fabric 1	front: 26 × 46 cm (10¼ × 18 in)	2
	back: 46 × 46 cm (18 × 18 in)	1
	sleeve: 38 × 42 cm (15 × 16½ in)	2
	lower pocket	2
	upper pocket	1
● fabric 2	collar	2
◐ lining	front: 29 × 49 cm (11 × 19 in)	2
	back: 49 × 49 cm (19 × 19 in)	1
	sleeve: 41 × 45 cm (16 × 17¾ in)	2
○ wadding	collar	1
	front: 29 × 49 cm (11½ × 19 in)	2
	back: 49 × 49 cm (19 × 19 in)	1
	sleeve: 41 × 45 cm (16 × 17¾ in)	2

FINISHED SIZE

For a child around age four / approximate height of 104 cm (41 in).
centre back: 44.5 cm (17½ in)
sleeve length: 37 cm (14½ in)

FABRIC

Note yardages are estimated for fabric 115 cm (45 in) wide.

> fabric 1: 1 m (1 yd)
> fabric 2: 0.5 m (½ yd)
> fabric 3: 0.25 m (¼ yd)
> fabric 4: 0.25 m (¼ yd)
> lining: 1 m (1 yd)

HABERDASHERY

> wadding: 1 m (1 yd)
> binding: 8 m (8¾ yards) of bias binding 1.2 cm (½ in) wide. If you have an overlocker (serger), you could overlock the internal seams instead of binding them.
> thread for piecing
> four 12-mm (½-in) snaps or buttons
> 2 × 40-m skeins of sashiko thread or 1 × 80-m spool of DMC perle 8 cotton for quilting
> white embroidery thread (floss) for the mushroom spots (optional; if you're using white sashiko thread you can use this instead)
> interfacing (optional; if using machine appliqué)

Continued overleaf →

Cutting out the appliqué pieces

Use your templates to cut out your appliqué pieces using the chart below.

fabric	piece	qty
● fabric 2	caps A and B	1 ea
● fabric 3	under cap C	1
○ fabric 4	stems D and E	1 ea
	circle F	6
	circle G	10

Marking out the pattern pieces

Lay your pattern pieces on their corresponding fabric rectangles, making sure that they are right in the middle. Secure the pattern pieces in place with pins or weights, then draw around them. You will use these traced lines later as a guide to position your appliqué and quilting lines.

Prepping the pockets

1. Press the bottom and side edges of the pockets to the wrong side, following the notches on the pattern.
2. Fold the tops of the pockets down to the first notch and press. Fold again, this time to the second notch, and press. (See illustrations overleaf.)
3. Set your sewing machine stitch length to 2.5 mm. Topstitch (see page 112) the fold down. Set aside.

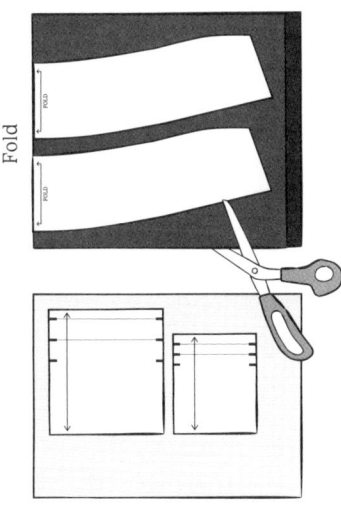

↑ *Getting started (step 3)*

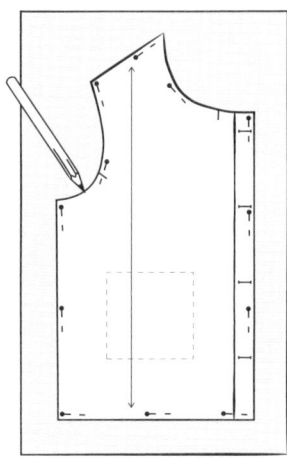

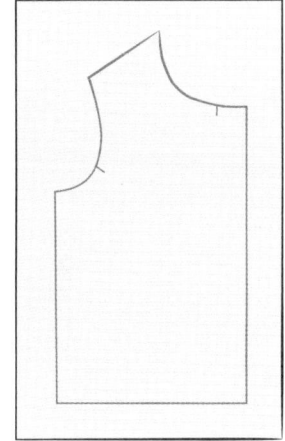

↑ *Marking out the pattern pieces*

Appliqué

1. Centre the mushroom appliqué on your back panel and secure in place by pin or stitch basting (see page 50).
2. Using your preferred method (see pages 43–5), appliqué the mushrooms onto the jacket back rectangle.
3. Next, appliqué the smaller mushroom design onto the upper pocket pattern piece.
4. The dots on the upper pocket mushroom are too small to appliqué. Instead, embroider French knots (see page 68) to create the tiny white spots on the smaller mushroom's cap.

Quilting

1. Baste (see page 50) each rectangle to its wadding and backing.
2. Next, mark and quilt your rectangles. I started on the jacket back, where I quilted around the mushroom, and then quilted straight, vertical lines 5 cm (2 in) apart over the rest of the jacket back and the remaining pieces.
3. Align your pattern pieces with the outlines that you traced onto your fabric rectangles. Pin. Cut them out, transferring all the notches and pocket placement.
4. Before you take out your basting, secure the edges of the pattern pieces so they're easier to work with.

   a. If you have an overlocker (serger), overlock the edges.
   b. If you don't have an overlocker, edge stitch (see page 112) each piece. Set your stitch length to 4 mm, and put a walking foot on your machine (if you don't have one, use a Teflon or invisible zipper foot for this step, as they drag the fabric less than a straight presser foot). Stitch 6 mm (¼ in) away from the edge of the fabric.

> basic quilt-making kit (page 73)
> overlocker (serger; optional)

NOTES

> A 1.2-cm (½-in) seam allowance is included in the pattern unless otherwise noted.
> Full-size templates are available to download at workingcloth.com

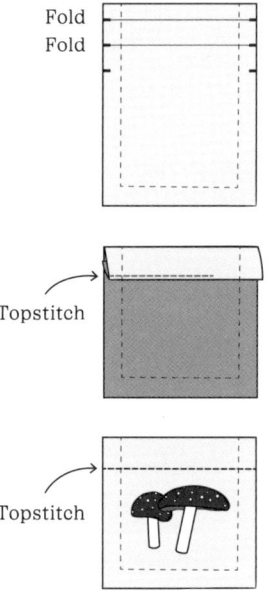

↑ *Prepping the pockets (steps 2–3)*

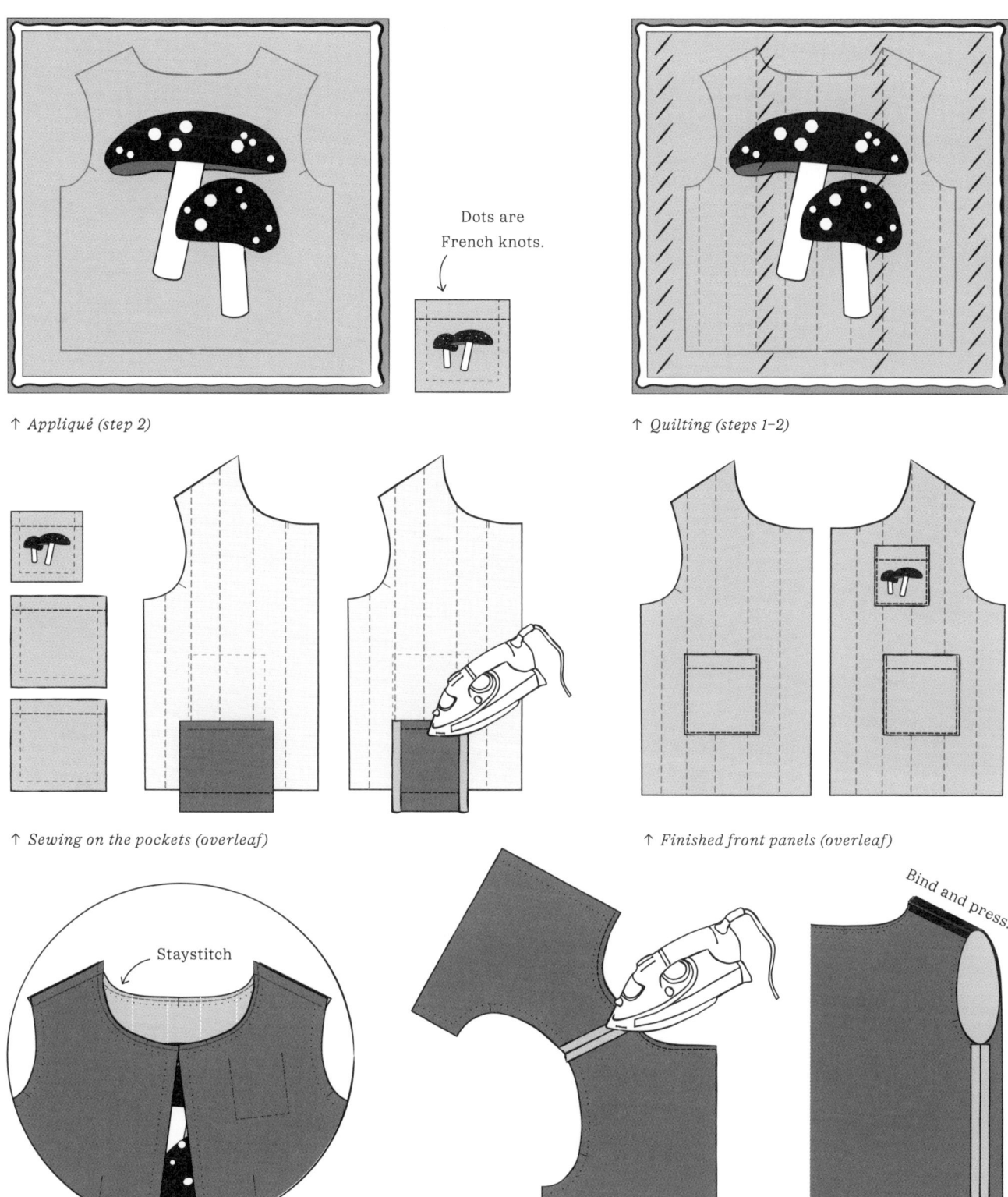

↑ *Appliqué (step 2)*

Dots are
French knots.

↑ *Quilting (steps 1–2)*

↑ *Sewing on the pockets (overleaf)*

↑ *Finished front panels (overleaf)*

Staystitch

↑ *Putting the jacket together (steps 1–2; overleaf)*

Bind and press.

Sewing on the pockets

1. Position your pockets on the front panels. Pin in place.
2. Stitch the pockets on, making sure that you backstitch securely at the beginning and end of each seam.

Putting the jacket together

1. With right sides together, pin the jacket fronts to the back at the shoulder seams. Stitch. Press the seam allowances open. If you've overlocked them, you're done. If not, bind (see pages 59–64) each seam allowance separately.
2. Pin and sew the side seams. Press the seam allowances open and finish them as you did the shoulder seams.
3. Fold the sleeves in half lengthwise, right sides together, and pin and sew the underarm seams. Press and finish as you did the shoulder and side seams. Turn the sleeves right side out.
4. Turn the body of the jacket wrong side out. Slot the sleeves into the armholes from the inside of the jacket, aligning the underarm seams with the jacket side seams, and sew in place. If they aren't overlocked, bind the armhole seam allowances separately. Turn the jacket right side out.
5. Starting near one side seam, apply bias binding all around the hem, centre fronts, and neckline of the jacket, mitring the corners (see page 64) at the bottom of each centre front.
6. Bind the cuffs of the sleeves, too.
7. Using a 1-cm (⅜-in) seam allowance, pin and sew around three sides of the collar as illustrated, leaving the bottom edge open. Trim the corners. Insert the wadding piece and snuggle it all the way up so that it lies flat and smooth within the collar. Quilt along the outside edge, as illustrated, making sure you don't quilt in the bottom-edge seam allowance.
8. From the outside of the jacket, stitch one of the collar's bottom seam allowances along the neckline.
9. Using sharp scissors, clip small Vs into your seam allowance, making sure you don't cut through the seam.
10. Flip the collar up, and ladder or whip stitch (see page 68) the collar's other bottom edge to the inside of the neckline.
11. Following the markings on your garment pieces, apply four snaps to the centre front of the jacket.

Set stitch length to 3 mm for topstitching.

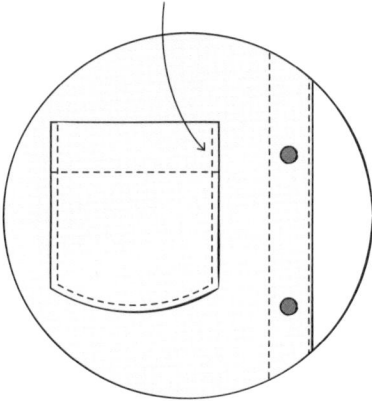

↑ *Example of topstitching on a shirt pocket and placket. Edge stitching and topstitching are cousins: edge stitching is sewn 3 mm (⅛ in) from the edge of a fabric, whereas topstitching is sewn 6 mm (¼ in) away or further.*

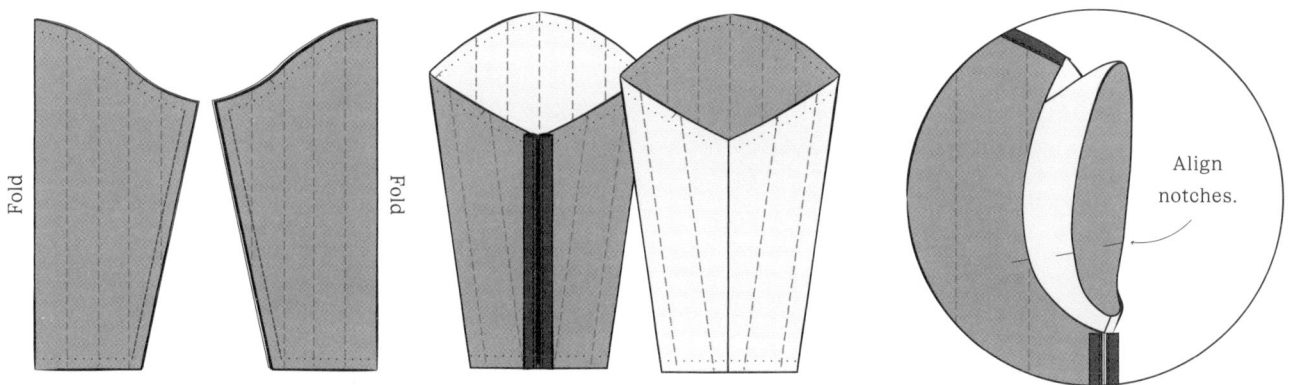

↑ *Putting the jacket together (step 3)*

↑ *Putting the jacket together (step 4)*

Align notches.

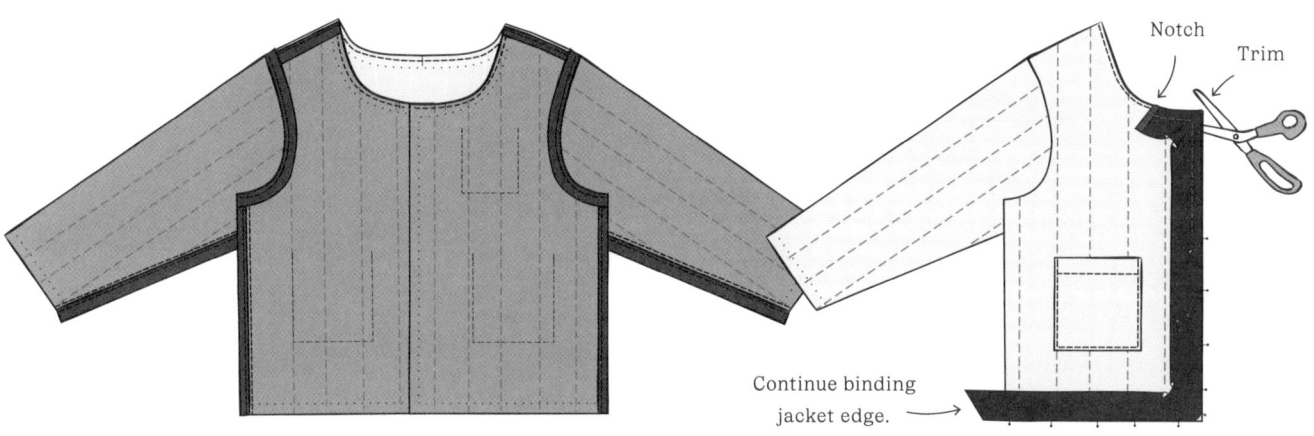

↑ *Putting the jacket together (steps 4–5)*

Notch

Trim

Continue binding jacket edge.

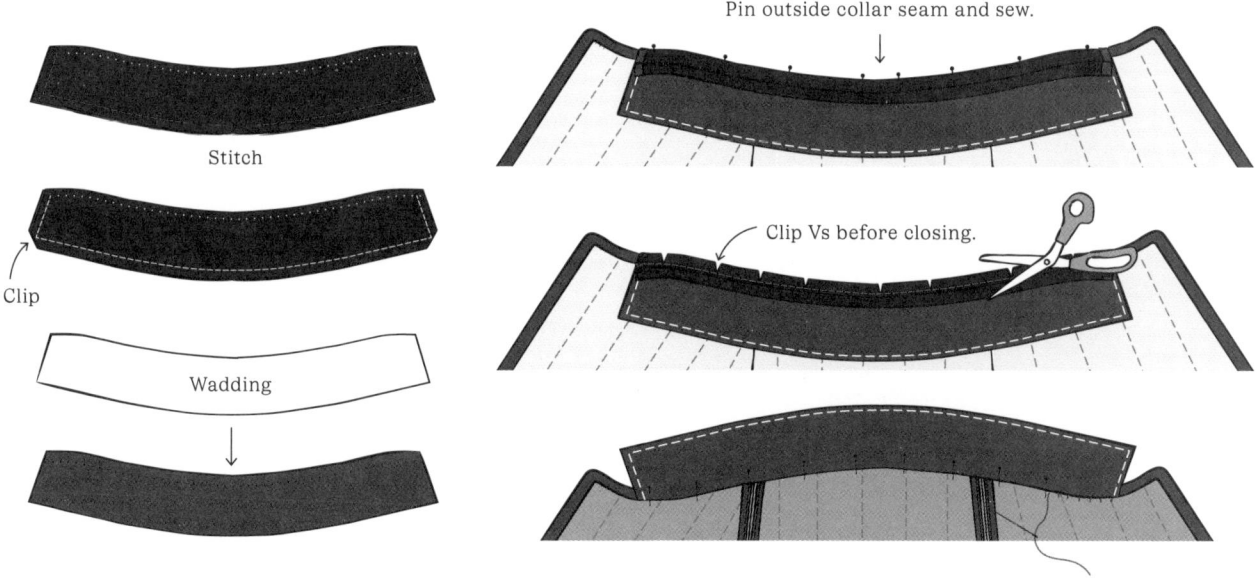

Stitch

Clip

Wadding

Pin outside collar seam and sew.

Clip Vs before closing.

↑ *Putting the jacket together (step 7)*

↑ *Putting the jacket together (steps 8–10)*

HOMEWARES

PINWHEEL CUSHION

Cushions are, traditionally, one of those projects that pepper the syllabi of 'learn to sew' classes. Alongside drawstring pyjama pants and a rectangular tote bag, they make up the trifecta of introductory sewing projects often shoved to the back of cupboards, never to be worn or used after they've been rustled up by their once-enthusiastic makers.

I worked long and hard on this pattern (and the two other cushions in this book) in the hope that they would escape this fate. It's simple enough for a complete beginner and small enough to sew and hand quilt the same day. The stripes add a little visual interest and patchwork skill-building without being overwhelming. And for those of you who are scared of putting in zips, you could add in ties or button loops instead. Or be brave, take the plunge and try your hand at a zip. You never know, you might like it.

⧙ METHOD ⧘

Cutting

If you are using fabric pieces that are 50 cm (19¾ in) wide or more, cut long strips 5 cm (2 in) wide across the whole width of the fabric. Sew alternating strips of fabric 1 and fabric 2 together to make long striped bars, and then cut your blocks from those. It will speed things up!

If you are using small pieces or scraps of fabric, cut each 5 × 25 cm (2 × 10 in) strip individually.

All together you will need:

fabric	piece	qty
○ fabric 1	5 × 25 cm (2 × 10 in) strip	24
● fabric 2	5 × 25 cm (2 × 10 in) strip	24

Piecing the top

1. Pin and sew the strips together, alternating fabrics 1 and 2. If you're using small scraps, you'll now have a block that is roughly square. It will be a little bigger than you need. If you're using long pieces of fabric, you'll have a long panel out of which you can now cut several squares.
2. Cut the panels into eight identically sized, neat squares measuring 24.5 × 24.5 cm (9¾ × 9¾ in). This means dividing up your long panel or trimming the edges of your individual squares. Use your quilt ruler to guide you, or make a 24.5 × 24.5 cm (9¾ × 9¾ in) template and trace around it.
3. Lay the blocks out as illustrated.
4. Stitch each row of blocks together, alternating the direction you press the seams.
5. Pin and sew the rows together, nesting your seams (see page 34). Press the patchwork.

FINISHED SIZE

45 × 45 cm (17¾ × 17¾ in)

FABRIC

Note yardages are estimated for fabric 115 cm (45 in) wide.

> fabric 1: 1 m (1 yd)
> fabric 2: 1 m (1 yd)
> backing fabric: 56 × 102 cm (22 × 40 in)

HABERDASHERY

> wadding: 56 × 102 cm (22 × 40 in)
> thread for piecing
> 1 × 40-m skein of sashiko thread or 1 × 80-m spool of DMC perle 8 cotton for quilting
> 45-cm (17¾-in) zip
> basting tape (optional)
> 45-cm (17¾-in) cushion pad

EQUIPMENT

> basic quilt-making kit (page 73)
> overlocker (serger) or pinking shears

NOTES

> A 1-cm (⅜-in) seam allowance is included in the pattern unless otherwise noted.

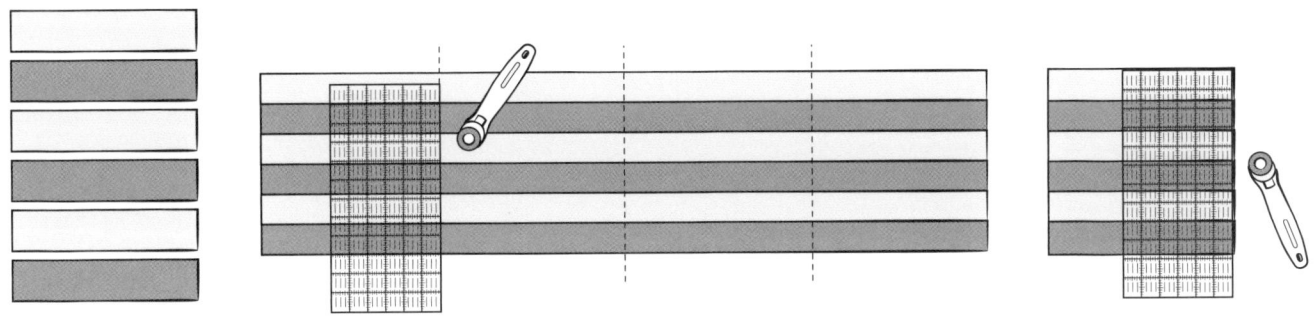

↑ *Piecing the top (step 1)*   ↑ *Piecing the top (step 2)*

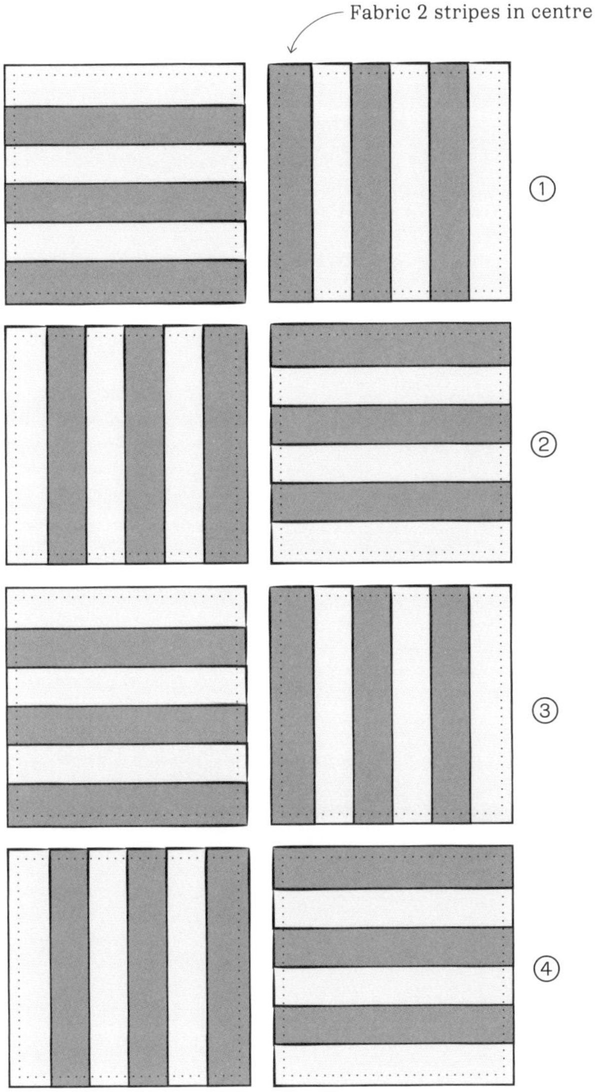

Fabric 2 stripes in centre

① ② ③ ④

↑ *Piecing the top (step 3)*

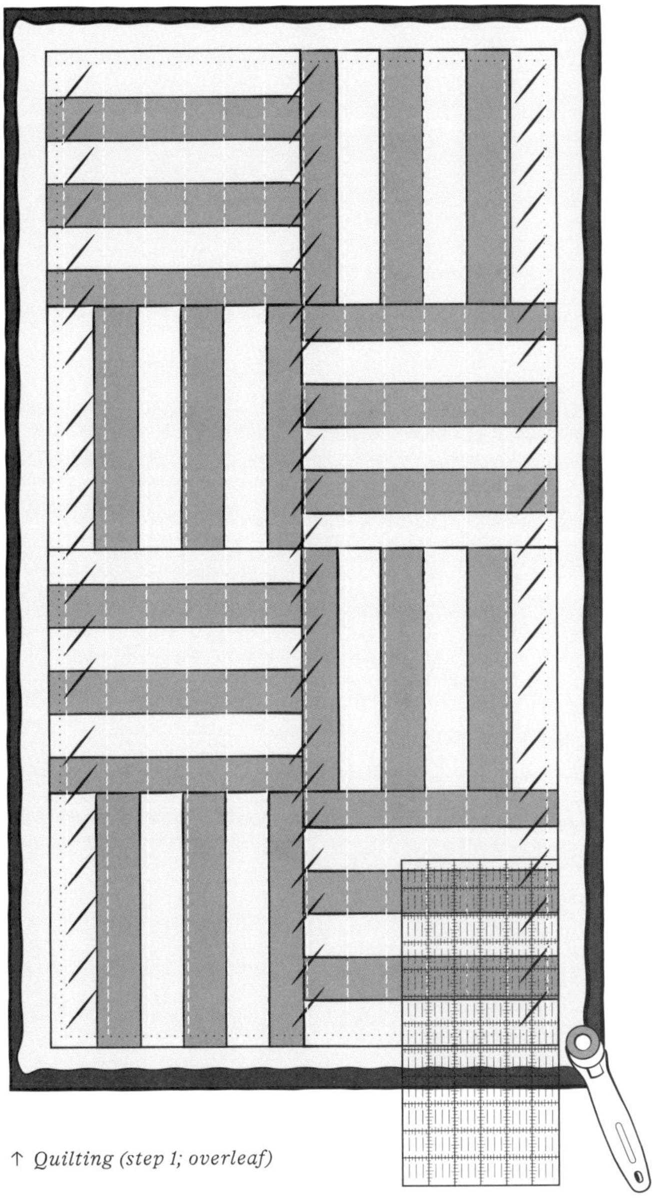

↑ *Quilting (step 1; overleaf)*

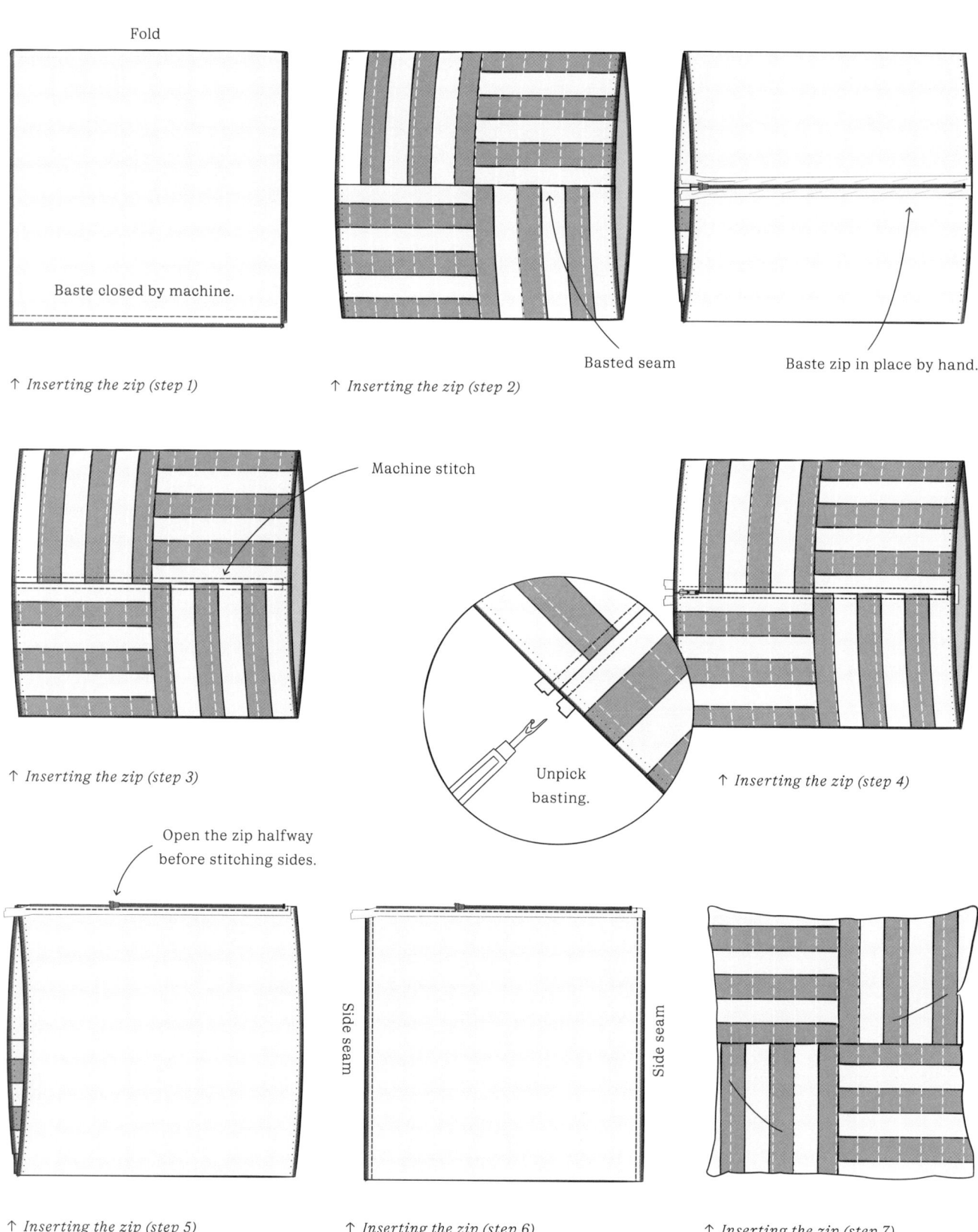

Fold

Baste closed by machine.

↑ *Inserting the zip (step 1)*

Basted seam

↑ *Inserting the zip (step 2)*

Baste zip in place by hand.

Machine stitch

↑ *Inserting the zip (step 3)*

Unpick basting.

↑ *Inserting the zip (step 4)*

Open the zip halfway before stitching sides.

↑ *Inserting the zip (step 5)*

Side seam

↑ *Inserting the zip (step 6)*

Side seam

↑ *Inserting the zip (step 7)*

Quilting

1. Following your preferred method (see Chapter 3), baste your layers together and quilt them. I stitched in the ditch (see page 51) along each of the vertical stripes and then extended these lines across the horizontal stripes by marking them out with my quilting ruler and a hera marker. You could also use a contrast thread or pattern to bring attention to the quilting. Trim your cushion cover so that all the edges are flush.
2. If you have an overlocker (serger), overlock all the edges.
3. Fold the cushion cover in half, with right sides together, to form a square.

Inserting the zip

1. Set your sewing machine to a 4 mm stitch length. Stitch along the edge opposite the fold. You'll remove this stitching after you've put in your zip (it's just there to hold everything together while you do so). Press the seam open.
2. Put your zipper foot on your sewing machine. Place your zip carefully along the basted seam, right side down, so that the zip's teeth are perfectly centred. Pin, stitch baste or use basting tape to secure the zip in place so that it doesn't move around while you sew.
3. Turn the cover right side out. Working from the right side, sew the zip along one side, close to the zip teeth. Then stitch across the zip's base (do this with the hand wheel of your sewing machine if you're using a metal zip, as your machine's needle will break if it hits the teeth). Finally, stitch up the other side of the zip.
4. Unpick the basting stitches so that you can see the zipper pull and teeth. Open the zip halfway.
5. Flip your cushion cover inside out.
6. Sew the sides of the cover shut. Press. Cut small V shapes into the corners so that they flip out neatly. I overlocked the edges, but you could simply trim them with a pair of pinking shears so that the seams don't fray.
7. Flip your cushion cover right side out, and slide your cushion pad in. Put it on your sofa, lie back and relax.

HOLLY QUILT

A souped-up version of the Ellen crib quilt (page 77), the Holly is a classic Irish chain variation. While it might look intimidating, it's deceptively simple to put together.

I made mine from earthy reds, gathered from a few years of sewing leftovers; a pair of cherry-red linen flares salvaged from a charity shop; and a red mini dress that I had owned for years and never wore. (My 178 cm/5 ft 10 in frame meant that the mini dress was more mini than it was meant to be. Whenever I put it on, I became a bit nervous about bending over, or indeed attempting to do anything other than standing up pencil-straight.)

I suggest using a range of tones here, whatever colour you decide to make this quilt out of. I think it has the effect of making a quilt that feels homemade and purposefully unstructured.

⅀ METHOD ⅀

Cutting

Both blocks in the Holly quilt can be made using either scrap fabric or yardage. If you are using scraps or fabric samples, cut the A, B, C and D rectangles individually. It takes longer, but it means you can include those diminutive pieces of linen and cotton lurking in your scrap bag that are just *too* good to throw away.

If you are using shop-bought fabric, cut it into strips and then subdivide the strips into squares afterwards to speed the cutting process along (see page 36).

fabric	piece		qty
○ fabric 1	A	28 cm (11 in) square	12
	B	10 cm (4 in) square	169
	C	10 × 28 cm (4 × 11 in) rectangle	48
● fabric 2	D	10 cm (4 in) square	204

Making block 1

Scrap patchwork

1. Gather together 48 fabric 2 squares (D), all the fabric 1 rectangles (C) and all the big fabric 1 squares (A).
2. Pin and stitch a fabric 2 square (D) to each of the short sides of 24 of the fabric 1 rectangles (C). This will be called unit 1.
3. Pin and stitch the long sides of the remaining fabric 1 rectangles to opposite edges of the big fabric 1 squares (A). Press the seam allowances towards the big fabric 1 squares. This will be called unit 2.
4. Continue to *For both scrap and stitch patchwork*.

Strip patchwork

1. Gather your fabric 1 strips 28 cm (11 in) wide and fabric 2 strips 10 cm (4 in) wide. Pin and stitch the long edge of one fabric 2 strip to each long edge of a fabric 1 strip.
2. Divide the fabric 1 and fabric 2 strips into strips 10 cm (4 in) wide. These will be called unit 1. Set aside.
3. Next, collect the rest of your fabric 1 strips 28 cm (11 in) wide and 10 cm (4 in) wide. Pin and stitch the long edge of one

FINISHED SIZE

200 × 200 cm (78¾ × 78¾ in)

5 × 5 blocks, each measuring 40 × 40 cm (15¾ × 15¾ in)

FABRIC

Note yardages are estimated for fabric 115 cm (45 in) wide.

> fabric 1: 6.25 m (7 yd)
> fabric 2: 3 m (3¼ yd)
> backing fabric: 2.5 × 2.5 m (2¾ × 2¾ yd; can be patchworked together)

HABERDASHERY

> wadding: 2.5 × 2.5 m (2¾ × 2¾ yd)
> binding: 10 m (11 yd) straight-grain binding 5 cm (2 in) wide
> thread for piecing
> 4 × 40-m skeins of sashiko thread or 2 × 80-m spools of perle 8 cotton thread for quilting

EQUIPMENT

> basic quilt-making kit (page 73)

NOTES

> A 1-cm (⅜-in) seam allowance is included in the pattern.
> Unless otherwise noted, press seam allowances towards the darker fabric where possible.
> Patchwork is sewn right sides together unless otherwise specified.

narrow fabric 1 strip to each long edge of the strip 28 cm (11 in) wide. Press the seam allowances towards the centre.

4. Divide the fabric 1 and fabric 2 strips into strips 28 cm (11 in) wide. These will be called unit 2. Set aside.

For both scrap and strip patchwork
1. Lay out your units so that you have 12 blocks consisting of: unit 1, unit 2, unit 1.
2. With right sides together, pin unit 1 to unit 2 so that the seams intersect, then sew them. Sew the second unit 1 of each block to the other side of unit 2 in the same way. Press the seams towards unit 1. Set aside.

Making block 2

Scrap patchwork
If you are using small scraps of fabric and have cut each of the squares individually, then do the following:

1. Gather together 13 fabric 1 squares (B) and 12 fabric 2 squares (D) for each block.
2. To create rows 1, 3 and 5 of your block, pin and sew five of your squares together, starting with fabric 1 (B) and alternating between the colours, as illustrated on page 127. This will be called unit 1. You'll need 39 of these when all is said and done.
3. To make rows 2 and 4, pin and sew five of your squares together, alternating colours, but instead of starting with a fabric 1 square (B), start with a fabric 2 square (D). (As in step 2, refer to the illustrations on page 127.) This will be called unit 2. You'll need 26 of these in total.
4. Lay out your units so that you have 13 blocks consisting of: unit 1, unit 2, unit 1, unit 2, unit 1.
5. Starting with the first block, pin unit 1 to unit 2 and sew together, nesting your seams (see page 34). Repeat until you have a neatly sewn block of five rows. Press.
6. Repeat for the remaining 12 blocks.

Strip patchwork
1. Gather the rest of your fabric 1 and fabric 2 strips 10 cm (4 in) wide. To make rows 1, 3 and 5 of each block, pin and sew three fabric 1 and two fabric 2 strips together lengthwise into long, stripy flags, alternating fabric 1, fabric 2, fabric 1, fabric 2, fabric 1.

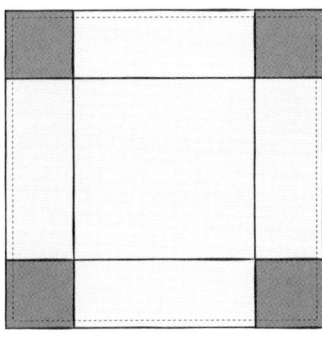

↑ *Block 1*

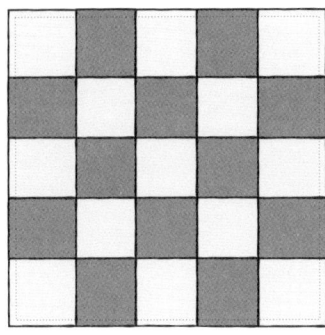

↑ *Block 2*

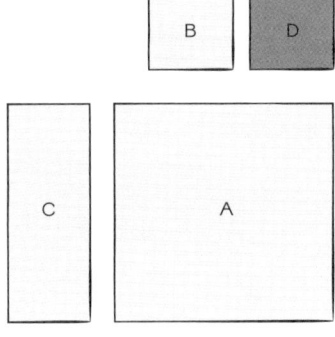

↑ *Scrap piecing block 1*

2. Divide the long stripy flags into strips 10 cm (4 in) wide. These will be called unit 1.

3. To make rows 2 and 4, pin and sew three fabric 2 and two fabric 1 strips together, alternating fabric 2, fabric 1, fabric 2, fabric 1, fabric 2.

4. Divide the long stripy flags into strips 10 cm (4 in) wide. These will be called unit 2.

5. Lay out your units so that you have 13 blocks consisting of: unit 1, unit 2, unit 1, unit 2, unit 1.

6. Starting with the first block, pin unit 1 to unit 2 and sew together, nesting your seams. Repeat until you have a neatly sewn block of five rows. Press.

Putting it together

1. Press and trim your blocks so that they are all the same size and are as perfectly square as you can make them.

2. Next, pin and sew the rows of your quilt. Go slowly and carefully with this step. It's worth taking the time and patience in this final leg of your big quilt-top journey (especially after all your effort sewing those little bits of fabric together).

3. Start by sewing rows 1, 3 and 5 of your quilt, each of which begins with block 2, then alternates with block 1. Press your seam allowances to the right.

4. Next, sew rows 2 and 4, which begin with block 1. Press your seam allowances to the left.

5. Pin and stitch the rows of the quilt together, nesting the seams. Remember to start pinning from the centre of the seams and work your way out (see page 46).

6. Press your quilt top.

7. Following your preferred method (see Chapter 3), baste your layers together, quilt them up, and then trim and bind your quilt. I used white sashiko thread to stitch in the ditch (see page 51) along the vertical seams, extending the stitch lines across the big white squares and rectangles with my quilting ruler and hera marker. I bound my Holly quilt with fabric 2 (red) scraps left over from the patchwork process.

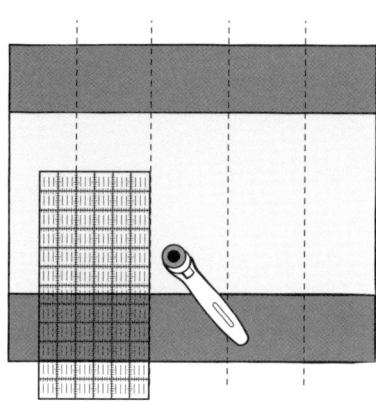

↑ *Strip patchwork (block 1, unit 1)*

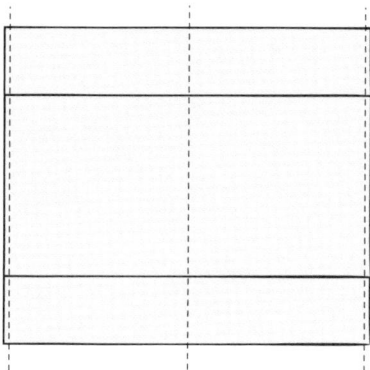

↑ *Strip patchwork (block 1, unit 2)*

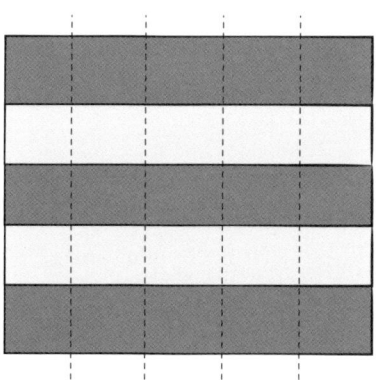

↑ *Strip patchwork (block 2, unit 2)*

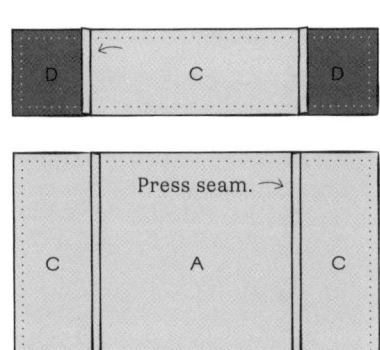

↑ *Making block 1 (unit layout)*

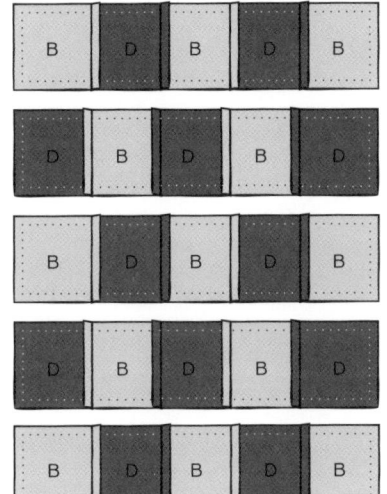

↑ *Making block 2 (unit layout)*

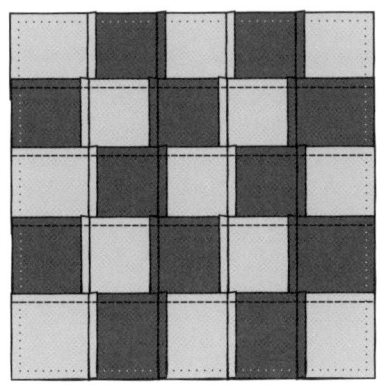

↑ *Making block 2 (full block)*

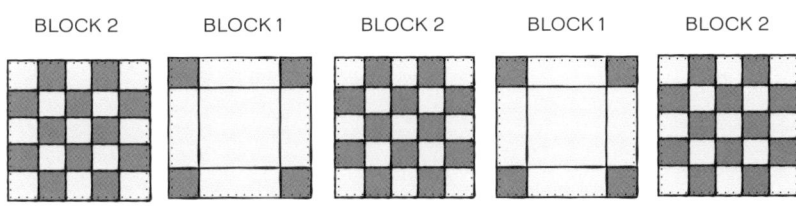

↑ *Putting it together (step 3; rows 1, 3 and 5)*

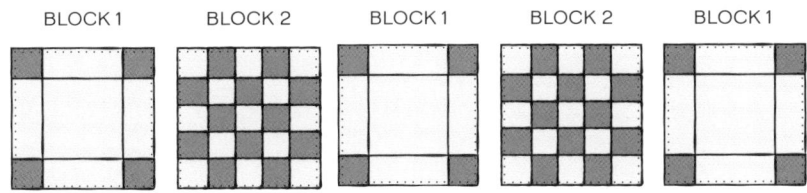

↑ *Putting it together (step 4; rows 2 and 4)*

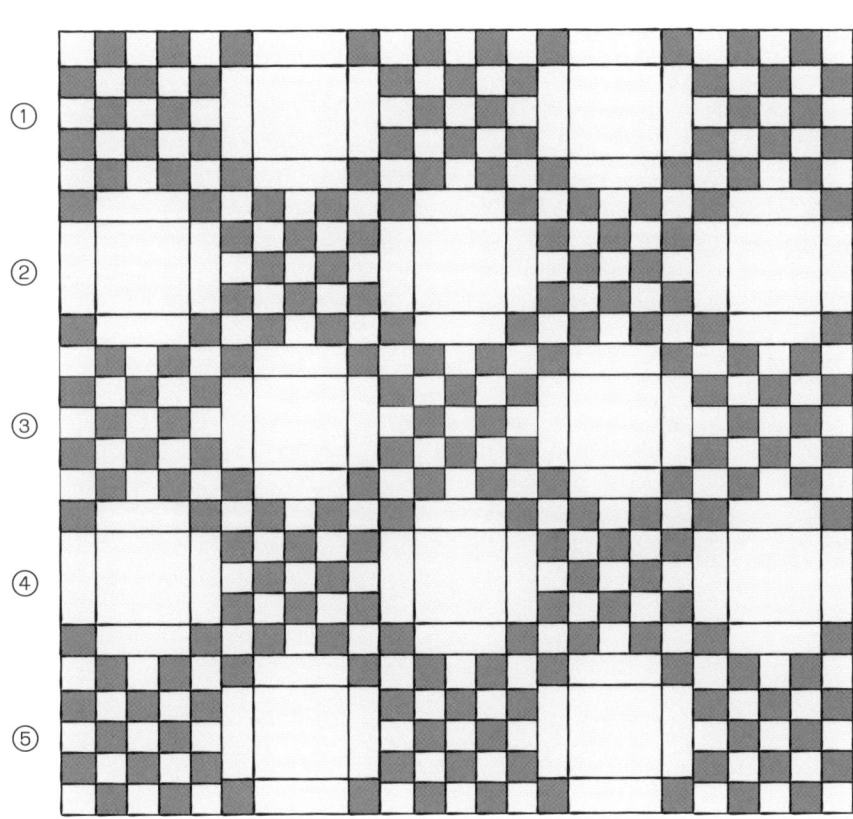

↑ *Putting it together (steps 5–6)*

ROMA BOLSTER

This bolster is properly scrappy. But beware: while it can suck up a hefty bag of leftover materials, it also sucks up a decent amount of time and no small amount of patience. It's not one for the faint of heart – minute slivers of patterned cotton are cut and sewn into tiny, perfect squares. I hope that you don't end up resenting its inclusion in this book, as it looks rather good when it is done.

I've made mine in white cotton that I cut from an old bedsheet and indigo-dyed fabrics I found on an online marketplace. I think the white complements the blue nicely, but if you were after something more subtle you could make this up using only shades of blue.

I haven't quilted this project – it's patchwork only to avoid bulk. If you want to quilt it, use the same method as for the Isobel tote bag (see page 174).

⸔ METHOD ⸕

Cutting

1. Draw a circle 23 cm (9 in) in diameter on thin card or paper and cut it out (see *Making the circle template*, page 96). This is your template for the bolster's end panels.
2. Fold the template in half three times. Unfold. Snip the template at your fold lines. Use these as notches.
3. For the lining, pin or trace the template onto your fabric and cut out two circles. Then cut out a 62 cm (24½ in) square.
4. Collect your fabrics for patchwork. Unless you are working from tiny scraps (less than 5 × 10 cm/2 × 4 in), cut strips 3 cm (1¼ in) wide of each fabric and follow the instructions for strip piecing. In total you will need:

fabric	piece	qty
○ fabric 1	3 × 5 cm (1¼ × 2 in) rectangle	328
● fabric 2	3 × 5 cm (1¼ × 2 in) rectangle	328

Creating the patchwork

Scrap piecing
1. Stitch a long side of each fabric 1 rectangle to a long side of each fabric 2 rectangle to form a square.
2. Trim off any excess fabric and square up the corners.

Strip piecing
1. Stitch one fabric 1 strip and one fabric 2 strip together.
2. Cut this fabric 1/fabric 2 strip into 5-cm (2-in) pieces, making sure your corners are square.

Both scrap and strip piecing
1. Repeat steps 1–2 (either scrap or strip piecing) until you have 328 striped units.
2. Take four striped units and lay them out as shown.
3. Stitch the top two units right sides together. Press the seam allowances to the right. Stitch the bottom two units right sides together. Press the seam allowances to the left.
4. Pin the top and bottom pieces right sides together, nesting the seams in the middle (see page 34). Stitch. Press. Set aside.

FINISHED SIZE

61 × 20 cm (24 × 8 in)

FABRIC

Note yardages are estimated for fabric 115 cm (45 in) wide.

> fabric 1: 0.75 m (¾ yd)
> fabric 2: 0.75 m (¾ yd)
> lining: 0.75 m (¾ yd)

HABERDASHERY

> binding: 1.5 m (1¾ yd)
> thread for piecing
> 60-cm (23½-in) zip
> 61 × 20.3 cm (24 × 8 in) bolster pad

EQUIPMENT

> basic quilt-making kit (page 73)

NOTES

> A 6-mm (¼-in) seam allowance is included in the pattern.
> Unless otherwise noted, press seam allowances towards the darker fabric where possible.

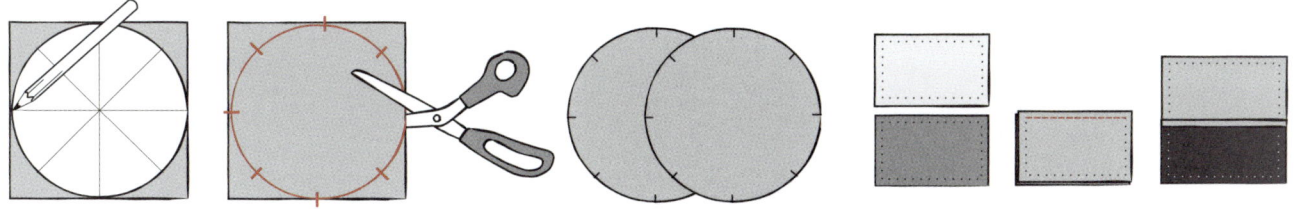

↑ *Cutting (steps 1–2)*   ↑ *Scrap piecing (steps 1–2)*

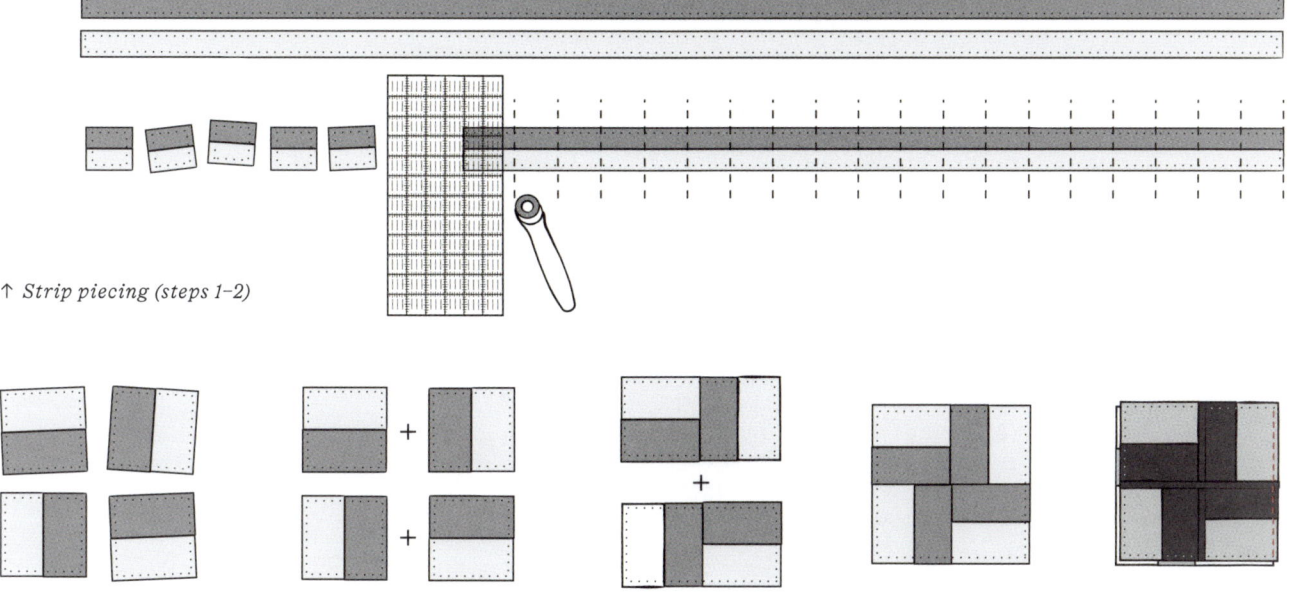

↑ *Strip piecing (steps 1–2)*

↑ *Both scrap and strip piecing (steps 2–6)*

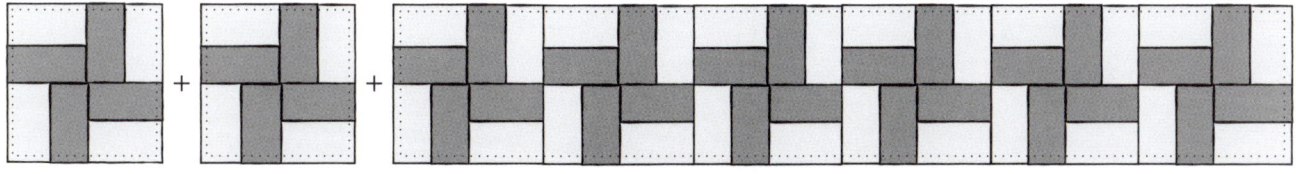

↑ *Both scrap and strip piecing (steps 2–4)*

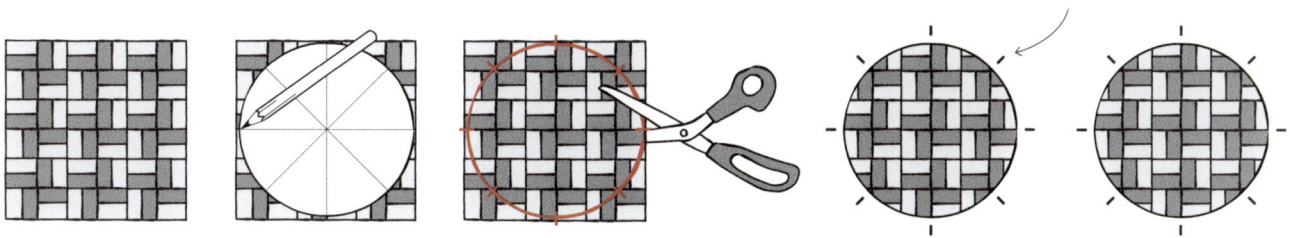

Mark notches.

↑ *Both scrap and strip piecing (step 11; overleaf)*

5. Repeat steps 2–4 until you have 82 square units.

6. Next, you'll create three panels: one big square (the cushion body) and two smaller squares (the ends).

7. To make the big square, arrange 64 units in an 8 × 8 grid.

8. Sew each row of your grid, pressing the seam allowances in alternate directions every row. Continue until you've stitched all the rows. (See *Making the play mat*, steps 2–4, page 95.)

9. Starting with rows 1 and 2, pin and sew the rows together, nesting your seams and pressing your seam allowances in one direction.

10. To make the smaller squares, arrange the remaining units into two 3 × 3 grids, and repeat steps 8–9 for each one.

11. Place your circular template in the centre of each smaller patchwork square, pin it or draw around it, then cut it out.

Inserting the zip and lining

1. Mark the centre points on the lining square, big patchwork square and zip.

2. Place the patchwork square right side up, with the zip right side down on top, aligning the edges. Place the lining square right side down on top, and pin along the zip, pinning the centre point first then working outwards.

3. Attach a zipper foot to your machine. Sew along the zip tape 6 mm (¼ in) from the edge, keeping your layers aligned.

4. Flip over and topstitch (see page 112) the lining to the zip.

5. Fold the opposite edge of the lining fabric up so that it aligns with the zip's other long edge. The right side of the lining fabric should be against the wrong side of the zip.

6. Line up the opposite edge of the patchwork with the right side of the zip, so you have two tubes (one lining, one patchwork) with the zip in the middle. Pin in place, starting from the centre.

7. Sew your zip in place 6 mm (¼ in) from the edge.

8. Flip the bolster. Topstitch the lining to the zipper, being careful not to catch any other fabrics (this is a bit fiddly; you can unzip the zipper to make the sewing easier).

9. Flip the tube so that the lining is on the outside.

10. Aligning your notches, pin the lining circles to either end of the lining tube (right sides together).

11. Sew. Clip small Vs into your seam allowance all the way around, making sure you don't cut through the seam.

12. Bind, overlock or pink the internal seams to reduce bulk, then insert the bolster pad.

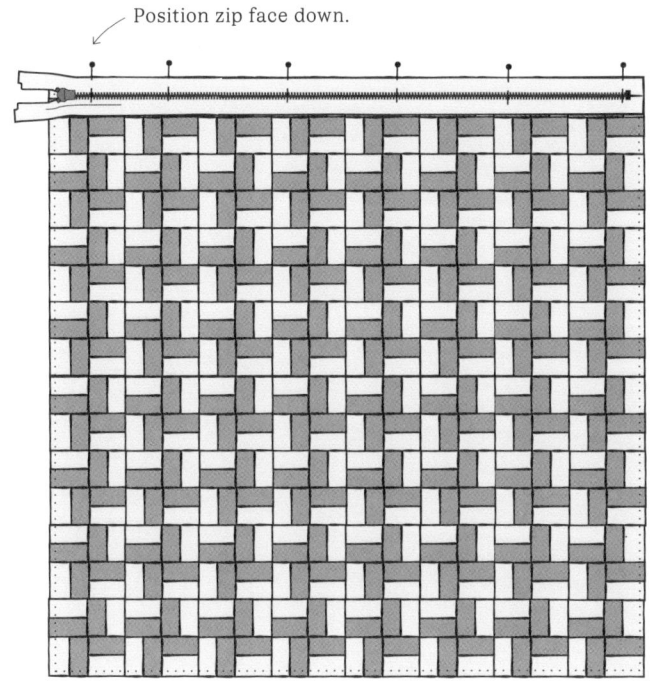

Position zip face down.

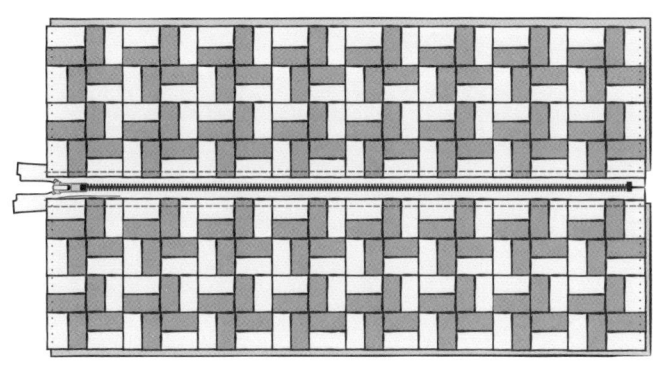

↑ *Inserting the zip and lining (steps 5–8)*

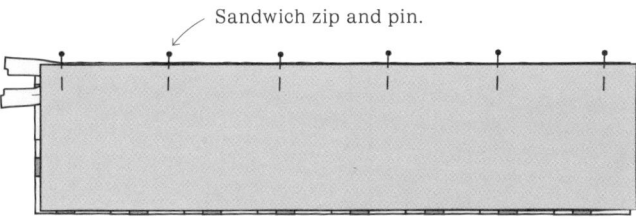

Sandwich zip and pin.

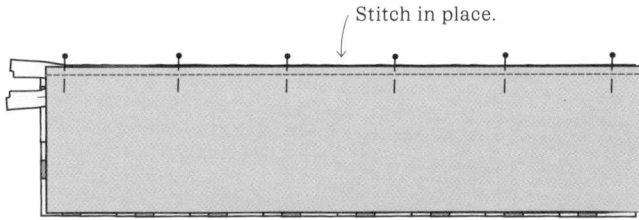

Stitch in place.

↑ *Inserting the zip and lining (steps 2–3)*

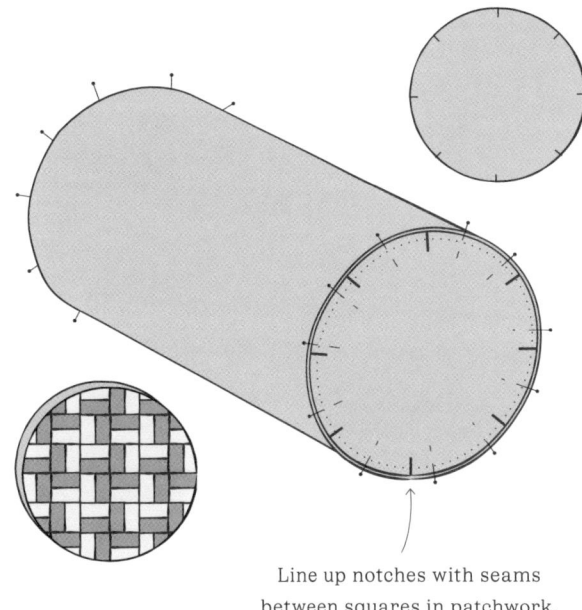

Line up notches with seams between squares in patchwork.

↑ *Inserting the zip and lining (step 10)*

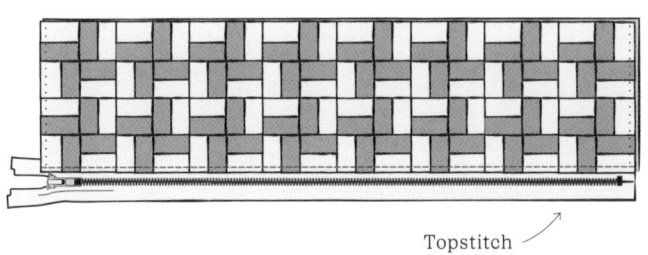

Topstitch

↑ *Inserting the zip and lining (step 4)*

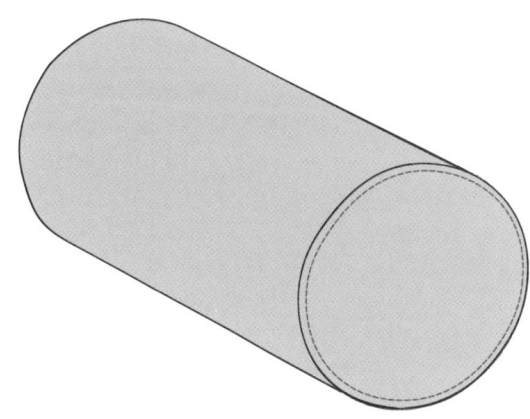

↑ *Inserting the zip and lining (steps 10–12)*

JESS QUILT

This quilt is based on one I made over the summer of 2019 and the early months of 2020 (with an autumnal pause when life and other projects got in the way). I received many compliments on it – the combination of simple shapes and shades of blue proved popular – so I decided to put a version of it in this book.

The original was patchworked from shades of indigo-dyed linen that I dipped into an inky blue vat in a workshop on a cloudy June day. When I ran out of those, I added gauzy pieces of cream-coloured cotton and a navy blue so dark it nearly tips into black.

The original was a work of improvisation. I laid out all the pieces on my living room floor and played around with the arrangement until I made something that I liked. This version is more structured so that you can easily follow along.

﹛ METHOD ﹜

Cutting

Cut the rectangles of fabric according to the sizes specified.

fabric	piece			qty
○ fabric 1	B	16.5 × 62 cm (6½ × 24½ in)		2
	C	11.5 × 103 cm (4½ × 40½ in)		1
	F	49.5 × 67 cm (19½ × 26½ in)		1
	H	35 × 88 cm (13¾ × 34½ in)		1
○ fabric 2	A	62 × 62 cm (24½ × 24½ in)		1
	G	14 × 67 cm (5½ × 26½ in)		1
	I	35 × 42 cm (13¾ × 16½ in)		1
	J	9 × 27 cm (3½ × 10¾ in)		1
● fabric 3	A	62 × 62 cm (24½ × 24½ in)		1
	E	62 × 88 cm (24½ × 34½ in)		1
● fabric 4	D	11.5 × 52 cm (4½ × 20½ in)		1
	K	27 × 27 cm (10¾ × 10¾ in)		1

Turn the page for instructions on how to put the quilt together.

FINISHED SIZE

152 × 165 cm (60 × 65 in)

FABRIC

Note yardages are estimated for fabric 115 cm (45 in) wide.

> fabric 1: 1.25 m (1⅜ yd)
> fabric 2: 1 m (1 yd)
> fabric 3: 1.4 m (1½ yd)
> fabric 4: 0.3 m (⅓ yd)
> backing fabric: 1.63 × 1.75 m (1¾ × 2 yd; can be patchworked together)

HABERDASHERY

> wadding: 163 × 175 cm (64 × 69 in)
> binding: 6.7 m (7⅓ yd) straight-grain binding 5 cm (2 in) wide
> thread for piecing
> 4 × 40-m skeins of sashiko thread or 2 × 80-m spools of perle 8 cotton thread for quilting

EQUIPMENT

> basic quilt-making kit (page 73)

NOTES

> A 6-mm (¼-in) seam allowance is included in the pattern.
> Unless otherwise noted, press seam allowances towards the darker fabric where possible.
> All panels are sewn right sides together unless otherwise specified.

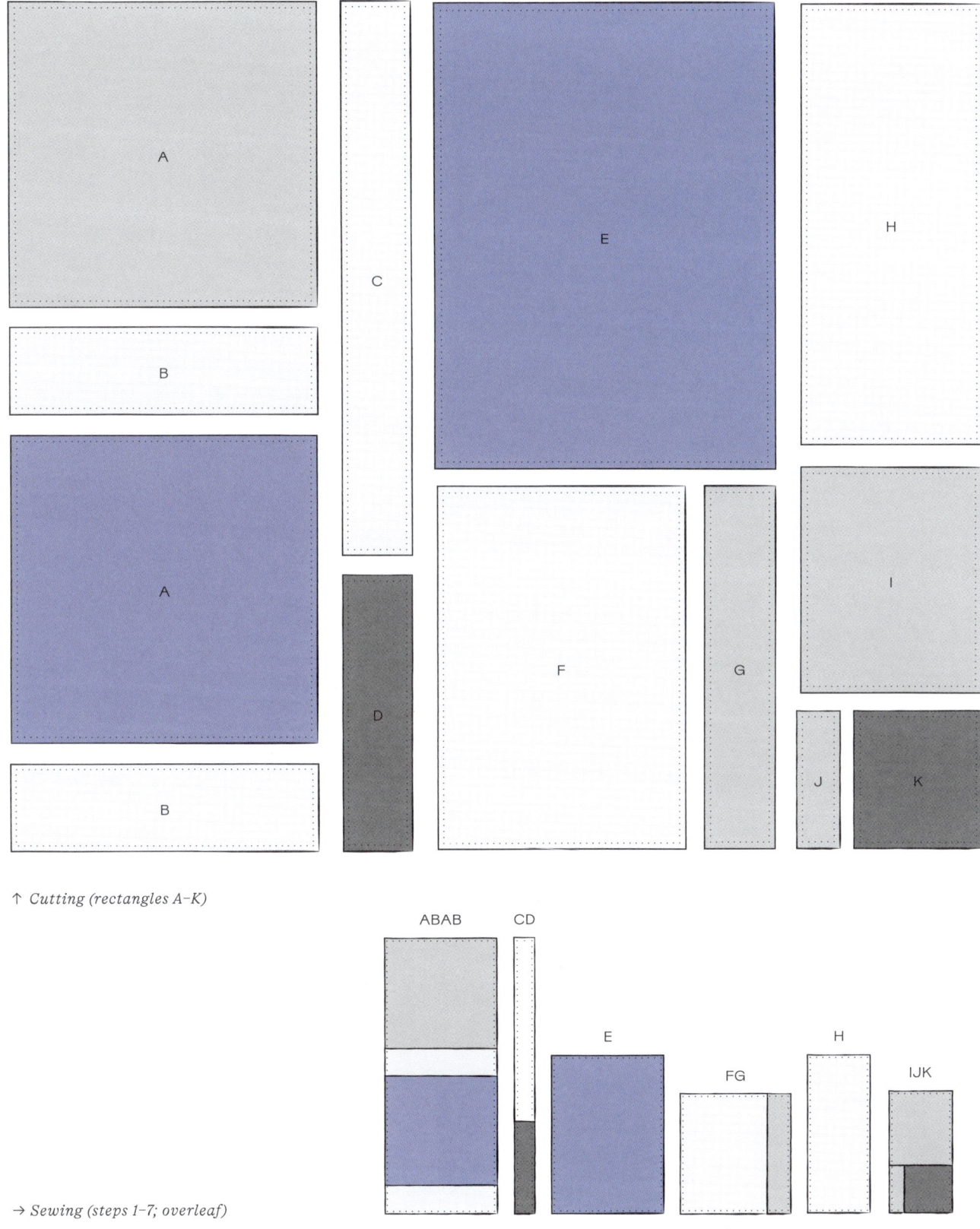

↑ *Cutting (rectangles A–K)*

→ *Sewing (steps 1–7; overleaf)*

Sewing

You'll sew this quilt together in rectangular panels, then join those up. Doing it this way means that you avoid sewing any dodgy corners or inserting pieces at tricky angles.

1. Take your A rectangle and one of the B rectangles. With right sides together, pin and sew the B strip to the bottom edge of each A square. Press.
2. Pin and sew one AB unit to the other. Press.
3. Stitch the C and D rectangles together. Press.
4. Pin and sew panel ABAB to panel CD. Press the seam allowances towards the ABAB panel. Set aside.
5. Pin and sew rectangle G to the right-hand side of rectangle F. Press.
6. Pin and sew the short side of rectangle E to the FG panel you've just made, making sure the G rectangle is on the lower right-hand side of the finished panel. Press. Set aside.
7. Pin and sew one of the long sides of rectangle J to the left-hand side of the K square. Press. Pin and sew the long side of the JK panel to rectangle I, making sure that the J rectangle (fabric 2) is on the lower left-hand side.
8. Attach rectangle H to the short side of the I rectangle (at the top of the panel you've just sewn), so that you have a long, skinny rectangular section.
9. Now join the three panels you've made (ABABCD, EFG and HIJK) together. Start by pinning and sewing the CD edge of the ABABCD panel to the EF edge of the EFG panel. Press. Pin and sew your ABABCDEFG (what a mouthful!) panel to your HIJK panel, along the EF and IJ edges. Press. Congratulations! You've finished your quilt top.
10. Following your preferred method (see Chapter 3) baste, quilt, trim and bind your quilt. I quilted lines 2.5 cm (1 in) apart for the first half of the quilt, then widened to 5 cm (2 in) for visual interest. I used all different blue scraps to create a variegated binding.

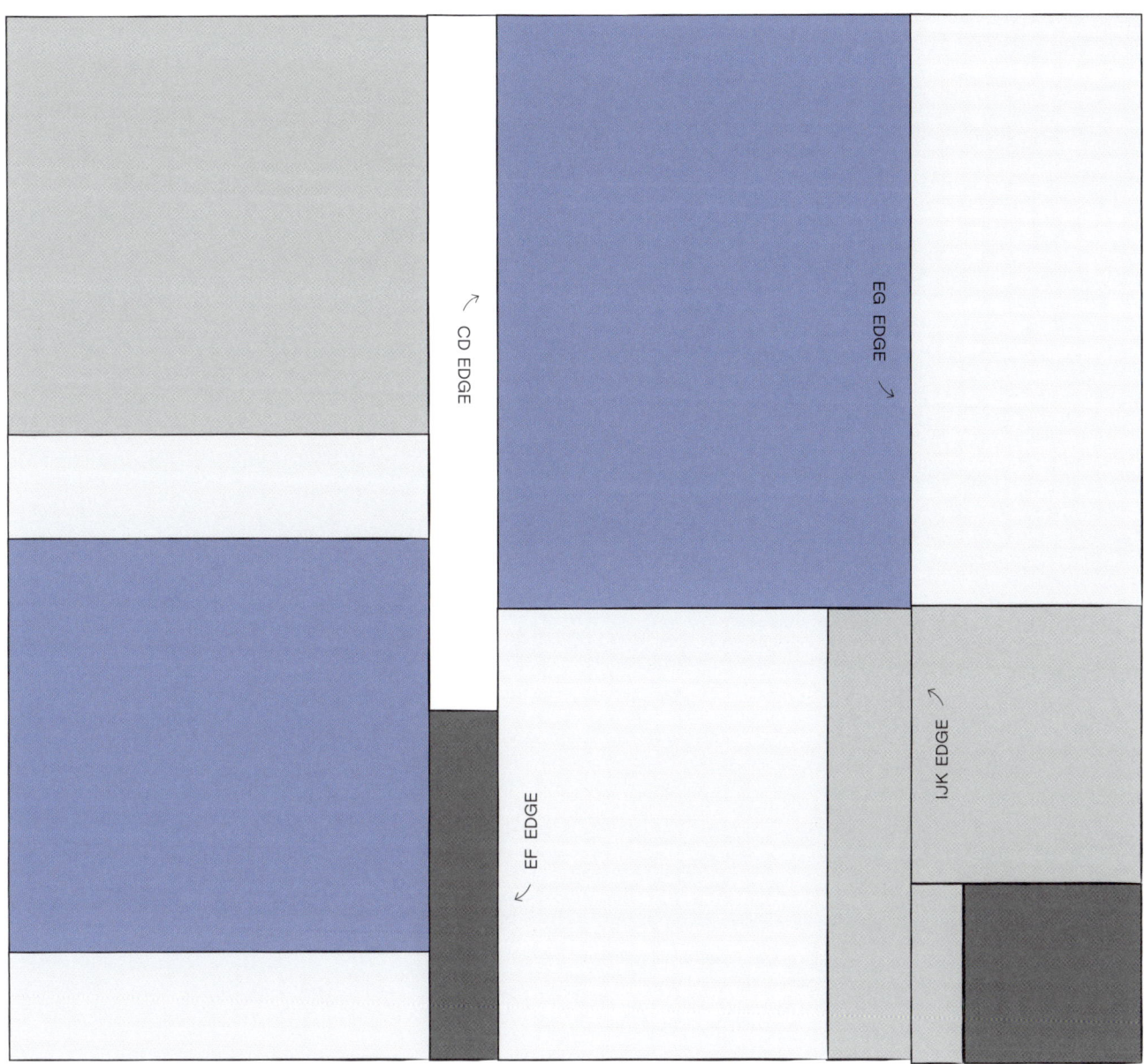

↑ Sewing (steps 9–10)

SARA CUSHION

This project combines patchwork and appliqué for a bold, graphic cushion. I was inspired by the colour work of the Bauhaus (a design movement that somehow still feels modern, despite its century-old tenure), though you could make your cushion in black and white to highlight the architectural angles of the appliqué, or play with subtle, neutral tones. You'll use a combination of big and small fabric scraps for this one, so raid your scrap bag accordingly.

⅋ METHOD ⅋

Cutting the rectangles

Mark and carefully cut out fabric rectangles using the table below.

fabric	piece		qty
○ fabric 1	A	42 × 6.5 cm (16½ × 2½ in)	1
	B	42 × 4 cm (16½ × 1½ in)	2
	C	18 × 6.5 cm (7 × 2½ in)	2
	D	36.5 × 32 cm (14½ × 12½ in)	1
	E	6.5 × 32 cm (2½ × 12½ in)	1
	F	4 × 32 cm (1½ × 12½ in)	1
	G	52.5 × 4 cm (20½ × 1½ in)	1
◔ fabric 2	B	42 × 4 cm (16½ × 1½ in)	1
	I	24.5 × 24.5 cm (9¾ × 9¾ in)	1
◑ fabric 3	B	42 × 4 cm (16½ × 1½ in)	1
	J	7.5 × 7.5 cm (3 × 3 in)	1
	K	52 × 52 cm (20½ × 20½ in)	1
● fabric 4	F	4 × 32 cm (1½ × 12½ in)	1
	H	24.5 × 13 cm (10½ × 5 in)	1
○ fabric 5	E	6.5 × 32 cm (2½ × 12½ in)	1

Cutting the appliqué pieces

1. Make a template by drawing a circle that is 24.5 cm (9¾ in) in diameter on card or paper and cutting it out (see *Making the circle template*, page 96). Lay it on top of fabric rectangle I, draw around the circumference, and cut out your circle.

2. Use the same template to make shape H. Lay the template on top of rectangle H and trace around it. Then, measure 7.5 cm (3 in) in from the top left-hand edge and mark a line all the way down from that point. Cut around the lines so you have a shape like the one in the illustration opposite.

FINISHED SIZE

50 × 50 cm (19¾ × 19¾ in)

FABRIC

Note yardages are estimated for fabric 115 cm (45 in) wide.

> This project is made up of such little pieces that giving you yardage seems futile. Instead, refer to the cut plan.

> backing fabric: 56 × 112 cm (22 × 44 in; will be inside the cushion)

HABERDASHERY

> wadding: 56 × 112 cm (22 × 44 in)
> thread for piecing
> 1 × 40-m skein of sashiko thread or 1 × 80-m spool of perle 8 cotton thread for quilting
> 50-cm (19¾-in) zip
> 50-cm (19¾-in) cushion pad

EQUIPMENT

> basic quilt-making kit (page 73)
> overlocker (serger) or pinking shears (optional)

NOTES

> A 6-mm (¼-in) seam allowance is included (3 mm / ⅛ in on the appliqué pieces).

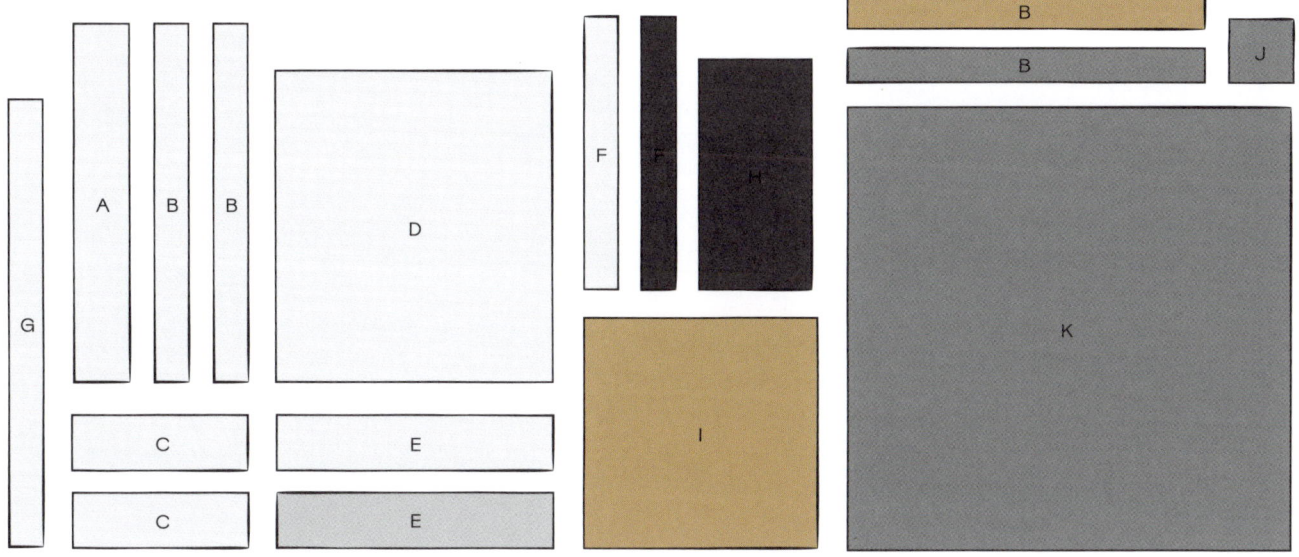

↑ *Cutting the rectangles*

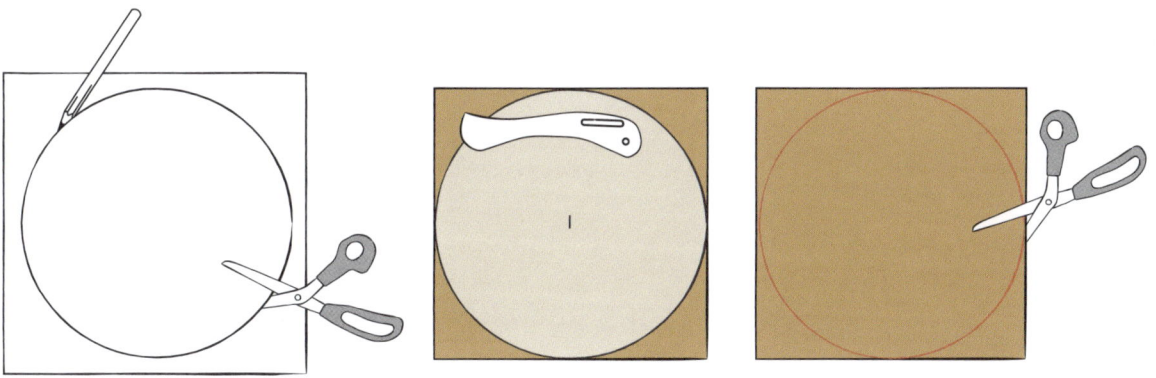

↑ *Cutting the appliqué pieces (step 1)*

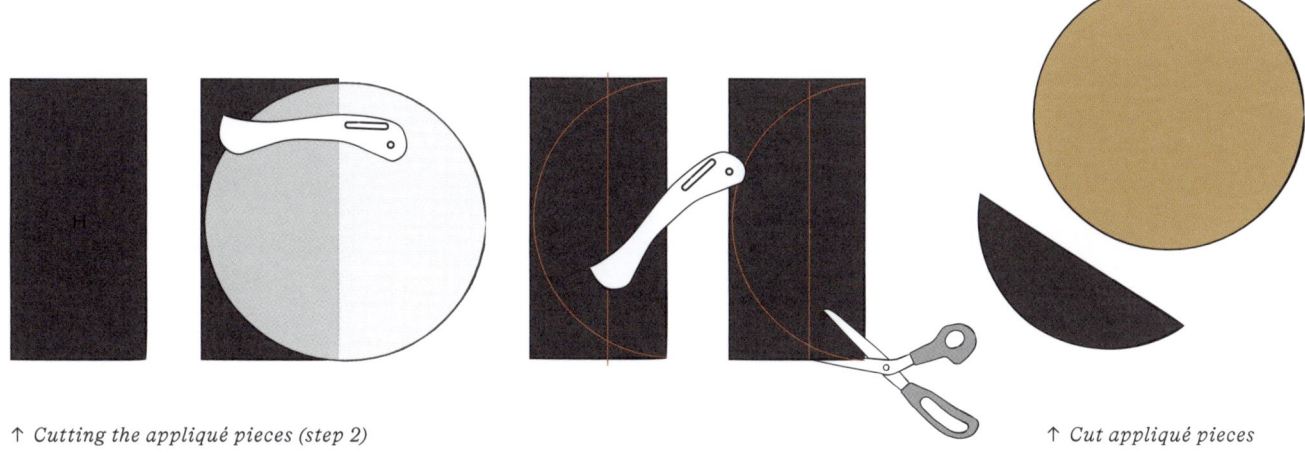

↑ *Cutting the appliqué pieces (step 2)*

↑ *Cut appliqué pieces*

Sewing

This is an easy project, but you have to be methodical when putting the cushion together. Start by piecing the right-hand side, then the left, then joining them. Finally, add the appliqué and backing piece to bring the whole thing together.

1. Stitch the A and B rectangles together following the illustration. You now have a panel of five strips.
2. Add the C rectangles to the top and bottom of your striped panel. Press the seam allowances towards the C panels. Trim the edges so that everything is nice and square.
3. Sew the D, E and F rectangles together following the illustration. You now have another striped panel.
4. Sew your ABC and DEF panels right sides together. Press the seam allowances towards the DEF panel.
5. Stitch the G rectangle to the right-hand side of the panel so that you have one neat, square patchwork. Press the seam allowances towards the DEF panel.

Appliqué and quilting

1. Position I, H and J on your cushion as illustrated, then use your favourite appliqué technique (see pages 43–5) to attach them to your cushion.
2. Press and trim your patchwork so it's 52 cm (20½ in) square.
3. Sew the K square to the upper edge of your patchwork (right sides together). Press.
4. Following your preferred method (see Chapter 3), baste your layers, then quilt and trim your cushion panel. Binding can add bulk to the inside of the cushion, so pink the edges, overlock them or add a lining.

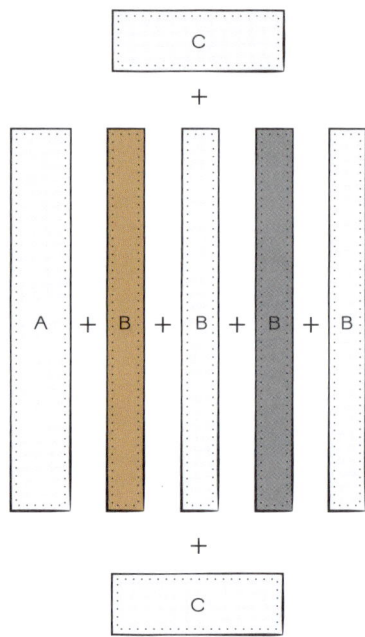

↑ *Sewing (steps 1–2)*

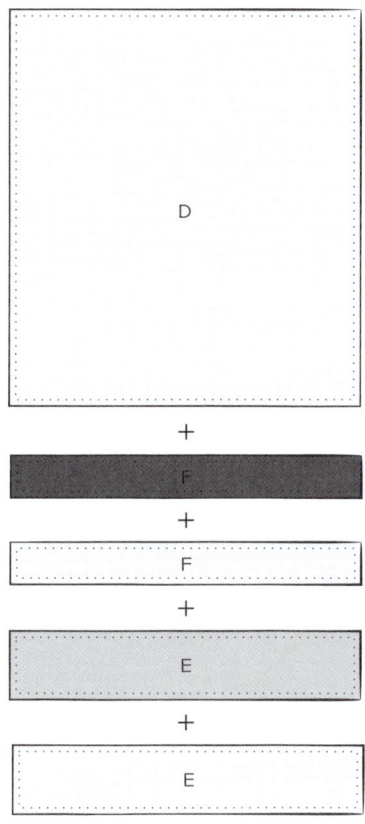

↑ *Sewing (step 3)*

ABC   DEF

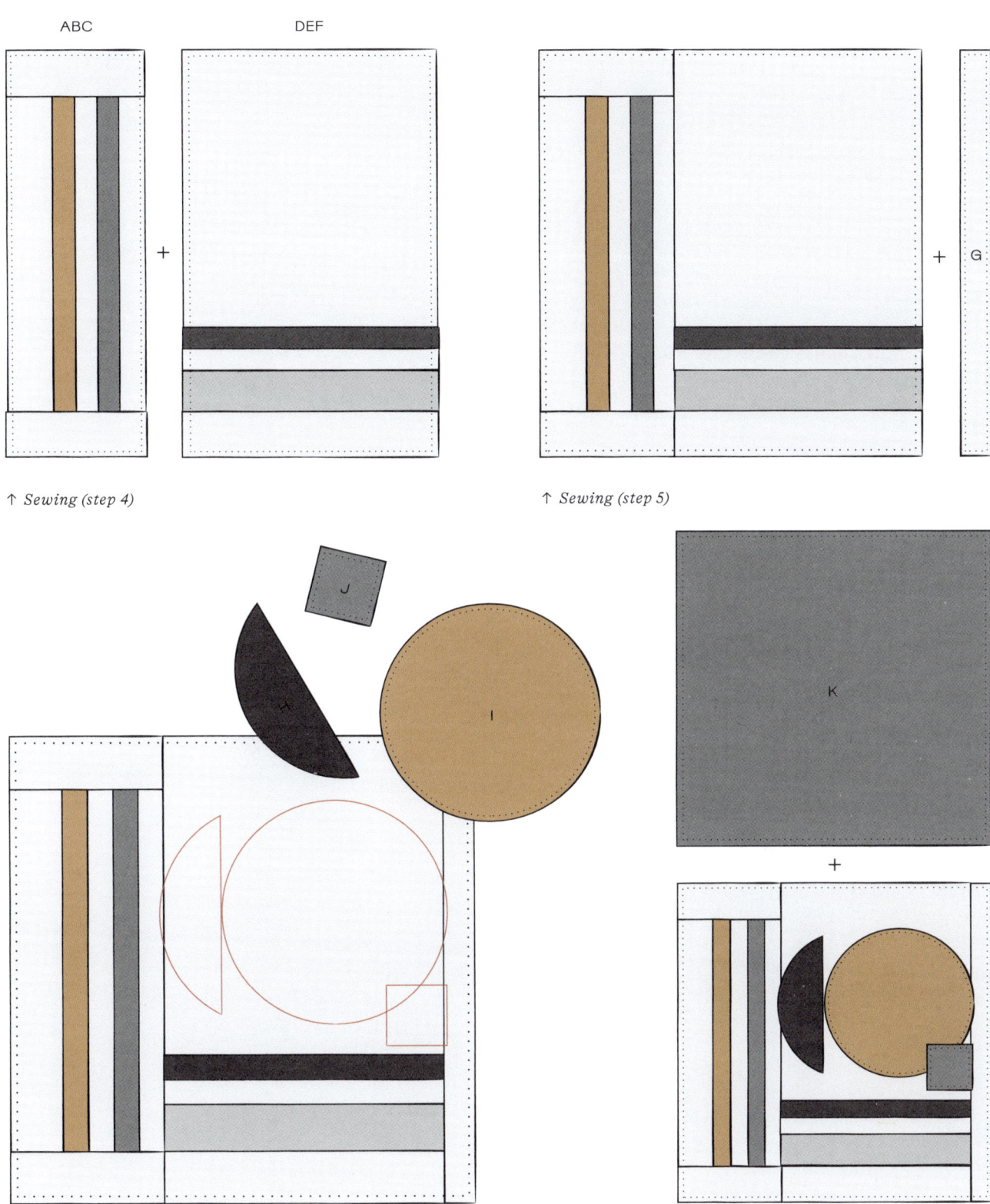

↑ *Sewing (step 4)*

G

+

↑ *Sewing (step 5)*

J

H   I

K

+

↑ *Appliqué and quilting (step 1)*

↑ *Appliqué and quilting (step 3)*

Adding the zip and finishing up

1. Fold the panel in half widthwise, right sides together. Baste the bottom of the cushion panel together on your sewing machine using a 4 mm stitch length and a 1-cm (⅜-in) seam allowance. Press the seam open.

2. Place the zip right side down on top of the basted seam so that the teeth line up with the seam line. Starting from the centre point and working your way to the outer edges of the cushion, pin the zip in place. Baste the zip in place by hand or use basting tape to secure it in position, so that it doesn't move around while you sew.

3. Put a zipper foot on your sewing machine, if you have one, and adjust the stitch length to 2.5 mm. Turn the cushion cover right side out and, from the right side, sew along one side of your basted line as close to the zip teeth as possible without catching them. Pivot with the needle down in the fabric and sew across the bottom of your zip tape (do this with the hand wheel of your sewing machine if you're using a metal zip, as your machine's needle will break if it hits the teeth). Finally, pivot one more time and sew along the other side of the zip, again stitching as close to the zip teeth as possible.

4. Unpick the basting stitches.

5. Unzip the zip and turn the cushion cover wrong side out again. Sew the sides of your cushion shut. Press. Cut a small V shape into the corners so that they flip out neatly.

6. Flip your cushion cover right side out. Insert the cushion pad.

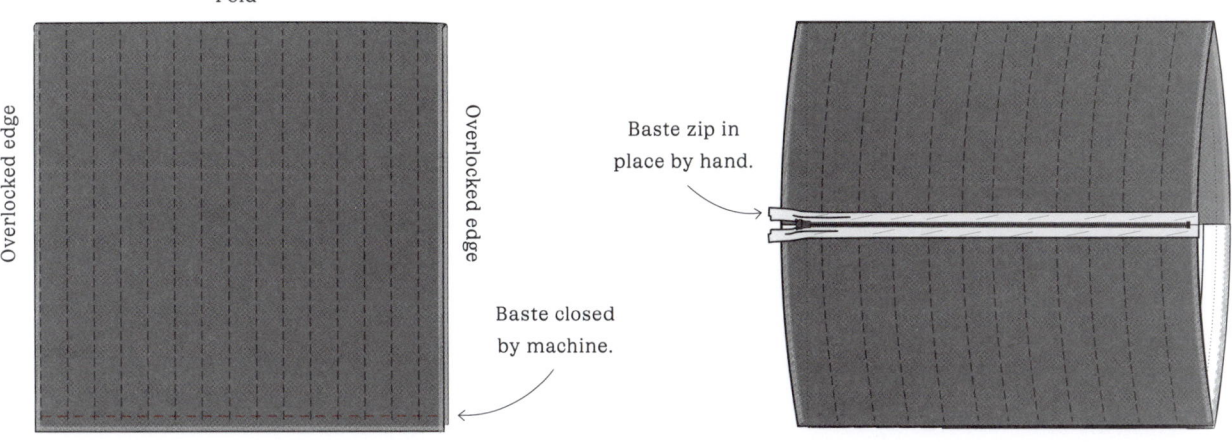

Fold

Overlocked edge

Overlocked edge

Baste zip in
place by hand.

Baste closed
by machine.

↑ *Adding the zip and finishing up (step 1)*

↑ *Adding the zip and finishing up (step 2)*

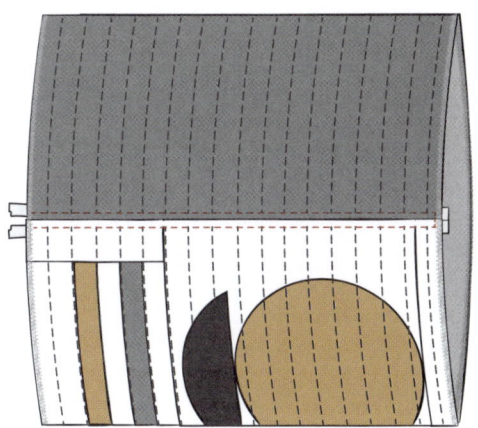

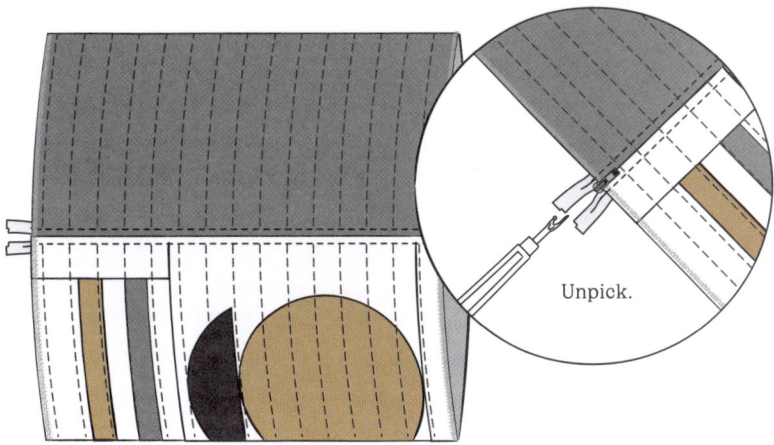

Unpick.

↑ *Adding the zip and finishing up (step 3)*

↑ *Adding the zip and finishing up (step 4)*

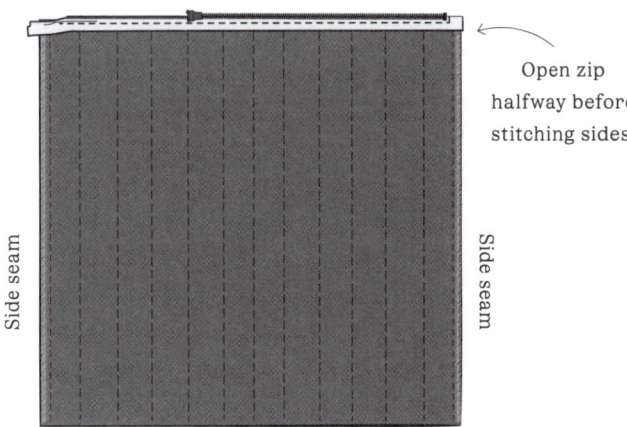

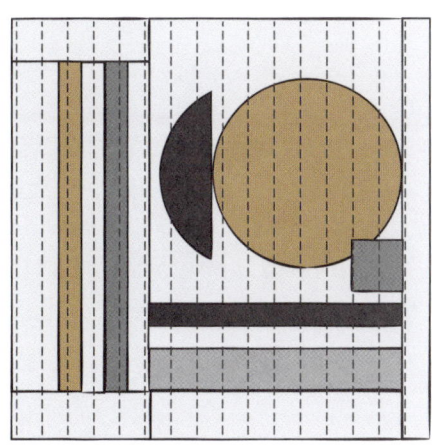

Open zip
halfway before
stitching sides.

Side seam

Side seam

↑ *Adding the zip and finishing up (step 5)*

↑ *Finished cushion*

CLARE QUILT

It took a lot of self-restraint for me not to open this introduction with a bad joke about 'life giving you lemons'. Instead, I'm going to get a little earnest and philosophical. I like lemons because they are sour, and sourness (while not universally loved) balances other flavours, offsetting tooth-hurting sweetness or sweat-inducing spiciness. In life, I think it is the same: you need some sour to make you appreciate the sweet.

The appliqué in this quilt, a simple abstracted lemon on a slender branch, is a tribute to that idea. I'd make it in linen, or cotton so old and soft that it wrinkles like linen. If you just want to appliqué and not quilt it, then this might also be used as a summertime tablecloth.

⧘ METHOD ⧙

Making the pattern and getting started

Scale up the appliqué templates on page 204 onto paper or card using your chosen method (see pages 72–3). Alternatively, full-size templates are available to download at workingcloth.com.

Cutting

1. Draw around the templates and carefully cut out your appliqué pieces as outlined in the table below.
2. Cut out your fabric 1 rectangle (see table below), then press it. If you are making up the 120 × 170 cm (47¼ × 67 in) background piece from multiple bits of fabric, do that patchwork now and press it so that you have a smooth quilt

fabric	piece	qty
◯ fabric 1	120 × 170 cm (47¼ × 67 in) rectangle	1
◗ fabric 2	lemon template	1
● fabric 3	stem templates	1 ea
	leaf template	1

top to work from.

Sewing

1. Position the appliqué pieces on your quilt top and stitch them in place, following the instructions for machine appliqué (pages 43–4) or needle-turned appliqué (page 45).
2. Press the quilt top.
3. Following your preferred method (see Chapter 3), baste, quilt, trim and bind your quilt. I quilted straight white lines, 7.5 cm (3 in) apart, and then I quilted around my appliqué pieces to give them a bit of a pop. I made the backing for this quilt from a burnt-orange-hued linen sheet, and bound the quilt with the same fabric.

FINISHED SIZE

120 × 170 cm (47¼ × 67 in)

FABRIC

Note yardages are estimated for fabric 115 cm (45 in) wide.

> fabric 1: 2 m (2¼ yd)
> fabric 2: 0.75 m (¾ yd)
> fabric 3: 0.25 m (¼ yd)
> backing fabric: 130 × 180 cm (51 × 71 in; can be patchworked together)

HABERDASHERY

> binding: 6.5 m (7¼ yd) straight-grain binding 5 cm (2 in) wide
> wadding: 130 × 180 cm (51 × 71 in)
> thread for piecing and appliqué
> 2 × 40-m skeins of sashiko thread or 1 × 180-m spool of perle 8 cotton thread for quilting

EQUIPMENT

> basic quilt-making kit (page 73)

NOTES

> A 6-mm (¼-in) seam allowance is included; add 3 mm (⅛ in) to the appliqué pieces if you're using the needle-turned method (see page 45).
> If you're using shop-bought fabric that is 115 cm (45 in) wide, use the width of the fabric. This will make the quilt a little narrower than the size listed, but you avoid having to patchwork the background.

↑ *Finished quilt*

PROJECTS / HOMEWARES

JANET QUILT

This version of a classic star patchwork pattern is the most complicated quilt in this section of the book. I named it after my mum (a complicated woman only in the best sense). She is who I inherited my crafty skills from, but hers are admittedly much cooler than mine, spanning everything from TIG welding to oil painting.

The central motif is the part of this quilt that might cause you problems. It's not too tricky, though you have to be careful where you put your sewn units. I suggest you clear a big section of your floor or a spare table so you can see that you're following the correct layout. If you're short on space, make up the quilt top in quarters, then sew those quarters together. If you're a hardcore quilter already, you may have a design wall. (For the uninitiated, a design wall is a flat surface usually covered with flannel so that the quilt top sticks to it. It's vertical, saving you floor space. You can make them or buy them, and they are very useful for those with limited mobility or room!)

As always, work slowly and methodically, and resist the urge (I know sometimes it's tough) to rush through the steps.

ξ METHOD ξ

Cutting

You're going to make a whopping 260 half-square triangles (HSTs), 12 squares with fabric 1 and 40 squares with fabric 2.

If you are using scraps, cut each square individually and use them to make the HSTs. There are different ways to make HSTs outlined on pages 38–9. My favourite way – and the quickest – is the magic 8 method. For this project, you'll need to cut 28 cm (11 in) squares.

If you are using fabric yardage, cut it into strips and then subdivide the strips into squares to speed the process along (see page 36).

MAGIC 8 METHOD

fabric	piece	qty
○ fabric 1	28 cm (11 in) square	33
	11.5 cm (4½ in) square	24
● fabric 2	28 cm (11 in) square	33
	11.5 cm (4½ in) square	40

TWO-AT-A-TIME METHOD

fabric	piece	qty
○ fabric 1	14 cm (5½ in) square	130
	11.5 cm (4½ in) square	24
● fabric 2	14 cm (5½ in) square	130
	11.5 cm (4½ in) square	40

FINISHED SIZE

180 × 180 cm (71 × 71 in)

FABRIC

Note yardages are estimated for fabric 115 cm (45 in) wide.

> fabric 1:
> *two-at-a-time*: 3 m (3¼ yd)
> *magic 8*: 3.1 m (3½ yd)
> fabric 2:
> *two-at-a-time*: 3.3 m (3¾ yd)
> *magic 8*: 3.3 m (3¾ yd)
> backing fabric: 190 × 190 cm (75 × 75 in; can be patchworked together)

HABERDASHERY

> wadding: 190 × 190 cm (75 × 75 in)
> binding: 5 m (5½ yd) straight-grain binding 5 cm (2 in) wide
> thread for piecing
> 4 × 40-m skeins of sashiko or 2 × 80-m spools of perle 8 cotton thread for quilting

EQUIPMENT

> basic quilt-making kit (page 73)

NOTES

> A 6-mm (¼-in) seam allowance is included unless otherwise noted.

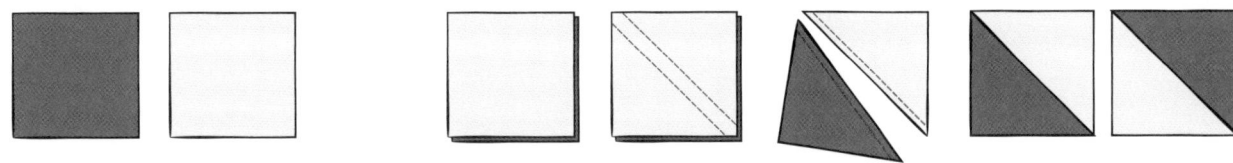

↑ *Cutting (squares)*   ↑ *Sewing (step 1; two-at-a-time method; overleaf)*

① ② ③ ④ ⑤ ⑥ ⑦ ⑧ ⑨

↑ *Sewing (step 3; quarter quadrant row plan; overleaf)*

Sewing

1. Sew 260 11.5-cm (4½-in) HSTs made of fabrics 1 and 2, using the method of your choice (see pages 38–9).
2. Press and trim each HST.
3. Following the illustration on page 155 very carefully, lay out the units in rows to create the top left quarter of the quilt.
4. Stitch the units in the first row, working methodically. Press the seam allowances to the left, then lay the row back down in its place.
5. Stitch the second row together, then press the seam allowances to the right. Lay it back below the first row.
6. Continue until you have completed all nine rows, alternating the direction you press the seams.
7. Double-check your layout before you start sewing. Starting with rows 1 and 2, pin and sew the rows together, nesting your seams (see page 34). Press the seams between the rows, alternating so that you can nest the seams when you put the quarters of the quilt together.
8. Set the completed section aside and repeat steps 3–7 for the other three quarters of the quilt.
9. Lay the four quarters out and rotate them to match the illustration.
10. When you're sure you've set them out correctly, pin and sew the top left and top right quarters together. Then pin and sew the bottom left and bottom right quarters together.
11. Pin and sew the two halves of the quilt top together. Press.
12. Following your preferred method (see Chapter 3), baste, quilt, trim and bind your quilt. I stitched in the ditch (see page 51) with white sashiko thread and then bound the quilt in a crisp, white cotton.

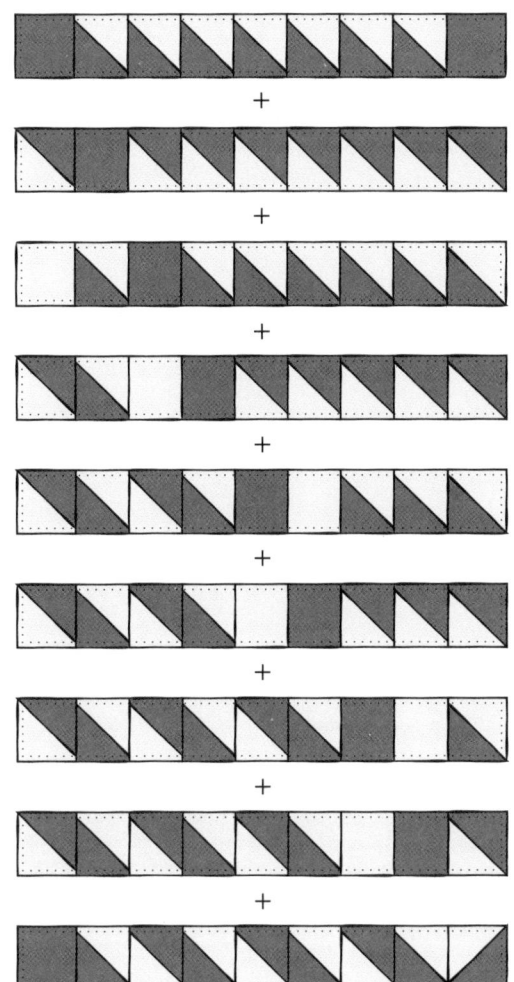

↑ *Sewing (step 6)*

↑ *Sewing (step 9)*

↑ *Sewing (step 12)*

CLOTHING AND ACCESSORIES

MARION DRAWSTRING BAG

I find these little bags endlessly useful. They're perfectly sized for stashing away everything from yarn to toiletries to snacks. You can find some in my sock drawer, sewing cupboard and tucked into my suitcase when I go on holiday.

The pattern has been designed for improvisational patchwork, so each bag will look a bit different.

I patchwork both the lining and the outer fabric to make the most of my fabric stash, but you could do only one (or neither). The lining piece ends up on the back, so it is worth paying it some attention in any case. I used a bit of curtain, a tablecloth with an existing (adorable) apple appliqué, and a piece of linen left over from another project.

⧘ METHOD ⧙

Making the patchwork panels

1. You're going to make an improvisational patchwork panel so have a riffle through your scrap bag and get sewing, following the instructions on page 42.
2. For the bag pictured, I patchworked my lining panel, too. You can do the same, or simply cut a piece of fabric for the lining that measures 30 × 60 cm (12 × 23½ in).
3. Square up the corners and edges of your panels so they measure exactly 30 × 60 cm (12 × 23½ in).

Making the bag

1. Fold your patchwork panel in half lengthwise. Press a crease into the centre. Unfold. Repeat for your lining fabric.
2. Lay your patchwork panel on top of your lining, right sides together, so that the edges are flush. Pin around the edges.
3. Starting 2.5 cm (1 in) from the centre fold, sew all around the edges of your panels using a 1-cm (⅜-in) seam allowance. Stop 2.5 cm (1 in) from the other side of the centre fold, so that you have a 5-cm (2-in) gap. Trim your threads.
4. Clip the corners, being careful not to cut through the seam.
5. Press the seam allowances open all the way around.
6. Turn the bag right side out through the 5-cm (2-in) gap, using a point turner to get the corners nice and crisp. (A chopstick or a mechanical pencil with no lead also works well.) Press.
7. Next, tidy up the edges of the 5-cm (2-in) gap, as it's going to become the opening that you thread your drawstring through. Press under the raw edges of the gap and stitch each side in place about 3 mm (⅛ in) from the edge.
8. Now comes a bit of fabric origami to push the lining layer into the top layer. Tease the two layers apart, then push the corner of one short end into the corner of the opposite short end, so the whole bag folds in on itself and you have a square. Press.
9. The hole will now be at the top of the bag and form a vertical split. This will be the opening for your drawstring.
10. Create a channel for your drawstring to go through by sewing all the way around the top edge, 2.5 cm (1 in) from the top.
11. Attach a safety pin to one end of your drawstring. Insert the safety pin into the channel and pull your drawstring all the way through, making sure each end extends the same length.

FINISHED SIZE

28.5 × 28.5 cm (11¼ × 11¼ in)

FABRIC

Note yardages are estimated for fabric 115 cm (45 in) wide.

> fabric 1: 0.25 m (¼ yd)
> fabric 2: 0.25 m (¼ yd)
> fabric 3: 0.25 m (¼ yd)
> lining fabric: 0.25 m (¼ yd)

HABERDASHERY

> thread for piecing
> 1 m (1 yd) grosgrain or ribbon for ties

EQUIPMENT

> basic quilt-making kit (page 73)
> point turner (optional)
> safety pins

NOTES

> I've used about 0.25 m (¼ yd) of each fabric, but one of the joys of improvisational patchwork is that you can make use of whatever you have to hand. Take the yardages above as a rough idea and not an exact formula.
> Use a 6-mm (¼-in) seam allowance for the improvisational patchwork panels and a 1-cm (⅜-in) seam allowance when sewing the bag.

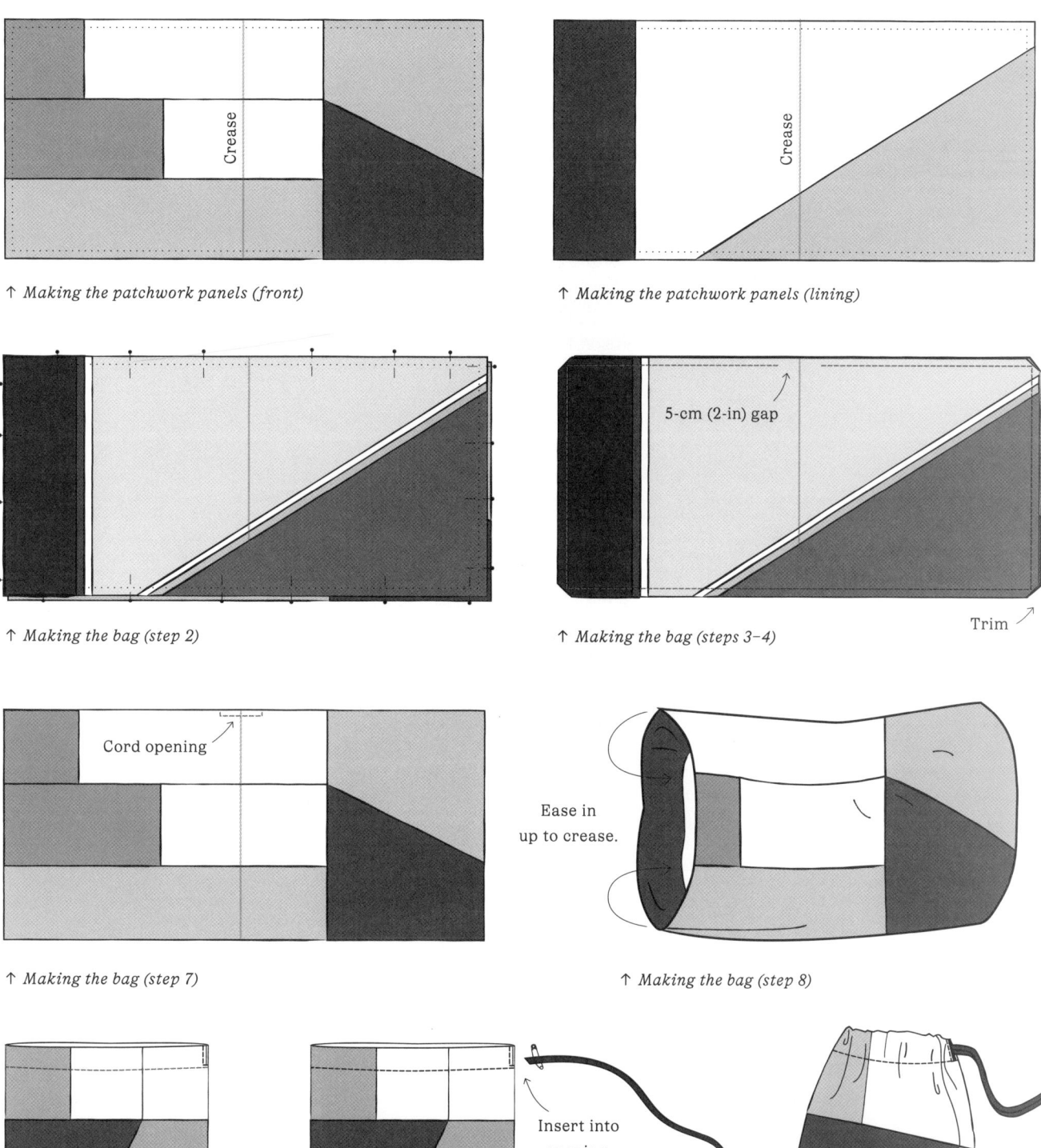

↑ *Making the patchwork panels (front)*

↑ *Making the patchwork panels (lining)*

Crease

Crease

↑ *Making the bag (step 2)*

5-cm (2-in) gap

↑ *Making the bag (steps 3–4)*

Trim

Cord opening

↑ *Making the bag (step 7)*

Ease in
up to crease.

↑ *Making the bag (step 8)*

↑ *Making the bag (step 10)*

Insert into
opening.

↑ *Making the bag (step 11)*

↑ *Finished bag*

PROJECTS / CLOTHING AND ACCESSORIES

ELEANOR ZIP POUCH

By virtue of having a zip, this pouch is a little more complicated (but only a little – don't let it scare you) than the Marion drawstring bag (page 161). In practice they play much the same role. Stash your pencils, tuck your toiletries away or use it (as I do) to organise your sewing kit.

I've made mine out of fabric strips – a simple way to use up small, leftover fabric scraps and make it look neat and purposeful. There are instructions for a plain version, but if you're feeling wild you could try some improvisational patchwork or a half-square triangle pattern.

⸙ METHOD ⸙

Cutting and prep work

Decide if you want to make a plain or striped pouch, then cut out your fabric and interfacing according to the table below.

version	fabric		piece	qty
plain	○	outer	32 × 38 cm (12½ × 15 in) rectangle	1
			7.5 cm (3 in) square tab	2
striped	○	fabric 1	6.4 × 38 cm (2½ × 15 in) rectangle	3
			7.5 cm (3 in) square tab	2
	●	fabric 2	6.4 × 38 cm (2½ × 15 in) rectangle	3
both	◗	lining	32 × 38 cm (12½ × 15 in) rectangle	1
	◗	binding	4 × 19 cm (1½ × 7½ in)	2
			4 × 13 cm (1½ × 5 in)	4
	⊙	interfacing	32 × 38 cm (12½ × 15 in) rectangle	1
			7.5 cm (3 in) square tab	2

Striped version only
Pin and sew your six rectangles together, starting with fabric 2 and alternating between the colours as illustrated. Press the seam allowances open. Check that your panel measures 32 × 38 cm (12½ × 15 in) and, if it doesn't, trim it to fit.

Both versions
Apply the interfacing to the wrong side of your striped panel or outer fabric rectangle and the two square tabs. Set aside.

Making the pouch

1. Mark the centre point of the shorter sides of the lining, the outer fabric panel and the zip.
2. Insert the zip using the technique shown for the Roma bolster (see pages 132–3).
3. Once your zip is in, your bag should be a tube. Flip the tube so that the lining is on the outside. Set aside.

FINISHED SIZE

L × W × H: 13 × 10 × 9 cm
(5 × 4 × 3½ in)

FABRIC

Note yardages are estimated for fabric 115 cm (45 in) wide.

Plain version
> outer fabric: 0.3 m (⅓ yd)

Striped version
> fabric 1: 0.25 m (¼ yd)
> fabric 2: 0.25 m (¼ yd)

Both versions
> lining/straight-grain binding fabric: 0.3 m (⅓ yd)

HABERDASHERY

> 25-cm (10-in) zip
> thread for piecing
> medium-weight iron-on interfacing: 50 × 50 cm (19¾ × 19¾ in)

EQUIPMENT

> basic quilt-making kit (page 73)

NOTES

> A 6-mm (¼-in) seam allowance is included in the pattern.

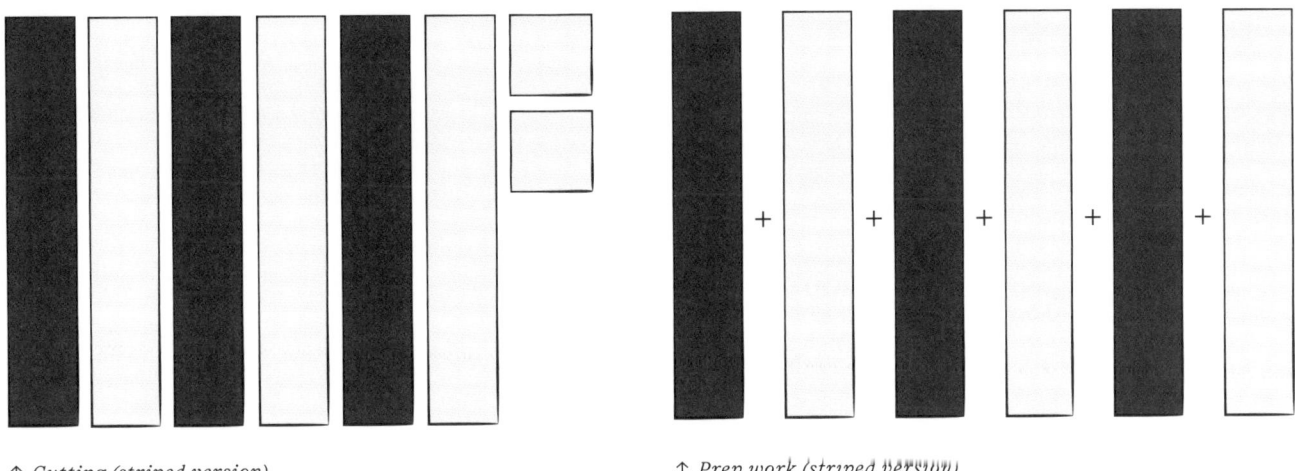

↑ *Cutting (striped version)*

↑ *Prep work (striped version)*

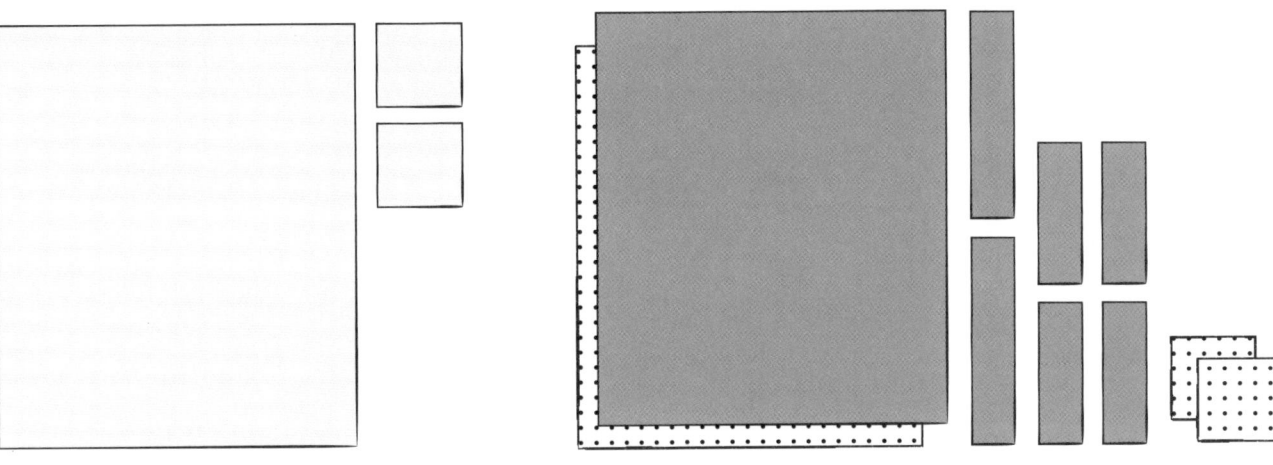

↑ *Cutting (plain version)*

↑ *Cutting (lining, binding and interfacing)*

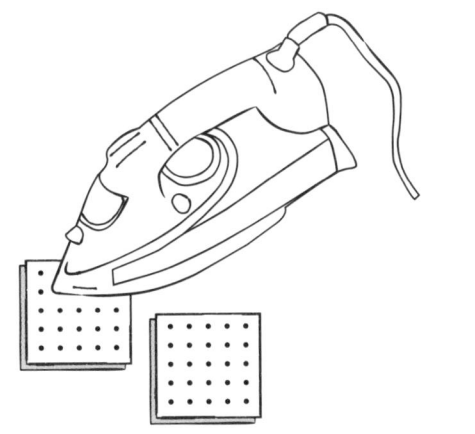

↑ *Prep work (interfacing your tabs)*

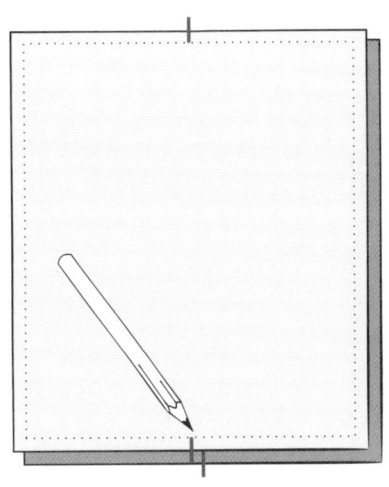

↑ *Making the pouch (step 1)*

PROJECTS / CLOTHING AND ACCESSORIES

Making the tabs and binding

1. Take your 7.5-cm (3-in) squares (these will be the tabs for your zip) and all of your small lining rectangles. Fold each one in half lengthwise. Open up and fold the outside edges into the middle as if you are making binding (see pages 59–64). Press.
2. Edge stitch (see page 112) around the perimeter of the two tabs.
3. Fold the tabs in half so they form a loop. Stitch the short edges together 3 mm (⅛ in) from the bottom edge.

Attaching the tabs

1. Lay the body of the bag flat so that the zip is centred in the middle, facing up.
2. Line up the first tab with the bottom centre of your bag (not on the zipper – halfway around the tube). Sew this short edge of the bag using a 1-cm (⅜-in) seam allowance, enclosing the end of the zip and the bag tab. Go slowly and carefully over the zip – you can use your hand wheel to help you with this. Repeat on the other side.
3. Bind the short edges of the bag (seam allowances together) with your 4 × 19 cm (1½ × 7½ in) rectangles (see pages 59–64).
4. At this stage, your bag should look like a flat rectangle, with the zip centred in the middle of one side. Starting at one corner and working your way around the bag, measure and mark 5 cm (2 in) along both the long and short edges of your bag, as illustrated.
5. On each corner, draw a square that connects the points that you marked in the last step.
6. Cut out each of the squares that you've just drawn.
7. Working your way around the pouch, pull the corner points of the cut-out squares apart until the cut edges become straight and you get a box shape. Pin the edges flush together. Stitch each corner edge with a 1-cm (⅜-in) seam allowance.
8. Bind each seam allowance with your 4 × 12.5 cm (1½ × 5 in) lining strips. Flip your bag right side out. You're all done!

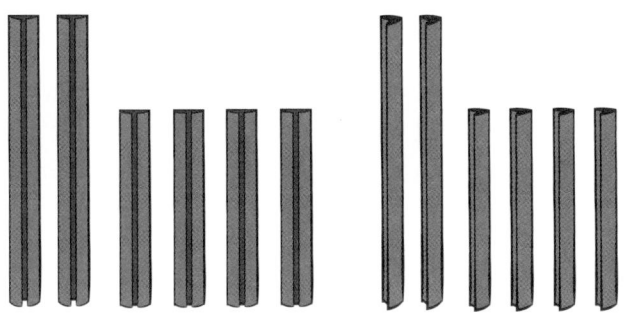

↑ *Making the tabs and binding (step 1)*

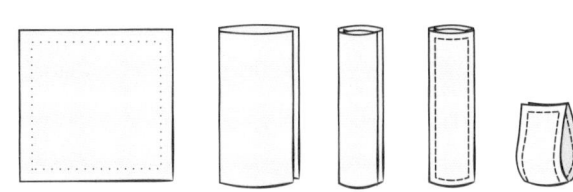

↑ *Making the tabs and binding (steps 2–3)*

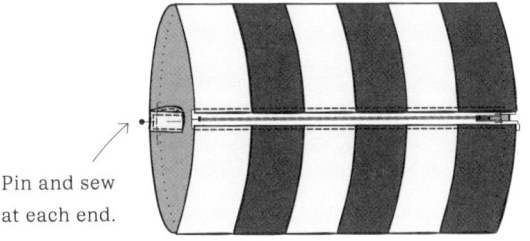

Pin and sew at each end.

↑ *Attaching the tabs (steps 1–2)*

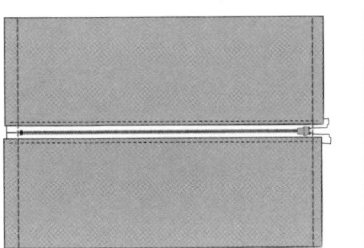

↑ *Attaching the tabs (step 3)*

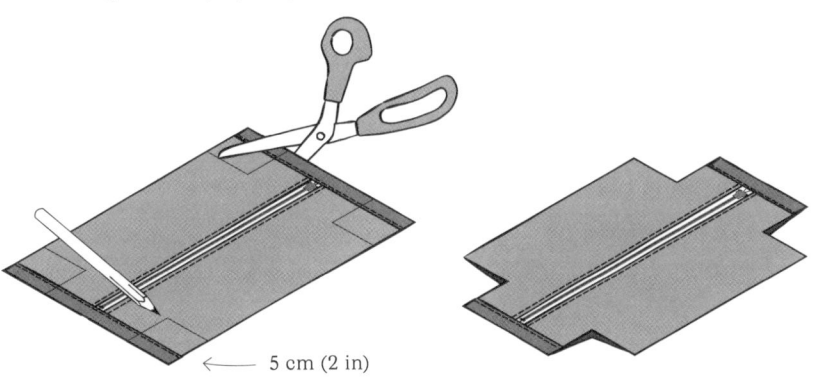

← 5 cm (2 in)

↑ *Attaching the tabs (steps 4–6)*

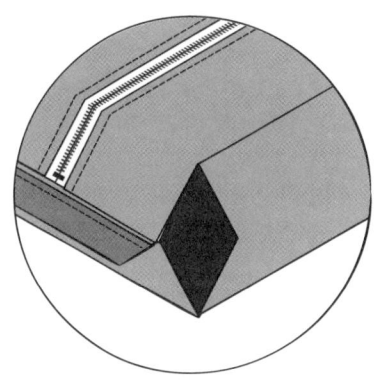

↑ *Attaching the tabs (step 7)*

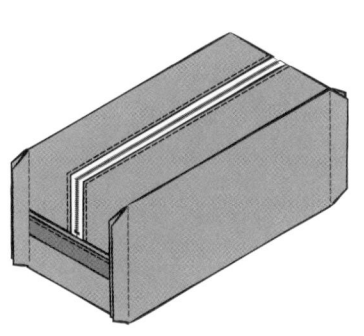

↑ *Attaching the tabs (steps 7–8)*

Fold over the top and bottom binding edges for a neat finish.

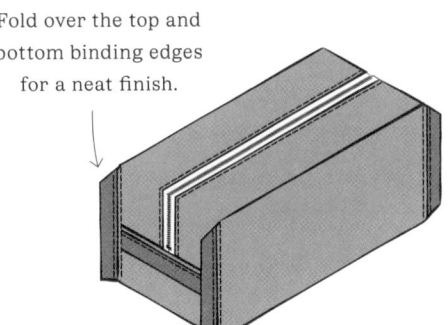

↑ *Finished striped pouch*

ISOBEL TOTE BAG

The Isobel is a catch-all weekend bag – it fits absolutely everything. Towels for the beach? Check. Bits for the gym? Check. A shapely stick your kid has found at the park and insists on bringing home? Check. Your kid themselves? Probably. But I am in no way recommending that this is how you get them from A to B.

The pattern I've used is an old one. It's often called the drunkard's path for its meandering curves, which slope and bend like a tipsy person trying very hard to walk in a straight line. Even though it

might look challenging, it's a pretty straightforward make. The only part that is somewhat difficult is sewing the curves – and with a bit of practice and patience you'll soon find that isn't so tricky either.

Still, if you're after a well-sewn bag, it's best not to take the pattern's name too literally. Don't go pouring yourself some boozy tipple before tucking into this project or your curves might wobble more than you'd like. You could make yours the same or try it in solid fabrics for a clean look instead.

⟨ METHOD ⟩

Cutting and prep work

Patchwork version
Trace the templates for the drunkard's path blocks on page 202, then cut out the quantities in the table below.

fabric	piece	qty
● fabric 1	templates A and B	31 ea
○ fabric 2	templates A and B	31 ea

Plain version
Cut out the pieces outlined in the table below.

fabric	piece	qty
● fabric 1	main: 64 × 94.5 cm (25¼ × 37¼ in)	1
	side: 12 × 42.3 cm (4¾ × 16⅔ in)	2

Both versions
1. Mark and cut out the zip panels, straps, lining, interfacing and wadding as outlined in the table below.
2. Interface your zip panels and straps.

fabric	piece	qty
● fabric 1	zip panel: 62 × 7.5 cm (24½ × 3 in)	4
	strap: 62 × 10 cm (24½ × 4 in)	2
◕ lining	main: 64 × 94.5 cm (25¼ × 37¼ in)	1
	side: 12 × 42.3 cm (4¾ × 16⅔ in)	2
⊙ interfacing	zip panel: 62 × 7.5 cm (24½ × 3 in)	4
	strap: 62 × 10 cm (24½ × 4 in)	2
○ wadding	62 × 146 cm (24½ in × 57½ in)	6

FINISHED SIZE

H × W × D: 40.6 × 61 × 10 cm
(16 × 24 × 4 in)

FABRIC

Note yardages are estimated for fabric 115 cm (45 in) wide.

Patchwork version
> fabric 1: 1.2 m (1⅜ yd)
> fabric 2: 0.8 m (1 yd)

Plain version
> fabric 1: 1.2 m (1⅜ yd)

Both versions
> lining fabric: 0.9 m (1 yd)

HABERDASHERY

> wadding: 1.2 × 1.2 m (1⅜ × 1⅜ yd)
> binding: 1.5 m (1¾ yd) straight-grain binding 5 cm (2 in) wide
> medium-weight iron-on interfacing: 0.5 m (½ yd)
> threads for piecing and sashiko or perle 8 cotton thread for quilting
> 53-cm (21-in) zip

EQUIPMENT

> basic quilt-making kit (page 73)

NOTES

> A 6-mm (¼-in) seam allowance is included for the patchwork version unless otherwise noted.
> A 1-cm (⅜-in) seam allowance is included for the plain version unless otherwise noted.

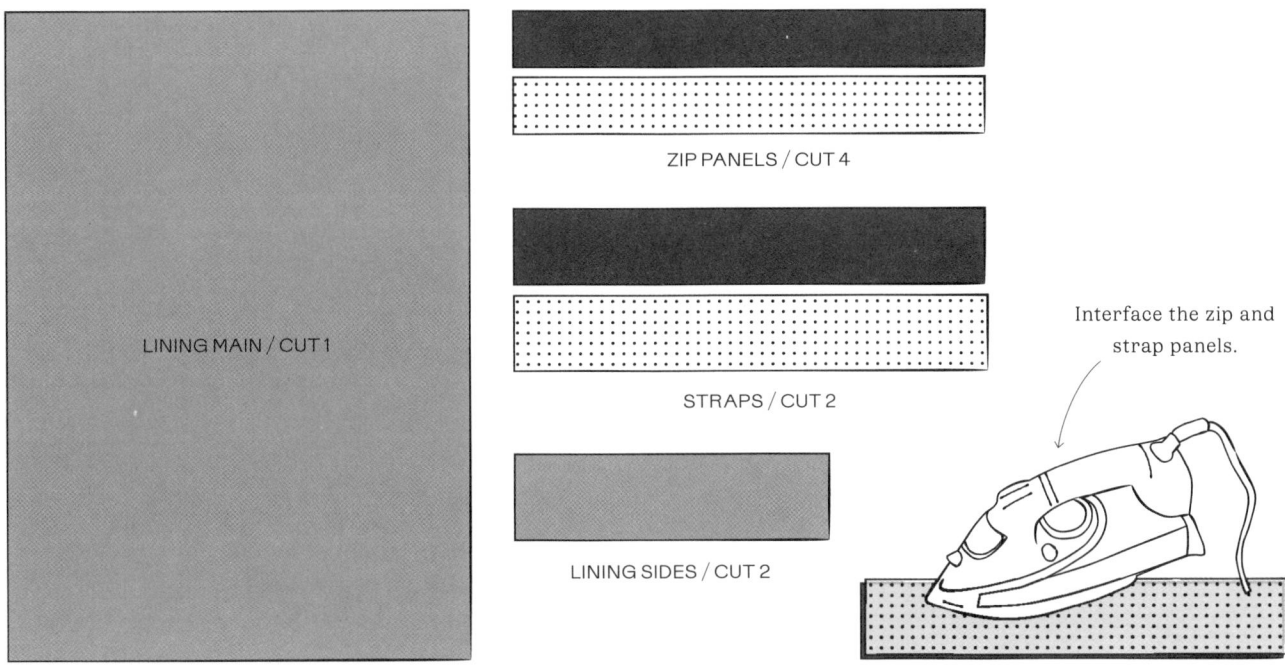

LINING MAIN / CUT 1

ZIP PANELS / CUT 4

STRAPS / CUT 2

LINING SIDES / CUT 2

Interface the zip and strap panels.

↑ *Cutting and prep work*

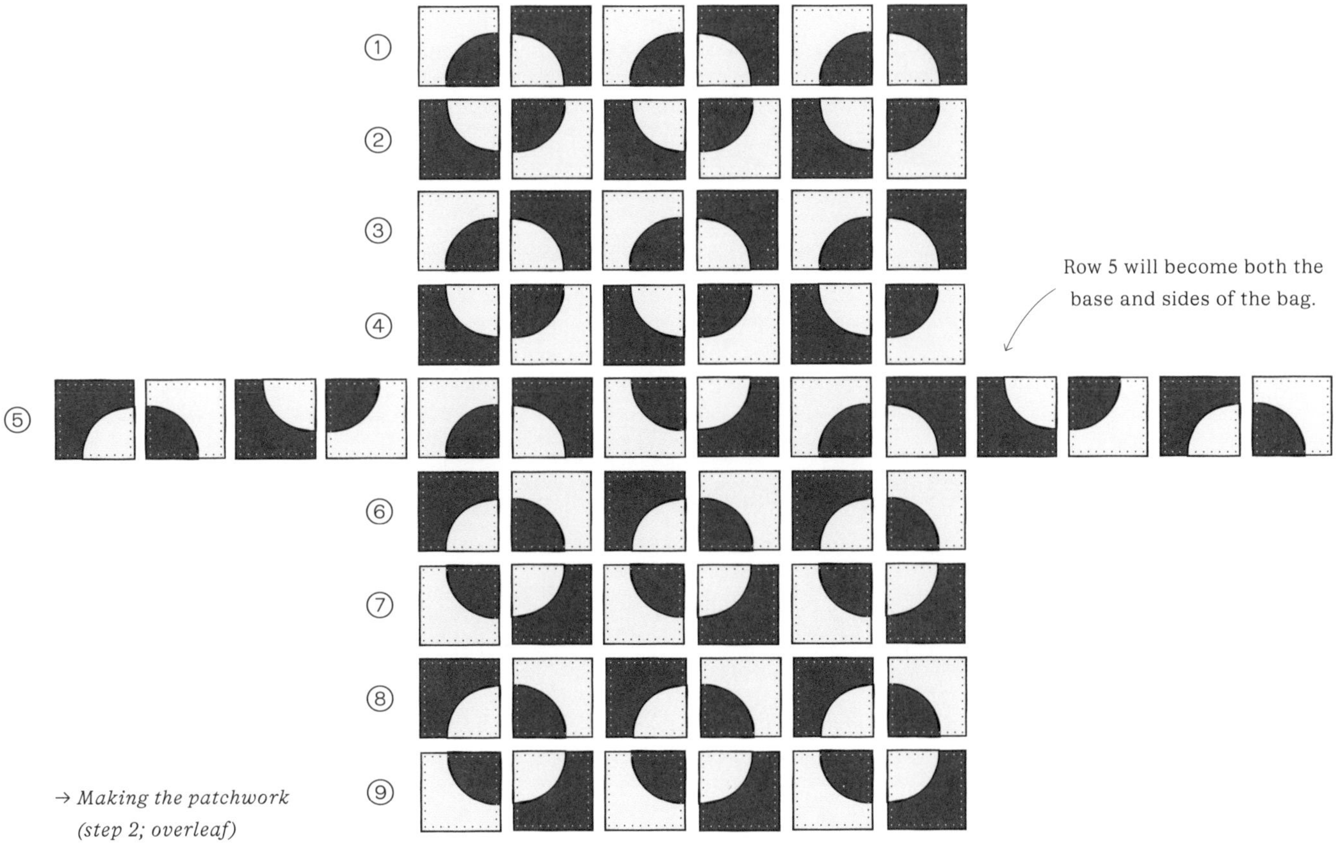

① ② ③ ④ ⑤ ⑥ ⑦ ⑧ ⑨

Row 5 will become both the base and sides of the bag.

→ *Making the patchwork*
(step 2; overleaf)

Making the patchwork

1. Sew 62 drunkard's path units, following the instructions for curved patchwork on page 41. Press and trim each one.
2. Following the illustration on page 173, lay out the units in rows to create the bag shape. Sew the rows together to create the outer bag.

Quilting the bag

1. For this bag, you'll quilt the patchwork to the wadding without a backing layer underneath because you're going to add a lining. Following your preferred method (see Chapter 3), baste your layers then quilt and trim them. I quilted parallel lines every 10 cm (4 in).
2. Carefully match up the side seams, then pin and stitch them together to create the outer body of the bag.

Making the lining and straps

1. Sew your lining pieces with right sides together using a 1-cm (⅜-in) seam allowance, following the illustration. Press the seams. Set aside.
2. Fold and press the rectangles of fabric for the straps in the same way as for making binding (see pages 59–64; illustrations overleaf).
3. Open the rectangles. Press the short ends to the wrong side of the fabric by 1.2 cm (½ in) so they are neatly tucked in.
4. Edge stitch (see page 112) along both edges of the handles.

Attaching the straps

1. Take your quilted bag panel. Mark a centre line, then mark 10 cm (4 in) on either side of the line you've just drawn, as shown on the illustration overleaf. Repeat on the other side of the bag.
2. Take one of your straps, and centre one end of it over one of these marks, so that it extends 7.5 cm (3 in) down the bag. Pin in place. Repeat for the other end of the strap, making sure it doesn't twist in the process.
3. Starting in the bottom right corner (about 3 mm/⅛ in away from the edge), topstitch (see page 112) across the width of the strap, then 5 cm (2 in) up the vertical edge of the strap, back across the width, and down the other vertical edge to create a box.

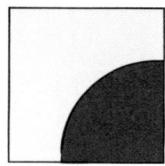 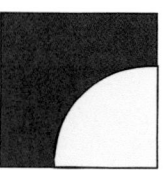

↑ *Making the patchwork (step 1)*

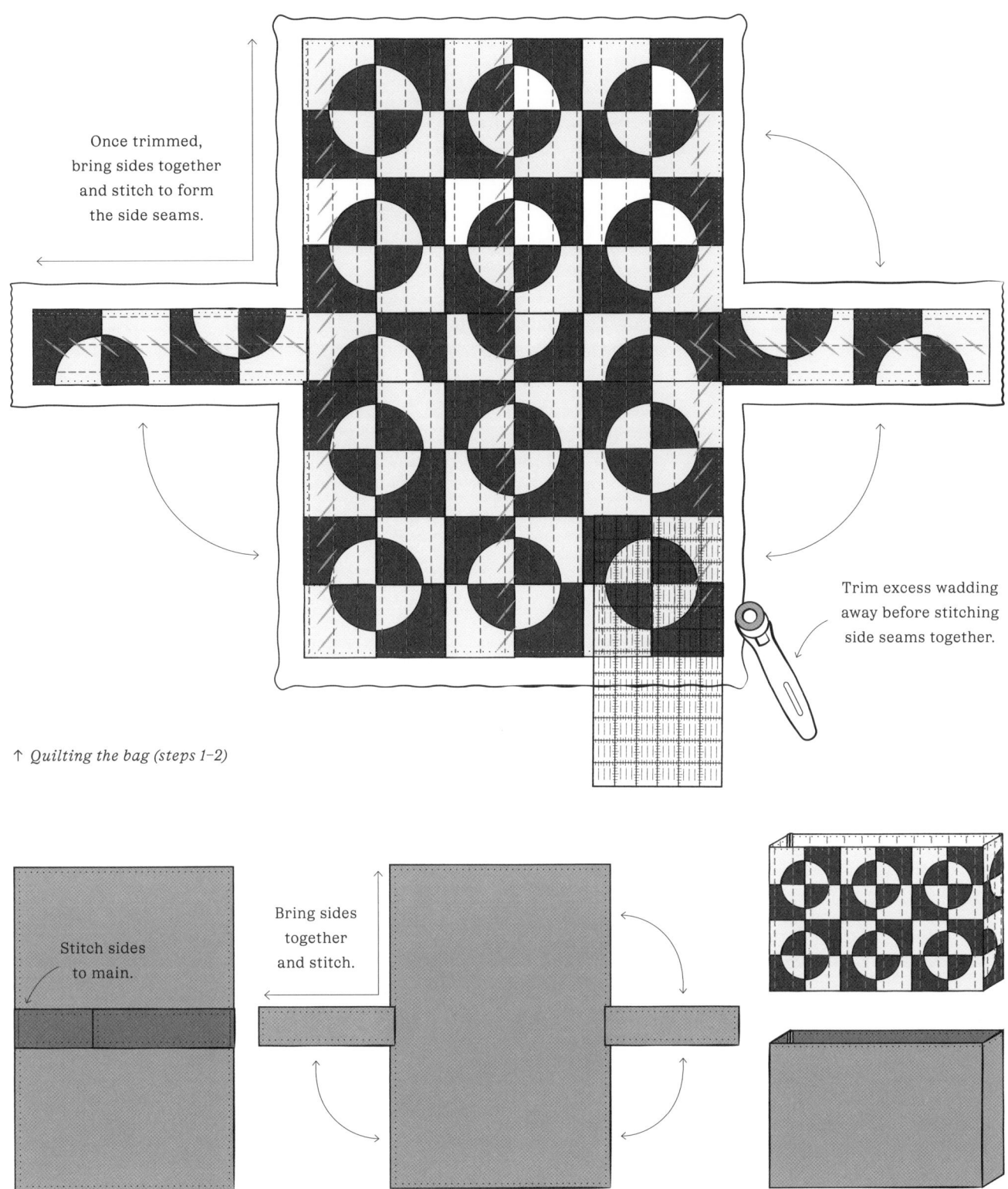

Once trimmed, bring sides together and stitch to form the side seams.

Trim excess wadding away before stitching side seams together.

↑ *Quilting the bag (steps 1–2)*

Stitch sides to main.

Bring sides together and stitch.

↑ *Making the lining and straps (step 1)*

4. Stitch diagonally up to the corner, across the width (stitching over your existing line), and diagonally down to the remaining corner to make an X. This creates a very secure strap, so you can lug around whatever you like in the bag.
5. Attach the other strap to the opposite side of the bag, following the same process.

Putting the lining in

1. Place the lining inside the patchwork bag with wrong sides together so that the top edges of both layers are flush with each other. Carefully match up and pin the corners, then pin the edges together all the way around.
2. Set your stitch length to 4 mm. Sew around the perimeter of the bag 6 mm (¼ in) from the top edge. This basting stitch will be covered up by binding, but it will help stabilise everything for now and make attaching your zip panel easier.

Adding the zip panel

1. Mark the centre point (widthwise) on each of the zip panels and the zip.
2. Sandwich the zip between two of the zip panels, right sides together. Pin the centre point first then work your way to the outside edges, using a 1.2-cm (½-in) seam allowance.
3. Sew 6 mm (¼ in) from the edge of the zipper teeth, being careful to keep your layers aligned and not to catch your zipper teeth in the process.
4. Sew the shorter ends of the zip panels right sides together, using a 1.2-cm (½-in) seam allowance. Clip your corners.
5. Flip over and topstitch the zip panels to the zip.
6. Match up the centre of the raw edges of the zip panel with the centre of the top edge of the bag's body. Pin. Work your way around the top edges, pinning the layers together. The zip panel should end neatly at the corner points of your bag.
7. Baste the zip panel in place, using a 4 mm stitch length, 6 mm (¼ in) from the top edge.

Binding the edge

Following the instructions on pages 59–64, bind the top edge of the bag to neatly enclose the lining, patchwork and zip panels.

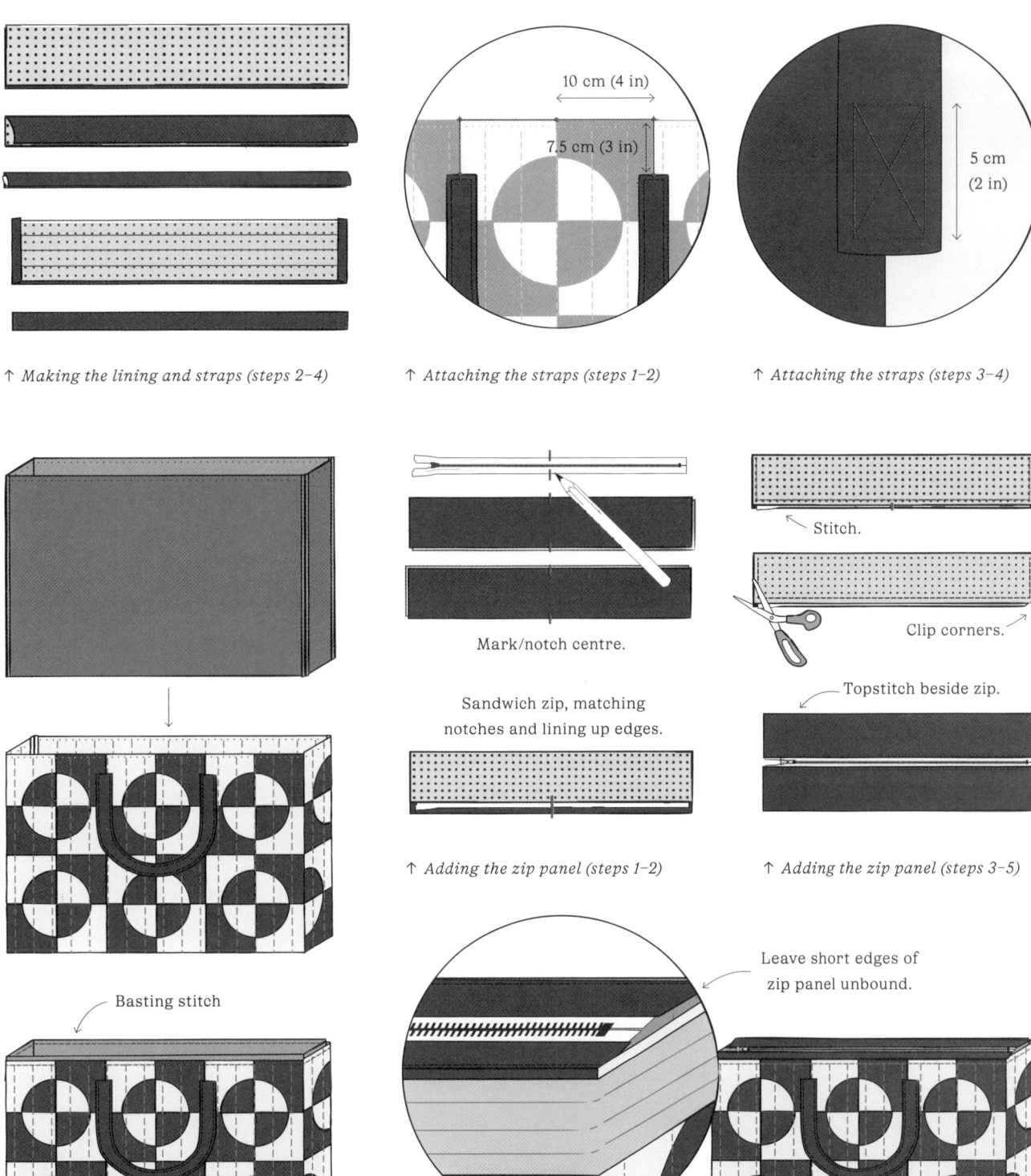

↑ *Making the lining and straps (steps 2–4)*

↑ *Attaching the straps (steps 1–2)*

10 cm (4 in)

7.5 cm (3 in)

↑ *Attaching the straps (steps 3–4)*

5 cm (2 in)

Mark/notch centre.

Sandwich zip, matching notches and lining up edges.

↑ *Adding the zip panel (steps 1–2)*

Stitch.

Clip corners.

Topstitch beside zip.

↑ *Adding the zip panel (steps 3–5)*

Basting stitch

↑ *Putting the lining in (steps 1–2)*

↑ *Binding the edge*

Leave short edges of zip panel unbound.

KNOT BAG PUZZLE / CATHEDRAL WINDOW

This bag is a good all-rounder. Its straps are two different lengths, so you can loop the long one around the short, which makes it easy to lug around. This style of patchwork is called cathedral window for its resemblance to the stained-glass panels that cast jewel-toned shadows on the floors of many churches. Each square is two fabrics – traditionally one is plain and the other a mix of colours and patterns. As I was playing around with versions of this project, I decided to make two jumps away from the original.

First, I fell in love with the way the patchwork looked when it was half done – folded and stitched into a crisp puzzle-like pattern – so I've provided instructions for stopping there. Then, I decided to make all the cathedral windows out of the same fabric, so the texture and intricacy of the patchwork are the heroes.

You can, as always, stray from the examples I've given.

⧙ METHOD ⧘

Cutting and pressing

1. If you're using scissors, rather than a rotary cutter or quilt ruler, take the time to make accurate card templates.
2. Cut twenty 30 cm (12 in) squares from fabric 1. Make sure they are cut on the grain.
3. Take one of your squares. On the wrong side, draw a line 1.2 cm (½ in) from either side of each corner.
4. Using your lines as a guide, press all the edges in towards the wrong side by 1.2 cm (½ in). Press over a piece of card for an extra-crisp edge. It is worth taking the extra time to do this. It really makes a difference!
5. Repeat steps 3–4 for all the 30 cm (12 in) squares.
6. For the cathedral window patchwork, repeat the process in steps 1–5 for all your small (14 cm/5½ in) squares: on the wrong side on each square, draw a line 1.2 cm (½ in) from either side of each corner. Press all the edges to the wrong side by 1.2 cm (½ in).

version	fabric	piece	qty
puzzle	⬤ fabric 1	30 cm (12 in) square	20
cathedral window	⬤ fabric 1	30 cm (12 in) square	20
	⬤ fabric 2	14 cm (5½ in) square	48

Making the squares

1. Take a 30 cm (12 in) square. Fold the square in half, wrong sides together. Press the fold to make a crease.
2. Fold the square in half again. Press the fold to make a crease. Unfold. The creases should cross at the centre of the square.
3. Using the creases that you've just pressed as a guide, fold all the corners into the centre to make a smaller square. Press the square again.
4. Fold the corners into the centre to make an even smaller square. Press once again.
5. Repeat for the other 19 squares.

FABRIC

Note yardages are estimated for fabric 115 cm (45 in) wide.

Puzzle version
> fabric 1: 2 m (2¼ yd)

Cathedral window version
> fabric 1: 1 m (1 yd)
> fabric 2: 0.5 m (½ yd; the second fabric is optional – you could use the main fabric again, a contrasting fabric or even many different kinds of fabrics.)

HABERDASHERY

> thread for piecing
> embroidery thread if you like a contrasting stitch when finishing patchwork by hand

EQUIPMENT

> basic quilt-making kit (page 73)

NOTES

> A 6-mm (¼-in) seam allowance is included in the pattern.

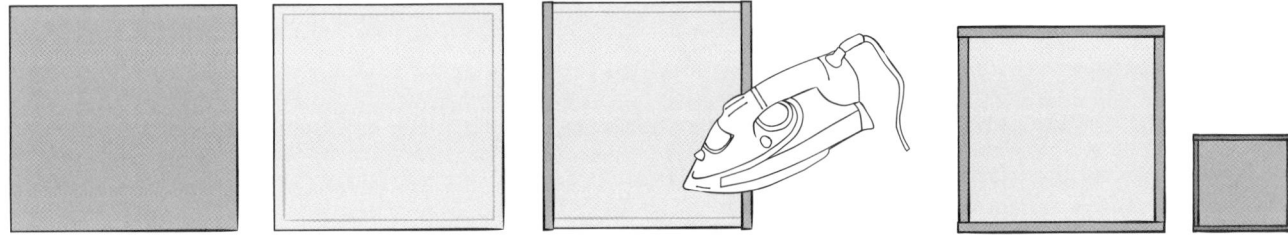

↑ *Cutting and pressing (steps 3–4)*

↑ *Cutting and pressing (step 5)*

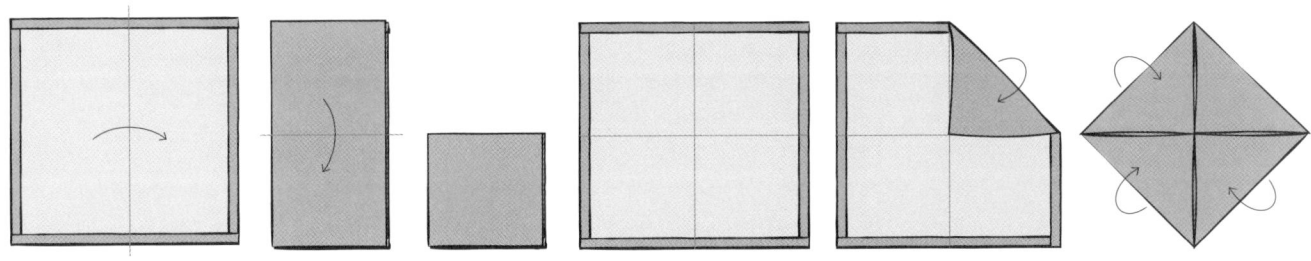

↑ *Making the squares (steps 1–3)*

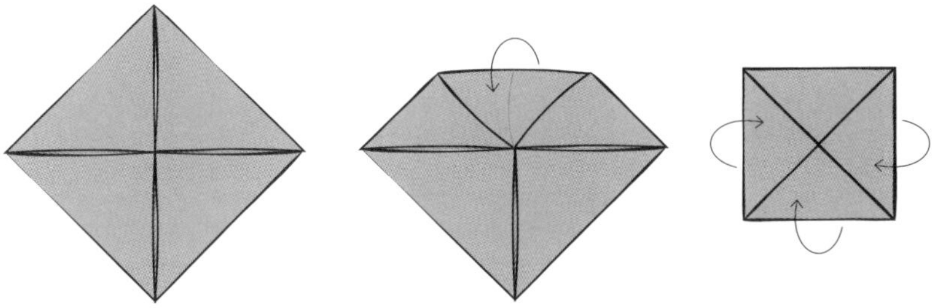

↑ *Making the squares (step 4)*

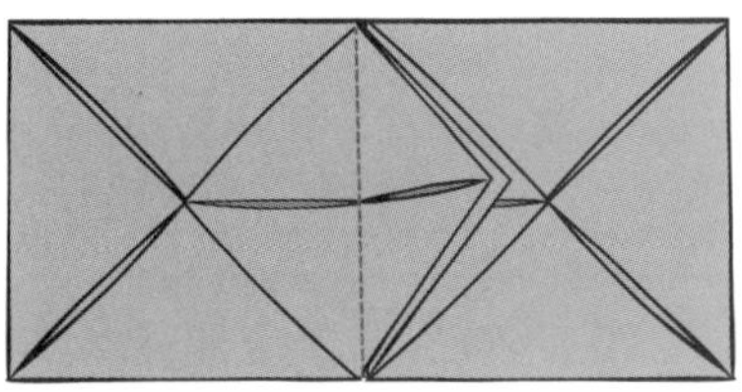

Stitch.

↑ *Sewing the bag together
(steps 1–2; overleaf)*

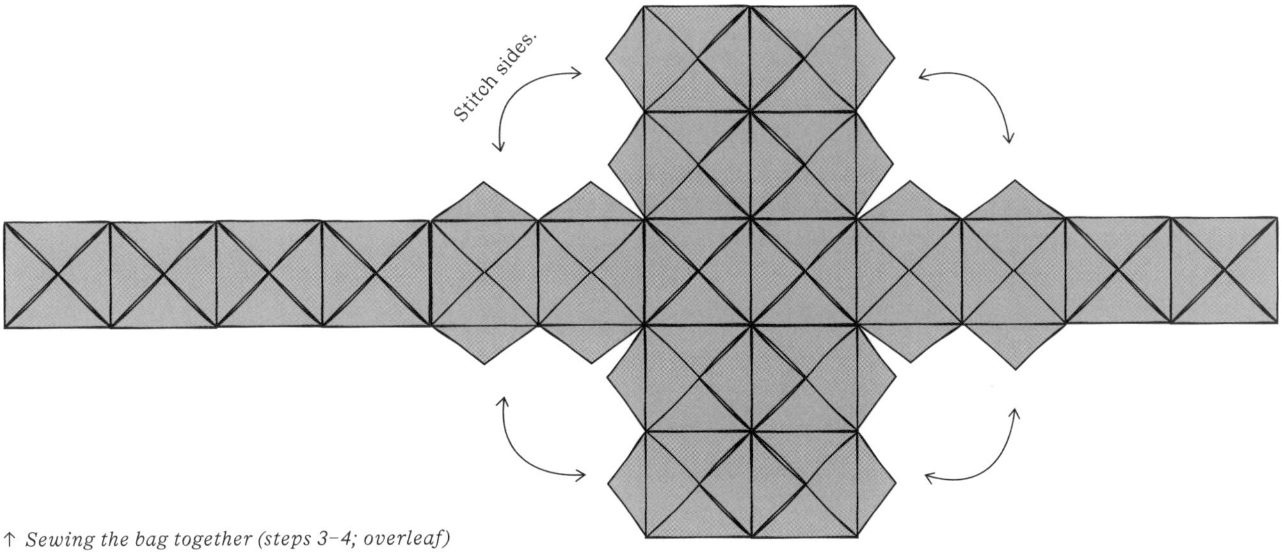

Stitch sides.

↑ *Sewing the bag together (steps 3–4; overleaf)*

PROJECTS / CLOTHING AND ACCESSORIES

Sewing the bag together

1. Take two folded, pressed 30 cm (12 in) squares and lay them side by side, with the triangular flaps facing up. Unfold one triangular flap from the centre of each square. Line up the triangles, wrong sides together, so the edges are flush. Pin.
2. Sew along the crease, following the stitch line marked on the illustration. Set the two squares aside.
3. Using the same technique, sew the remaining squares together into a flat panel, following the illustration.
4. Next, you'll create the sides and bottom of your bag. Using the same technique and following the illustration, unfold the triangular flaps and stitch the sides of the panel together. You'll now have a boxy bag with two tabs (one made of two squares, one made of four), which you'll turn into handles.
5. To make the bag's shorter handle, start with the tab made of two squares. Unfold the triangular flap at the top of the tab, then unfold the triangular flap on the square next to it. Line these up, pin them together and stitch as illustrated, so that the handle forms a loop.
6. To make the bag's longer handle, repeat the process in step 5 for the tab made of four squares.
7. Carefully press the squares one final time, then hand tack the centre of each square where the triangles meet so that all the triangle flaps are secured down.
8. Stop here if you want a puzzle bag. You're done!

Cathedral window patchwork

1. Centre one of the pressed small squares right side up in the middle of a large square, so that each corner point lines up with one of your hand-tacked stitches. Pin in place.
2. Fold the folded edges of the large square over the edge of the small square so that they curve. Pin them in place.
3. Ladder or whip stitch (see page 68) the folded edges down, overlapping the corners and working methodically from one window to the next. Take care not to go through all the layers of the bag.
4. Repeating the process in steps 1–3, continue working methodically around the bag until you have filled the centres of the windows. On the straps and top opening, this means tucking one half of the small square into the inside of the bag and stitching it down.

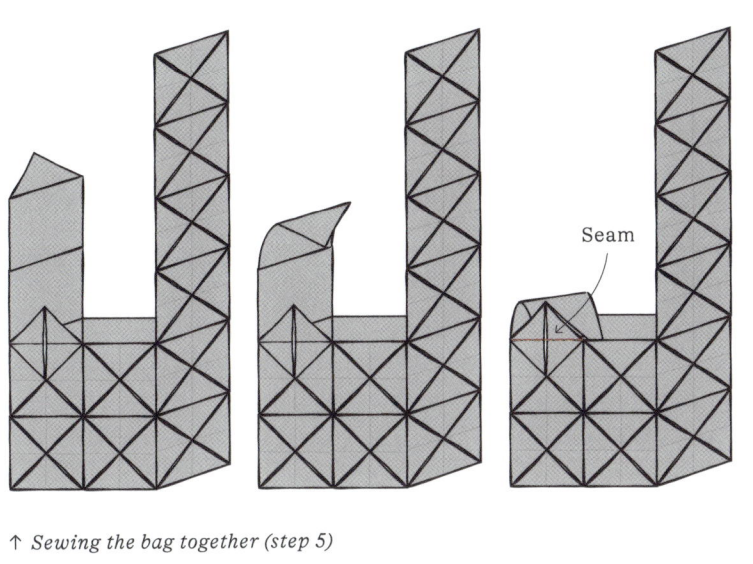

↑ *Sewing the bag together (step 5)*

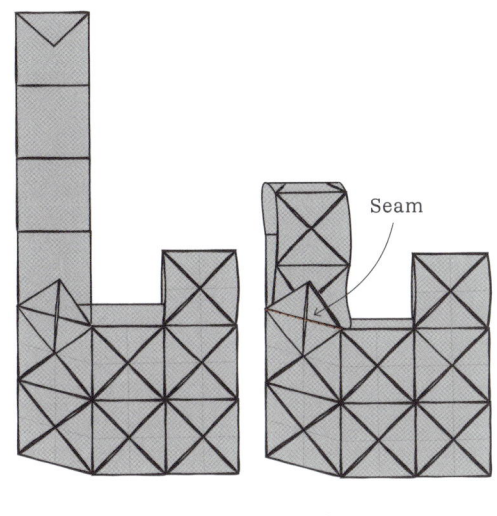

↑ *Sewing the bag together (step 6)*

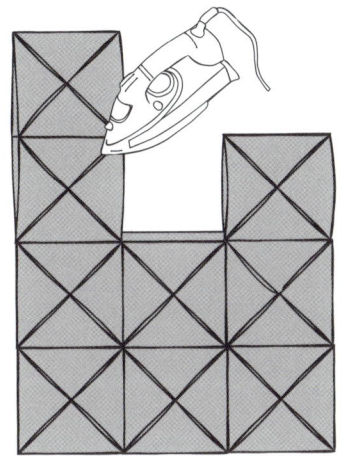

↑ *Sewing the bag together (step 7)*

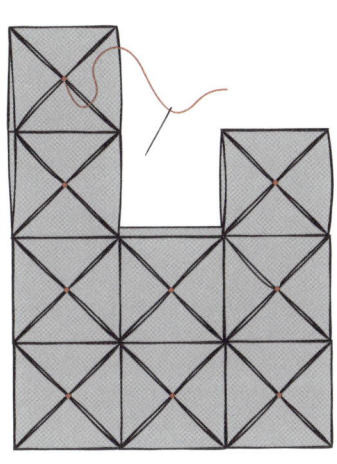

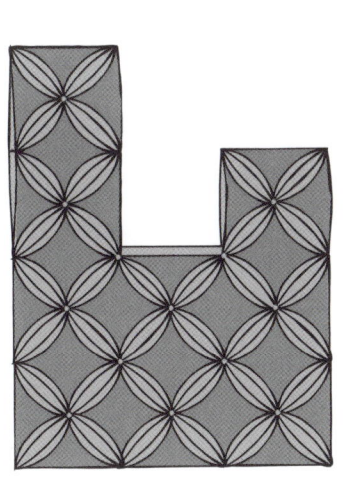

↑ *Finished bag (puzzle)*   ↑ *Finished bag (cathedral window)*

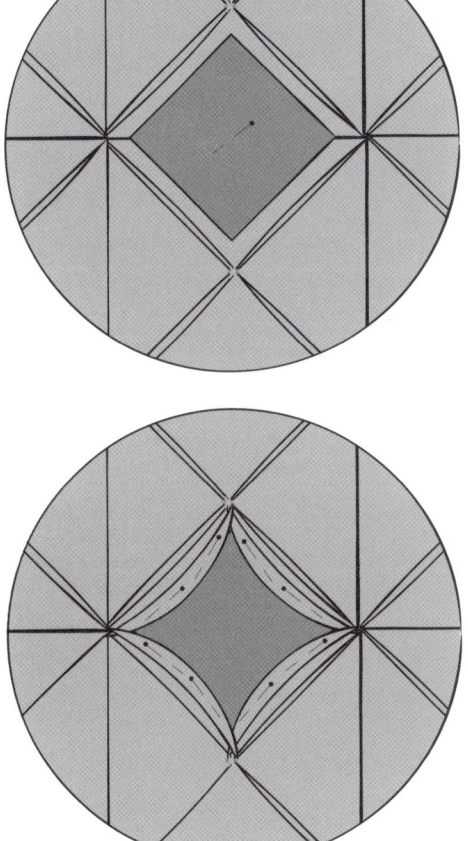

↑ *Cathedral window patchwork (steps 1–2)*

ROSE DRESS

There is a strong argument for the 'everything' dress: something you can throw on and instantly feel a boost but that also works for going about your daily life. It's a lot of expectation for a single garment, but it's what I was aiming for with this pattern. I wanted something slouchy, cool and comfortable.

And so I followed the logical route, looking for the comfiest garment made in the past 500 years. I settled on a version of a seventeenth-century Italian chemise, a riff on the one Dorothy K Burnham supplied in her book *Cut my Cote*.

I made mine out of an old sheet. If you don't have fabric scraps big enough to cut each of the rectangles from, you could patchwork together smaller pieces until they're the right dimensions. Improvisational patchwork (page 42) would look interesting, as would a simple stripe. If you do decide to try out patchwork, I recommend using a flat felled seam (see page 69) so the inside of the garment looks neat.

Alternatively, you could use the floral appliqué templates to embellish or mend something you already own.

⸙ METHOD ⸙

Cutting

1. This is so simple that you may not even want to make a paper pattern. Instead make a note of the rectangles then mark them directly onto your fabric. In either case, always double-check the measurements. It's a cliché for a reason: measure twice, cut once.

fabric	piece	qty
◯ main	body: 115 × 105 cm (45 × 41½ in) rectangle	2
	sleeve: 76 × 61 cm (30 × 24 in) rectangle	2
	gusset: 23 cm (9 in) square	2

2. Once you have cut the gusset pieces, cut them again diagonally corner to corner to make four triangles from each square.

Sewing the dress

1. First, you're going to sew the gussets to the sleeves. The following process uses a French seam so the seams are enclosed and no raw edges are visible, but if you're after a quick finish you could overlock (serge) the edges. If you're overlocking, ignore the directions for 'wrong sides together' and go 'right sides together' instead. In either case, pin the short edges of a gusset triangle to each side of the shorter edges (61 cm/24 in) of the sleeves, with wrong sides together (for a French seam) or right sides together (for overlocking).
2. Sew the pinned edges of one sleeve with gussets using a 6-mm (¼-in) seam allowance. Trim seam to 3 mm (⅛ in). Press.
3. Fold the seam so the cut edge is trapped between the gusset triangle and the sleeve rectangle.
4. Sew your second seam using a 1-cm (⅜-in) seam allowance, so the cut edge is trapped between the two seams. Press.
5. Repeat steps 2–4 for the remaining sleeve and gussets.
6. Next, attach the sleeves to the body. Pin and sew the sleeves to the sides of the front body panel so that the top edges of the front panel are 5 cm (2 in) above the gusset seams. For a French seam, make sure you start with wrong sides together, using a 6-mm (¼-in) seam allowance.

This dress is made to fit a size M, but it's a generous fit and suits a wide range of bodies. The finished bust is 205 cm (81 in). Adjust the fit by adding length or width.

FABRIC

Note yardages are estimated for fabric 115 cm (45 in) wide.

> main fabric: 3.5 m (3¾ yd)
> appliqué fabrics: 20 × 10 cm (8 × 4 in) scraps in the following colours: green, pink, orange and red

HABERDASHERY

> binding: 1.75 m (2 yd) bias binding 5 cm (2 in) wide to make three pieces (95 cm/37½ in for neckline and 40 cm/15¾ in per wrist)
> interfacing (if using machine appliqué)
> thread to match your main fabric, plus threads to match your appliqué fabrics

EQUIPMENT

> basic quilt-making kit (page 73)

NOTES

> A 6-mm (¼-in) seam allowance is included for all patchwork.
> A 1.5-cm (⅝-in) seam allowance is included for all structural garment seams (unless otherwise noted).
> Full-size templates are available to download at workingcloth.com

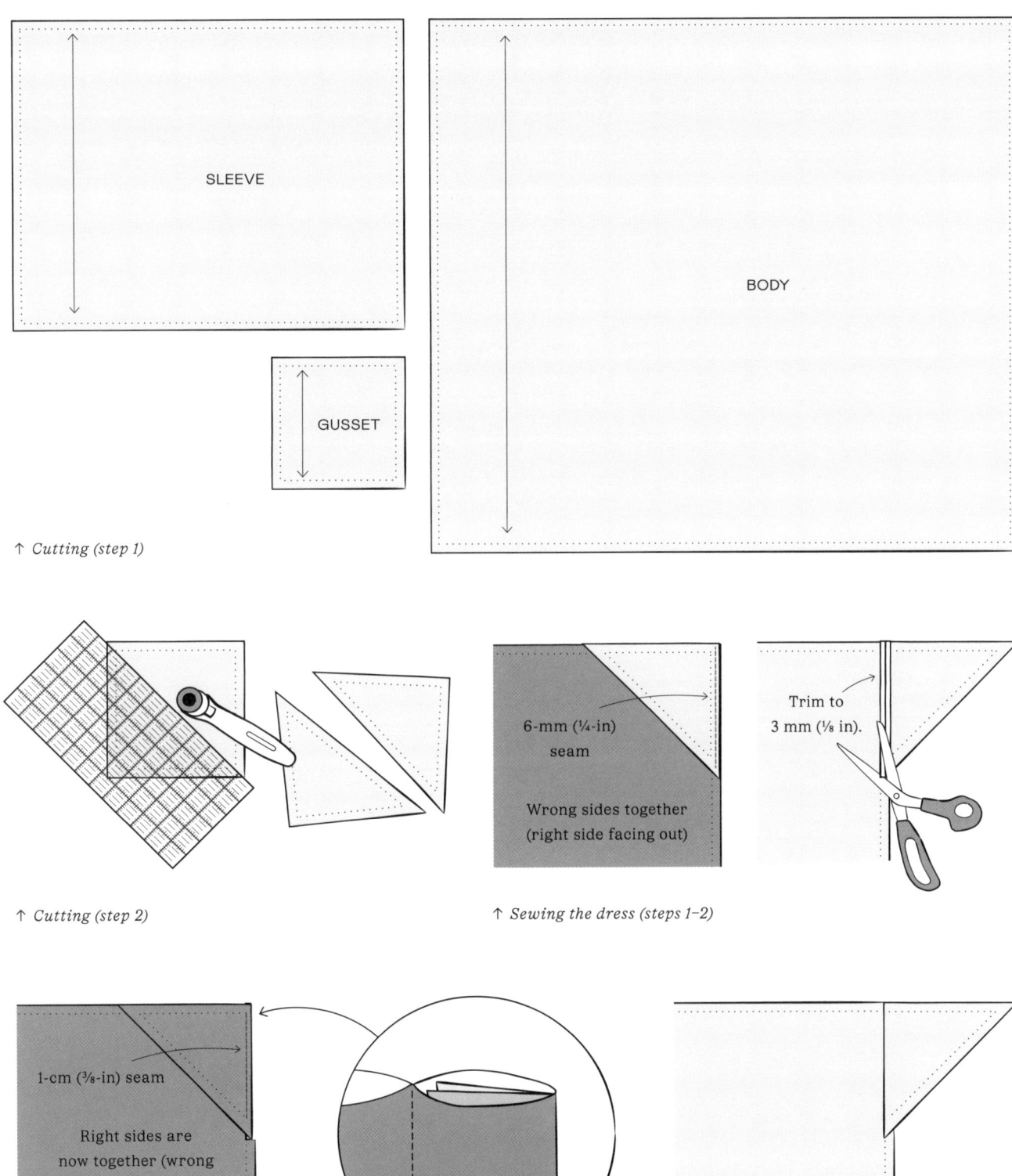

SLEEVE

BODY

GUSSET

↑ *Cutting (step 1)*

↑ *Cutting (step 2)*

6-mm (¼-in) seam

Wrong sides together (right side facing out)

Trim to 3 mm (⅛ in).

↑ *Sewing the dress (steps 1–2)*

1-cm (⅜-in) seam

Right sides are now together (wrong side now facing out).

Seam will go here.

↑ *Sewing the dress (steps 3–4)*

↑ *Sewing the dress (steps 4–5)*

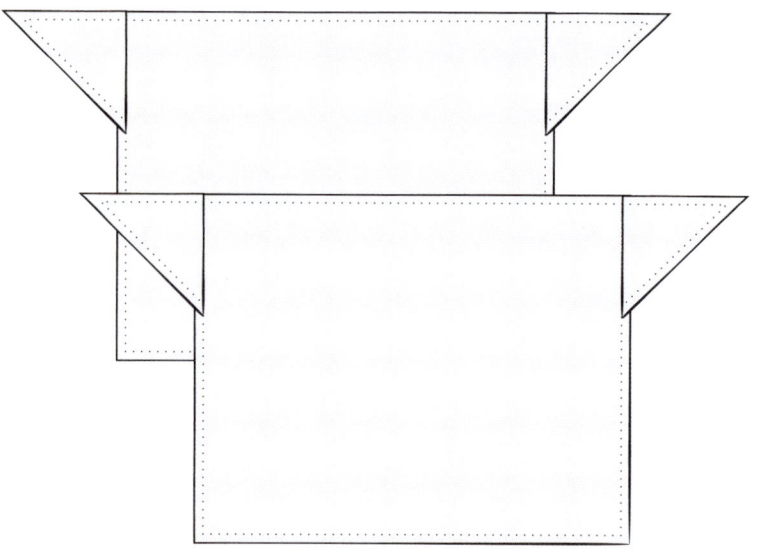

↑ *Sewing the dress (finished sleeve/gusset panels)*

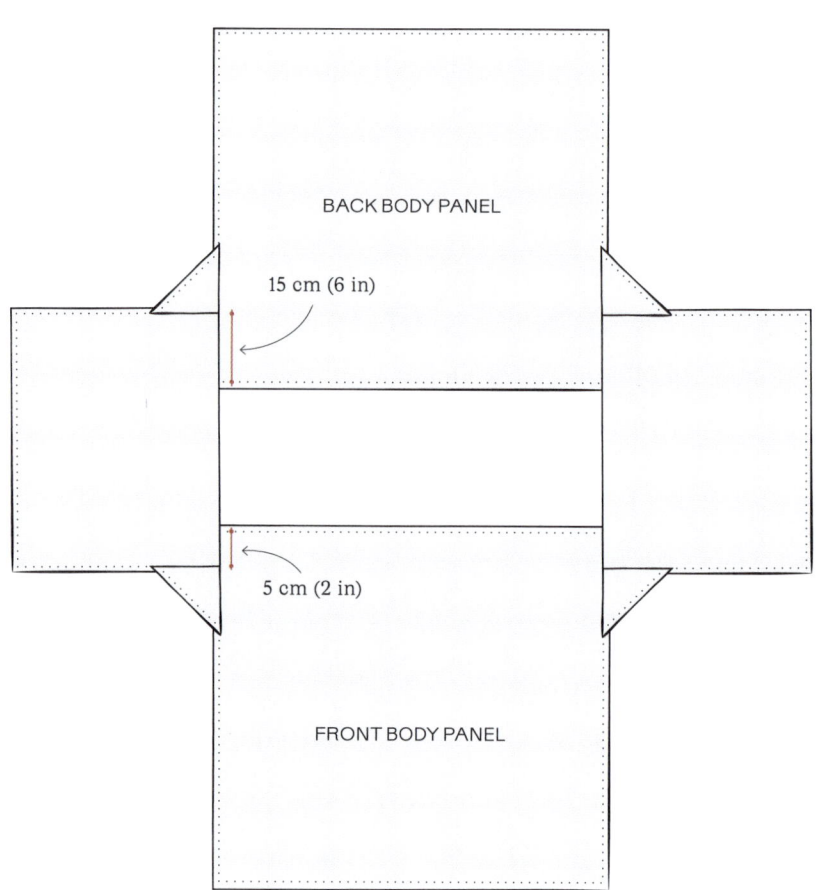

BACK BODY PANEL

15 cm (6 in)

5 cm (2 in)

FRONT BODY PANEL

↑ *Sewing the dress (steps 6–7)*

↑ *Finishing the neckline and sleeves (steps 1 and 3)*

↑ *Finishing the neckline and sleeves (steps 1 and 3)*

7. Pin and sew the sleeves to the sides of the back body panel so that the top edge of the back panel is 15 cm (6 in) above the gusset. Again, keep wrong sides together, using a 6-mm (¼-in) seam allowance.

8. Returning to the gusset and sleeve pieces, trim the seam allowances, fold the pieces right sides together along the seam line, and sew a second seam to complete the French seam.

9. Fold your garment in half down the sleeve so that it makes a big T shape. Pin the side seams wrong sides together, sew them up, then French seam them as before.

Finishing the neckline and sleeves

1. Sew two rows of gathering stitches (machine stitch length 4 mm) around the neckline, 6 mm (¼ in) and 1 cm (⅜ in) from the edge. Gather the neckline so that it measures 75 cm (29½ in) around. Try on the dress and adjust the neckline as you'd like (less gathering will make it bigger, more will make it smaller – just make sure you can still get it over your head).

2. Once you're happy with the size of the neck opening, bind the neckline (see pages 59–64).

3. Sew two rows of gathering stitches around each of the sleeve hems, using the same method as for the neckline. Gather each sleeve so it measures roughly 25 cm (10 in) around. Try on the dress and adjust as you'd like, making sure that you can still get your hands through!

4. Bind each sleeve hem.

5. Press the hem of the dress to the wrong side by 6 mm (¼ in). Press and pin the hem again 4 cm (1½ in) so that you have a double fold.

6. Hem the dress. Now you're ready to appliqué.

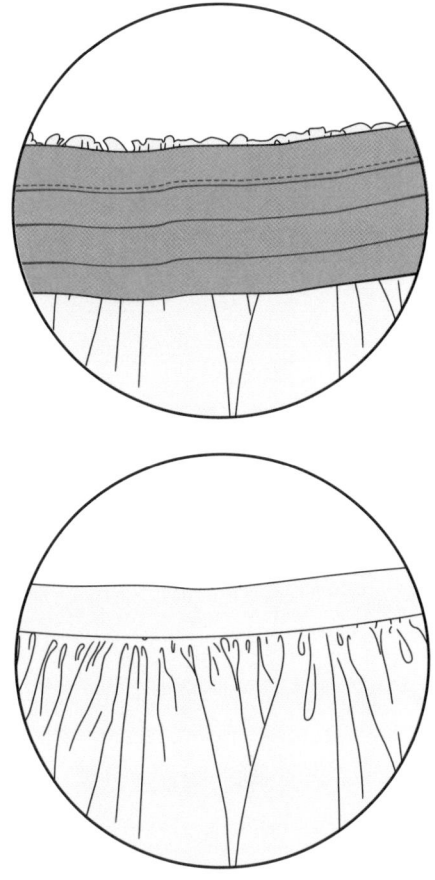

↑ *Finishing the neckline and sleeves (steps 2 and 4)*

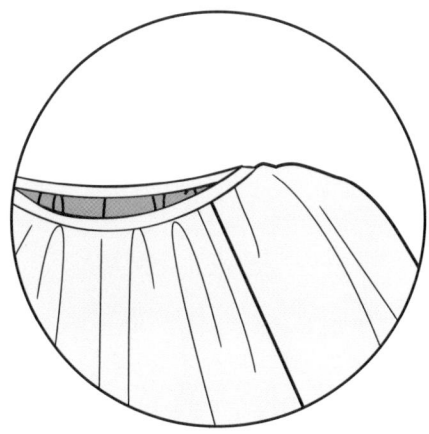

↑ *Finished neckline with binding*

Adding the appliqué

1. Scale up (see pages 72–3) the rose appliqué templates (page 207) onto thick paper or card and then cut them out.
2. Cut the quantities indicated on the template pieces, adding a 3-mm (⅛-in) seam allowance around each piece if you're doing needle-turned appliqué.
3. Position the appliqué pieces on the dress. I started on the centre front of the skirt, 5 cm (2 in) up from the bottom edge of the hem, but you might want to experiment with positioning.
4. Following the instructions for machine appliqué (pages 43–4) or needle-turned appliqué (page 45), stitch the pieces onto the dress.

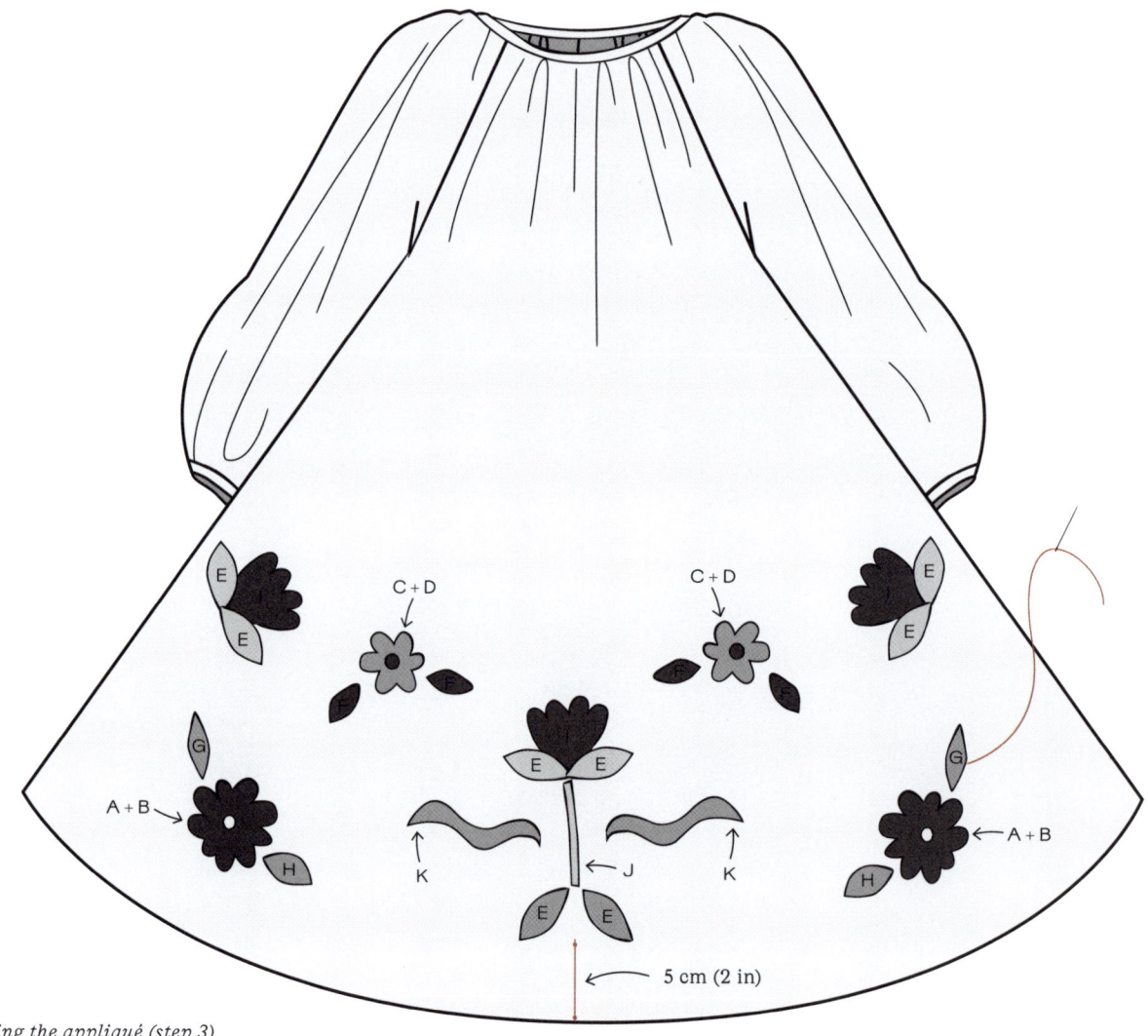

↑ *Adding the appliqué (step 3)*

↑ *Adding the appliqué (step 1)*   ↑ *Adding the appliqué (step 2)*

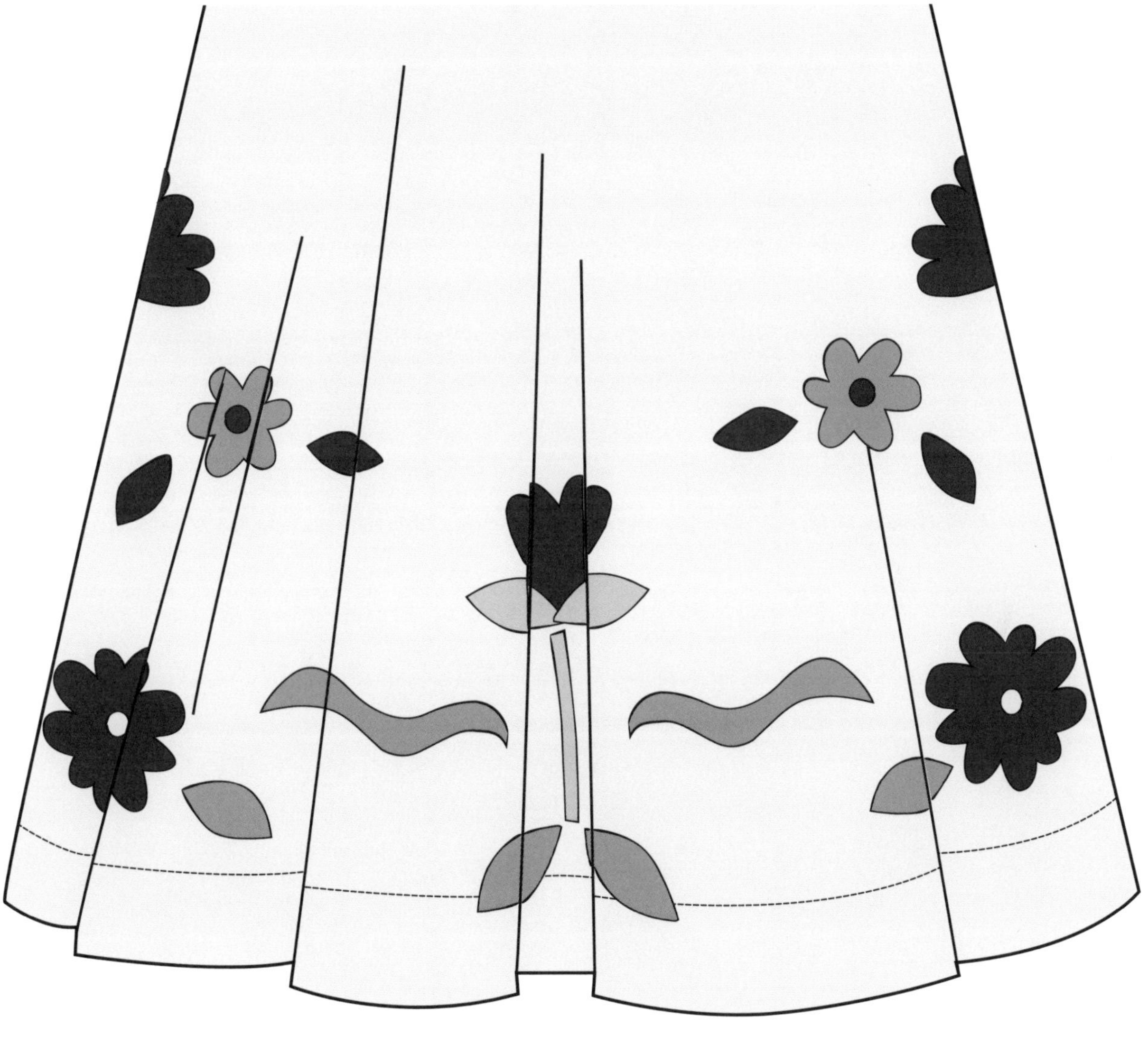

→ *Finished appliqué*

PATCHWORK JACKET ALICE / FRAN

What is better than a slouchy, oversized housecoat? Almost nothing, in my opinion. These are cosy, quilted and inspired by Japanese Hanten jackets. I named them after the models wearing them: my best friend, Alice, and her sister, Frances. I made the star patchwork (*Alice*; see photo left) from two old skirts, an oxford shirt and a sheet. For the colour-block patchwork (*Fran*; see photo page 158), I used a buttery

soft, tobacco coloured linen sheet that had a hole worn through the middle, some orange fabric offcuts, the leftover bit of white sheet from the *Alice* jacket, and a bit of soft pink, madder-dyed cotton.

These jackets don't need a pattern. Instead, they're made from a series of rectangles. Like the toadstool jacket (page 107), you cut, patchwork and quilt larger rectangles first, then trim them to shape afterwards.

≋ METHOD ≋

PART 1: ALICE

Cutting

1. For this pattern, you'll use both half-square triangles (HSTs) and quarter-square triangles (QSTs). The methods for these are outlined on pages 38–40.
2. Once you've chosen a method, use the relevant table below to cut your squares to the sizes specified.
3. Using the table at the top of page 195, mark and cut out your lining pieces, pockets and wadding (batting). The sleeves in this pattern are measured and cut directly out of the sleeve rectangles, so there are no pattern pieces to scale for them.

MAGIC 8 METHOD

fabric	piece	qty
○ fabric 1	27 cm (10¾ in) square	10
	25 cm (10 in) square	8
	15 cm (6 in) square	8
● fabric 2	25 cm (10 in) square	8
	15 cm (6 in) square	5
	11.2 cm (4½ in) square	22
◐ fabric 3	27 cm (10¾ in) square	10
	15 cm (6 in) square	3

TWO-AT-A-TIME METHOD

fabric	piece	qty
○ fabric 1	12.7 cm (5 in) square	32
	14 cm (5½ in) square	37
	7.5 cm (3 in) square	30
● fabric 2	12.7 cm (5 in) square	32
	7.5 cm (3 in) square	20
	11.2 cm (4½ in) square	22
◐ fabric 3	14 cm (5½ in) square	37
	7.5 cm (3 in) square	10

FINISHED SIZE

These jackets loosely fit a size M (bust approx. 135 cm/53 in; length approx. 76 cm/30 in). Grade up or down by adjusting the number of rows or block units.

FABRIC

Note yardages are estimated for fabric 115 cm (45 in) wide.

Alice jacket
> fabric 1: 1.6 m (1¾ yd)
> fabric 2: 1.1 m (1¼ yd)
> fabric 3: 0.9 m (1 yd)

Fran jacket
> fabric 1: 0.75 m (¾ yd)
> fabric 2: 0.75 m (¾ yd)
> fabric 3: 0.45 m (½ yd)

Both jackets
> pocket fabric: 0.25 m (¼ yd)
> lining fabric: 3.2 m (3½ yd)

HABERDASHERY

> wadding: 3.2 × 1.2 m (3½ × 1⅜ yd)
> binding: 3.5 m (3¾ yd) bias binding 5 cm (2 in) wide
> internal binding (optional): 13.5 m (14¾ yd) bias binding 1.2 cm (½ in) wide
> thread for piecing
> 3 × 40-m skeins of sashiko or 2 × 80-m spools of perle 8 cotton thread for quilting

Continued overleaf →

POCKETS, LINING AND WADDING

fabric	piece	qty
● pocket	20 × 23 cm (8 × 9 in) rectangle	2
○ lining	body: 160 × 80 cm (63 × 31½ in) rectangle	1
	sleeve: 75 × 55 cm (29½ × 21½ in) rectangle	2
○ wadding	body: 160 × 80 cm (63 × 31½ in) rectangle	1
	sleeve: 75 × 55 cm (29½ × 21½ in) rectangle	2

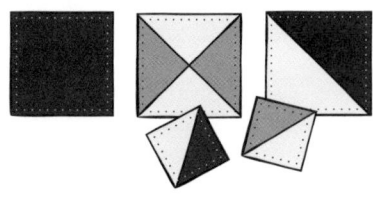

↑ Alice (Sewing, step 1)

Sewing

1. If you're following the magic 8 method:

    a. Use your 27 cm (10¾ in) squares (fabrics 1 and 3) to make 74 big (11.2 cm/4½ in) QSTs.

    b. Use your 25 cm (10 in) squares (fabrics 1 and 2) to make 64 big (11.2 cm/4½ in) HSTs.

    c. Use five 15 cm (6 in) fabric 1 squares and all the 15 cm (6 in) fabric 2 squares to make 40 small (6.2 cm/2½ in) HSTs.

    d. Use three 15 cm (6 in) fabric 1 squares and all the 15 cm (6 in) fabric 3 squares to make 20 small (6.2 cm/2½ in) HSTs.

    e. Go to step 3.

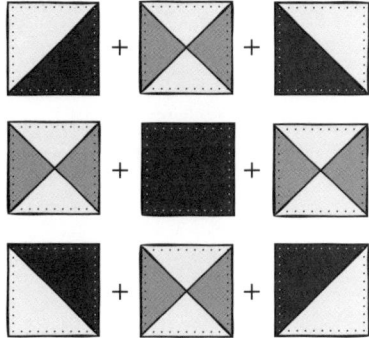

↑ Alice (Sewing, step 3)

2. If you're following the two-at-a-time method:

    a. Use your 14 cm (5½ in) squares (fabrics 1 and 3) to make 74 big (11.2 cm/4½ in) QSTs.

    b. Use your 12.7 cm (5 in) squares (fabrics 1 and 2) to make 64 big (11.2 cm/4½ in) HSTs.

    c. Use twenty 7.5 cm (3 in) fabric 1 squares and all the 7.5 cm (3 in) fabric 2 squares to make 40 small (6.2 cm/2½ in) HSTs.

    d. Use ten 7.5 cm (3 in) fabric 1 squares and all the 7.5 cm (3 in) fabric 3 squares to make 20 small (6.2 cm/2½ in) HSTs.

    e. Go to step 3.

↑ Alice (finished star block)

3. Press and trim each unit, then lay them out and sew them together to create 14 star blocks, as illustrated (you'll have some HSTs and QSTs left over after this – we'll get to them soon).

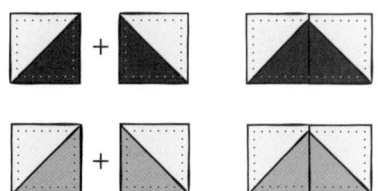

↑ Alice (Making the body rectangle, step 2)

Making the body rectangle

1. Sew ten star blocks into a 5 × 2 grid (see *Assembling your quilt top*, pages 46–7). This will be your main body piece.
2. Make a border for the main body piece that you've just put together. Take your small HSTs. Start with the HSTs made of fabric 1 and 2, and sew two together so that fabric 2 creates a bigger triangle (called a flying geese unit). Repeat for all the small HSTs.
3. Starting with a fabric 1 and 3 flying geese unit, sew 15 of the units into a long strip, alternating colours as you go but keeping the points in the same direction.
4. Repeat to make a second strip.
5. Carefully pin and stitch a flying geese border panel to the long edge of each of your main body pieces. Press. Set aside.

Making the sleeves

1. Each sleeve panel is made up of two full star blocks (you've already put these together) plus two partial star blocks and a centre patchwork panel, which you'll make now. First, assemble the centre panel of the sleeves using three QST units and two 11.2 cm (4½ in) squares, as illustrated.
2. Make four partial star block panels, as illustrated. (They are like the full star blocks but missing the bottom row.)

NOTES

> A 6-mm (¼-in) seam allowance is included for all patchwork.
> A 1.5-cm (⅝-in) seam allowance for all structural garment seams (unless otherwise noted).
> Unless otherwise noted, press seam allowances towards the darker fabric where possible.

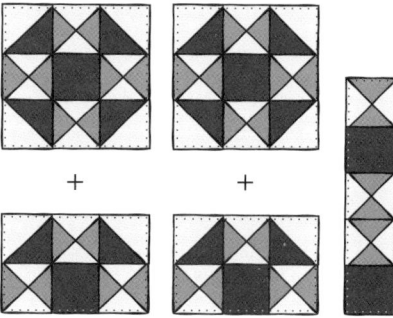

↑ *Alice (Sewing; Making the sleeves, steps 1–3)*

↑ *Alice (finished sleeve panel)*

↑ *Alice (Sewing; Making the body rectangle, steps 3–5)*

3. Take one full star block and one partial star block. Sew the partial block to the full one, making sure that the centre square (fabric 1) is positioned on the edge of the panel. Repeat three more times.

4. Assemble each sleeve panel by sewing a centre panel between two star/partial star blocks.

5. Go to part 2.

PART 1: FRAN

Cutting

This colour-block version of the jacket is much simpler than the star patchwork. For mine, I patched smaller scraps together to make colour-block rectangles, as I didn't have quite the right ones in my stash.

fabric	piece	qty
○ fabric 1	main body: 70 × 91.2 cm (27½ × 36 in)	1
● fabric 2	lower body: 70 × 30.6 cm (27½ × 12 in)	2
	lower sleeve: 70 × 20.6 cm (27½ × 8⅛ in)	2
● fabric 3	upper sleeve: 70 × 30.6 cm (27½ × 12 in)	2
● pocket	20 × 23 cm (8 × 9 in) rectangle	2
○ lining	body: 160 × 80 cm (63 × 31½ in) rectangle	1
	sleeve: 75 × 55 cm (29½ × 21½ in) rectangle	2
○ wadding	body: 160 × 80 cm (63 × 31½ in) rectangle	1
	sleeve: 75 × 55 cm (29½ × 21½ in) rectangle	2

Sewing

Making the body rectangle
Pin and sew the long sides of your lower body rectangles to the short sides of your main body rectangle. Press.

Making the sleeves
For each sleeve, pin and sew one long side of your upper sleeve rectangle to a long side of your lower sleeve rectangle. Press.

↑ *Fran (Sewing; Making the body rectangle)*

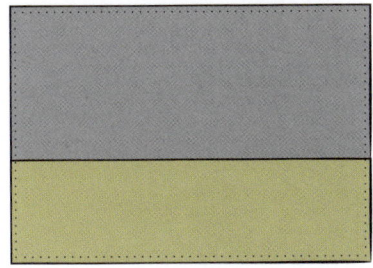

↑ *Fran (Sewing; Making the sleeves)*

Now you'll draw the final sleeve shape onto your rectangular sleeve panels. Measure 45 cm (17¾ in) down from the top edge and draw a horizontal line across the width of your sleeve. Along the line you've just drawn, mark the centre point of the width of your sleeve panel, then measure 20 cm (8 in) on either side of it. Connect each of the top corners down to this mark on the horizontal lines. Use these points to position your quilted lines.

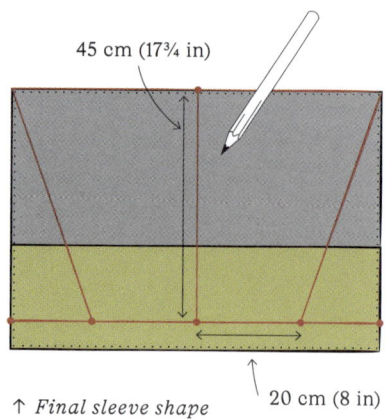

45 cm (17¾ in)

↑ *Final sleeve shape*   20 cm (8 in)

Quilting

1. Baste, quilt and trim your panels following your preferred method (see Chapter 3). I used white sashiko thread and quilted in straight lines along the length of the jacket.
2. If you have an overlocker, overlock the edges of the sleeve and body panels. If not, don't worry. You'll bind them later.

Adding the pockets

1. Press all the pocket edges 1 cm (⅜ in) towards the wrong side. Fold the top edges another 2 cm (¾ in) towards the wrong side. Press.
2. Set your stitch length to 2.5 mm. Topstitch the top fold down.
3. Mark a line on your body rectangle to make it easy to position your pocket. Measure 10 cm (4 in) in from the long side of the body panel, and 7.5 cm (3 in) up from the short side. Draw an 18-cm (7-in) horizontal line from this point.
4. With right sides together, position your pockets on the body panel, lining up the crease in the bottom edge with the line you've just marked (the pockets will be upside down). Topstitch along that bottom line, backstitching at each end.
5. Flip your pockets up. Pin them in place. Stitch around the side and bottom edges 3 mm (⅛ in) from the edge to secure them in place, remembering to backstitch.

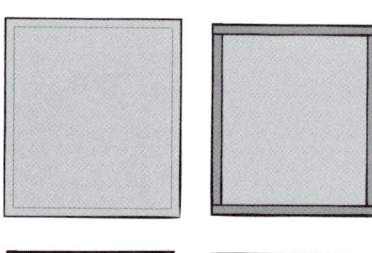
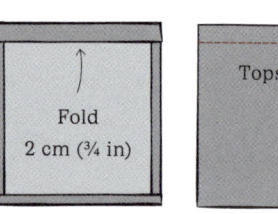

Fold
2 cm (¾ in)

Topstitch

↑ *Adding the pockets (steps 1–2)*

> ### TIP
>
> If you like to keep heavy things in your pockets, add another row of stitching.

Adding the centre front opening

Next you'll cut the centre front opening. I have designed this to be smooth and sloping, but you might prefer a little more space in your opening. I recommend you follow the steps on the next page, then try it on and adjust once you've attached the sleeves – you can always cut more away, but you can't add it back on!

↑ *Adding the pockets (step 3)*

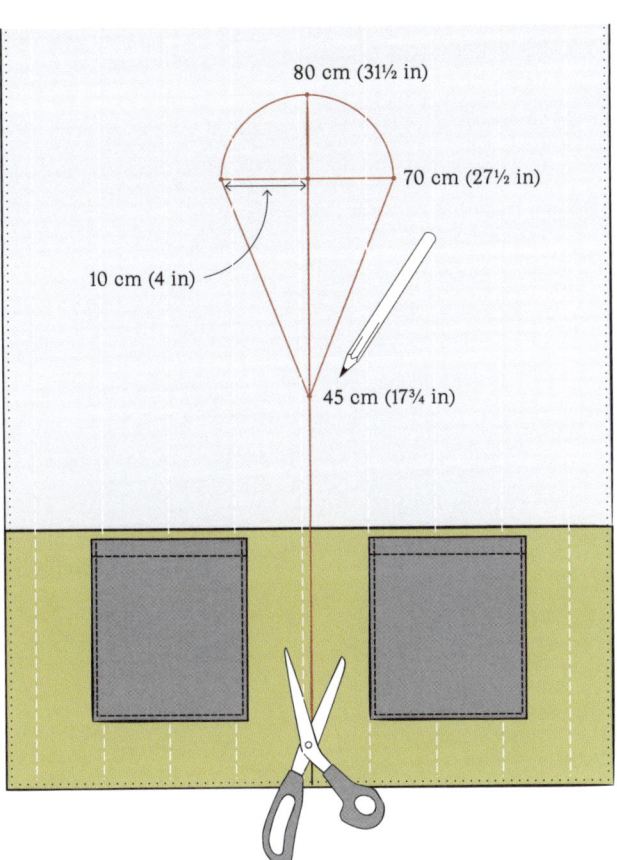

↑ *Adding the centre front opening (steps 1–5; overleaf)*

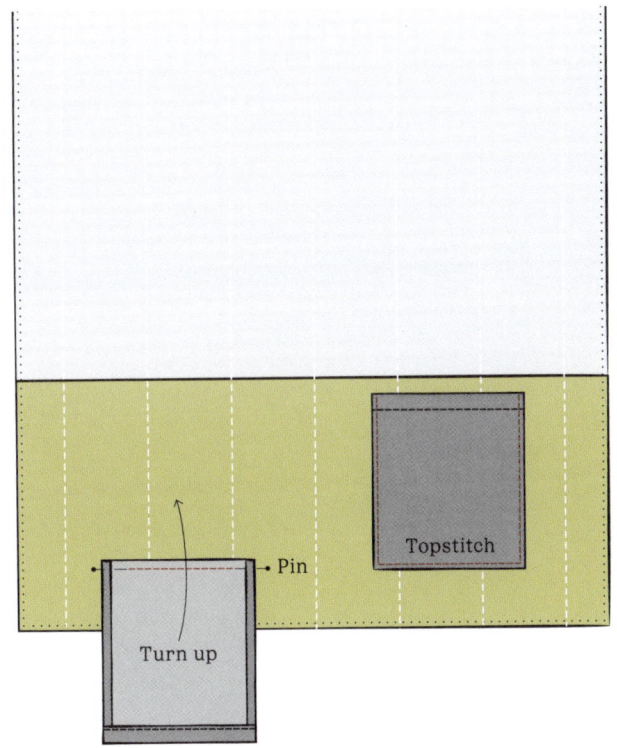

↑ *Adding the pockets (steps 4–5)*

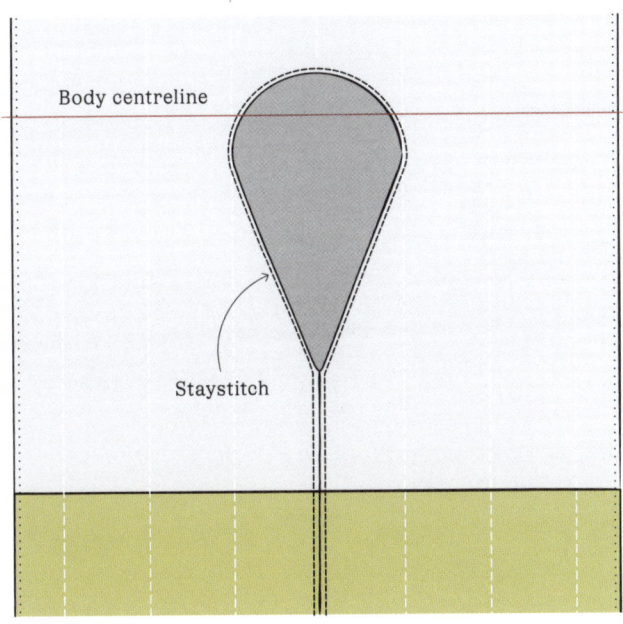

↑ *Adding the centre front opening (step 6; overleaf)*

1. Mark the centre back of your neckline. Find the centre of the short side of your body rectangle. Measure 80 cm (31½ in) straight up the centre, marking a line as you go.

2. Make two marks on your line: one at 45 cm (17¾ in) up (this is where your neckline will start to curve) and one at 70 cm (27½ in) up (this is where your neckline will be at its widest).

3. At the second mark, draw a 10-cm (4-in) perpendicular line either side. This is the width of your neckline.

4. Draw a line connecting the mark at 45 cm (17¾ in) to each end of the line you just made, creating a V shape.

5. Draw two identical curved lines connecting the top of your V to your centre back neckline point (fold the panel in half to make this easier).

6. Cut along the lines to create your neckline opening. Set your sewing machine to 4 mm and staystitch 6 mm (¼ in) away from the edge, all the way around your opening. This will prevent the neckline from stretching while you try it on.

Putting the jacket together

1. Make a guide for your sleeve position. Fold the body panel in half lengthwise. Press the fold to create a crease. Unfold.

2. Next, do the same for your sleeve. Fold each sleeve in half widthwise and press the folds to crease them. Unfold.

3. Match your sleeve creases to the body rectangle pins (right sides together). Pin and stitch the sleeves to the body, stopping 1.5 cm (⅝ in) before the end of the seam.

4. If you didn't overlock them, bind the seam allowances of the top of the sleeves separately using narrow bias binding (see pages 61–4). Leave the body panel edge raw for now.

5. Fold the jacket in half lengthwise, wrong side out. Starting from the underarm, match the seam and pin in place. Working outwards, pin the sleeves then the body.

6. Starting at the wrist, stitch the sleeves and underarm seams.

7. If you haven't overlocked the panels individually, bind the seam allowances separately to reduce bulk.

8. Try on your jacket to make sure you are happy with the length and neckline. Adjust as necessary.

9. If you've overlocked the panels, fold the hem up 2 cm (¾ in), press, pin and blind stitch (see page 68) in place. If you haven't, bind the hem.

10. Using your wide bias binding, bind the neckline and sleeve cuffs. You're done!

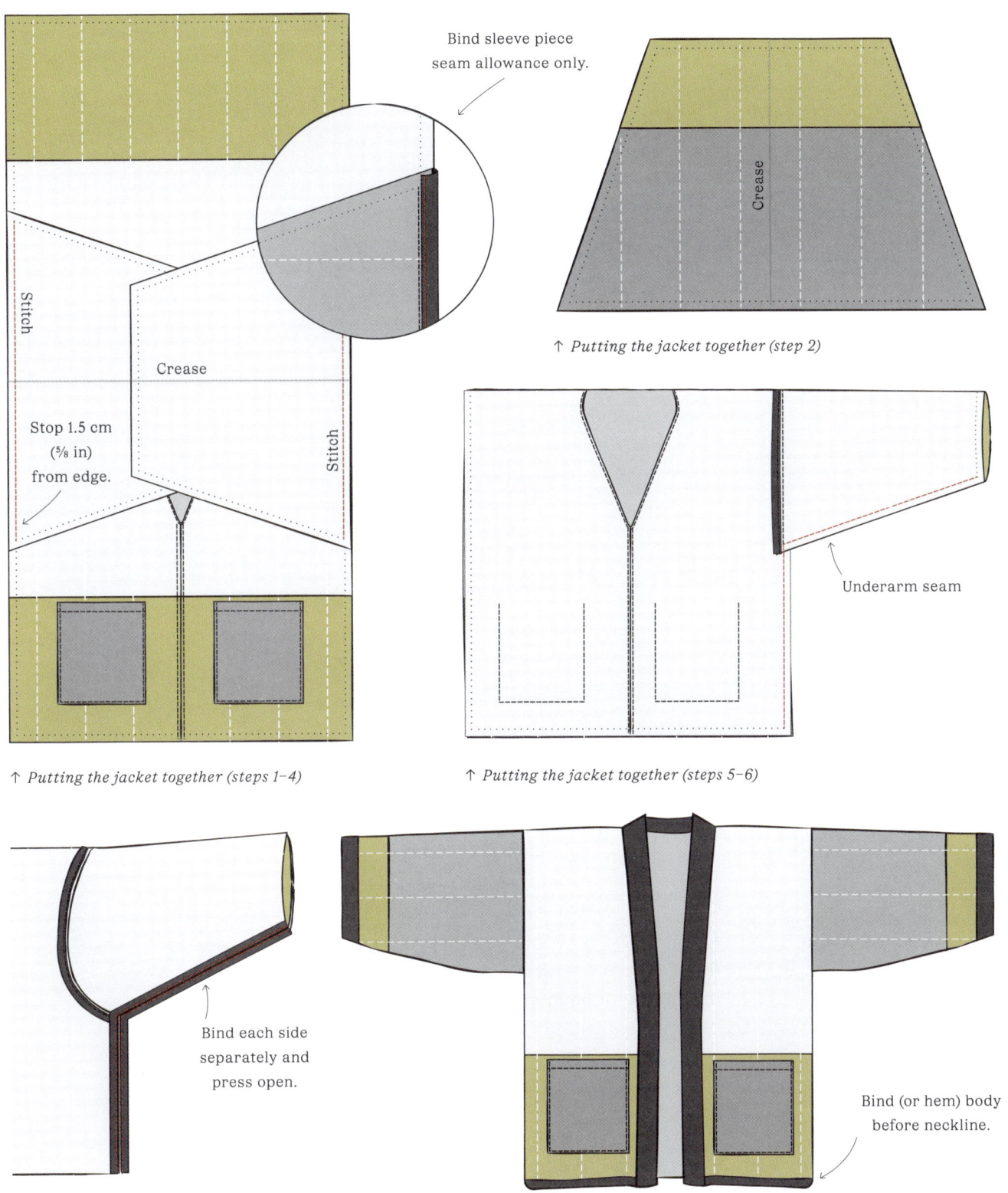

Bind sleeve piece seam allowance only.

Crease

Stitch

Stitch

Crease

Stop 1.5 cm (⅝ in) from edge.

↑ *Putting the jacket together (steps 1–4)*

↑ *Putting the jacket together (step 2)*

Underarm seam

↑ *Putting the jacket together (steps 5–6)*

Bind each side separately and press open.

↑ *Putting the jacket together (step 7)*

Bind (or hem) body before neckline.

↑ *Putting the jacket together (steps 9–10)*

TEMPLATES

————————————— cut edge

——————————→ grain line

↓ ————————— ↓ fold grain (place on fold)

▬ notch

☐ ☆ ○ markings to align details (e.g. pockets)

⊢———⊣ buttonhole

TIP

To help with scaling, templates are centred on a grid line or aligned at two edges wherever possible. See pages 72–3 for more information on how to scale up your pattern and appliqué templates.

ISOBEL TOTE BAG

Drunkard's path templates
Scale 1:1 (full size)
6-mm (¼-in) seam allowance included

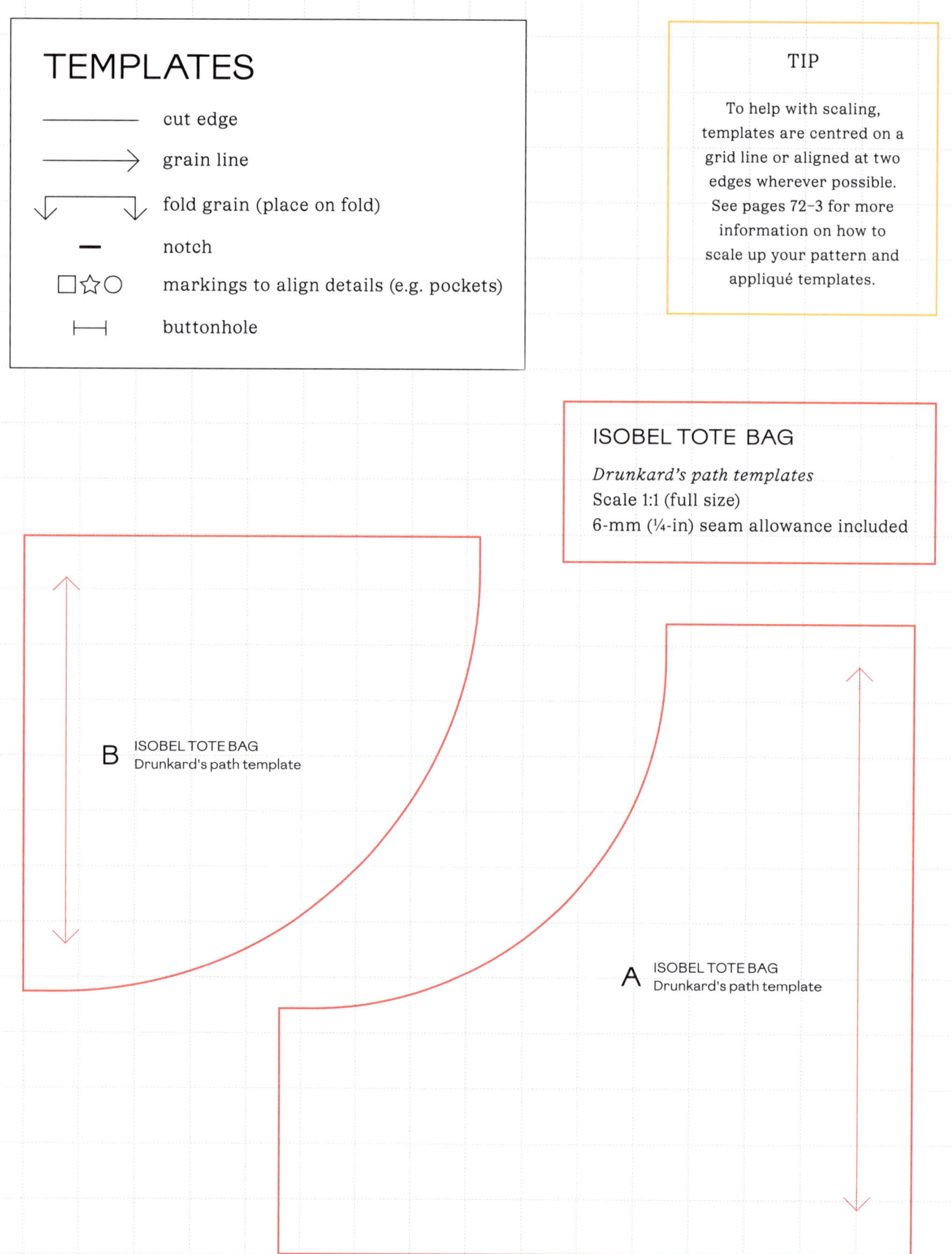

B ISOBEL TOTE BAG
Drunkard's path template

A ISOBEL TOTE BAG
Drunkard's path template

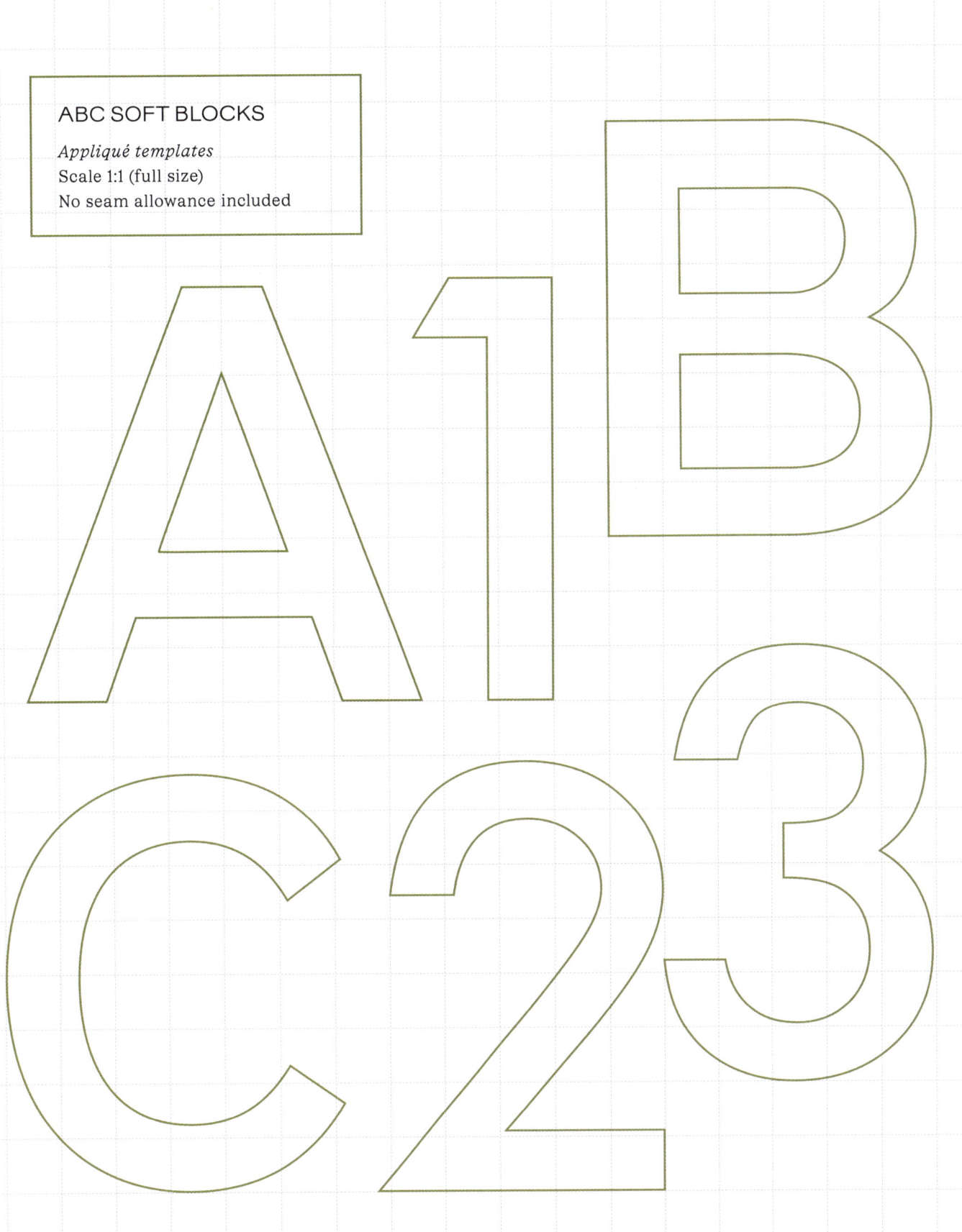

ABC SOFT BLOCKS

Appliqué templates
Scale 1:1 (full size)
No seam allowance included

ELLIE QUILT

Appliqué templates
Scale 1:10
No seam allowance included

Full-size templates are available to
download at workingcloth.com

CLARE QUILT

Appliqué templates
Scale 1:10
No seam allowance included

Full-size templates are available to
download at workingcloth.com

PATCHWORK BEAR

Pattern templates
Scale 1:2
6-mm (¼-in) seam allowance included

Full-size templates are available to
download at workingcloth.com

ELLIE QUILT
Elephant ear
CUT 1
Fabric 3

ELLIE QUILT
Elephant eye
CUT 1
Fabric 4

ELLIE QUILT
Elephant body
CUT 1
Fabric 2

CLARE QUILT
Stem pieces
CUT 1 EACH
Fabric 3

CLARE QUILT
Leaf
CUT 1 Fabric 3

CLARE QUILT
Lemon
CUT 1
Fabric 2

J

PATCHWORK BEAR
Hand paw pad
CUT 1 PAIR
Fabric 2

Position ear here

Eye placement

Nose embroidery
placement

a

A

PATCHWORK BEAR
Lower face
CUT 2
Fabric 1

Leave one side
open for stuffing

b

Dart

F

PATCHWORK BEAR
Inner arm
CUT 1 PAIR
Fabric 1

C

PATCHWORK BEAR
Ear
CUT 2 PAIRS
Fabric 1

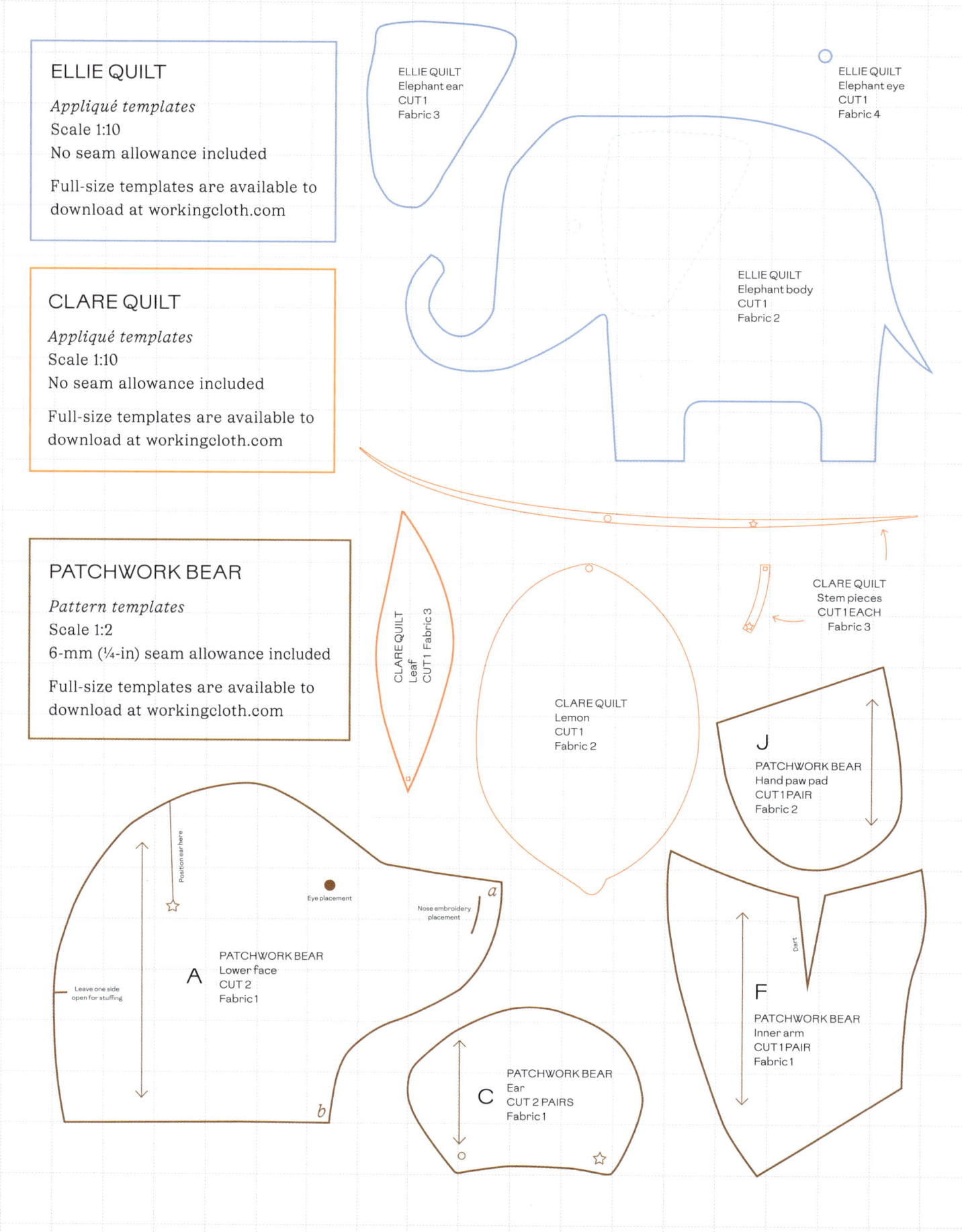

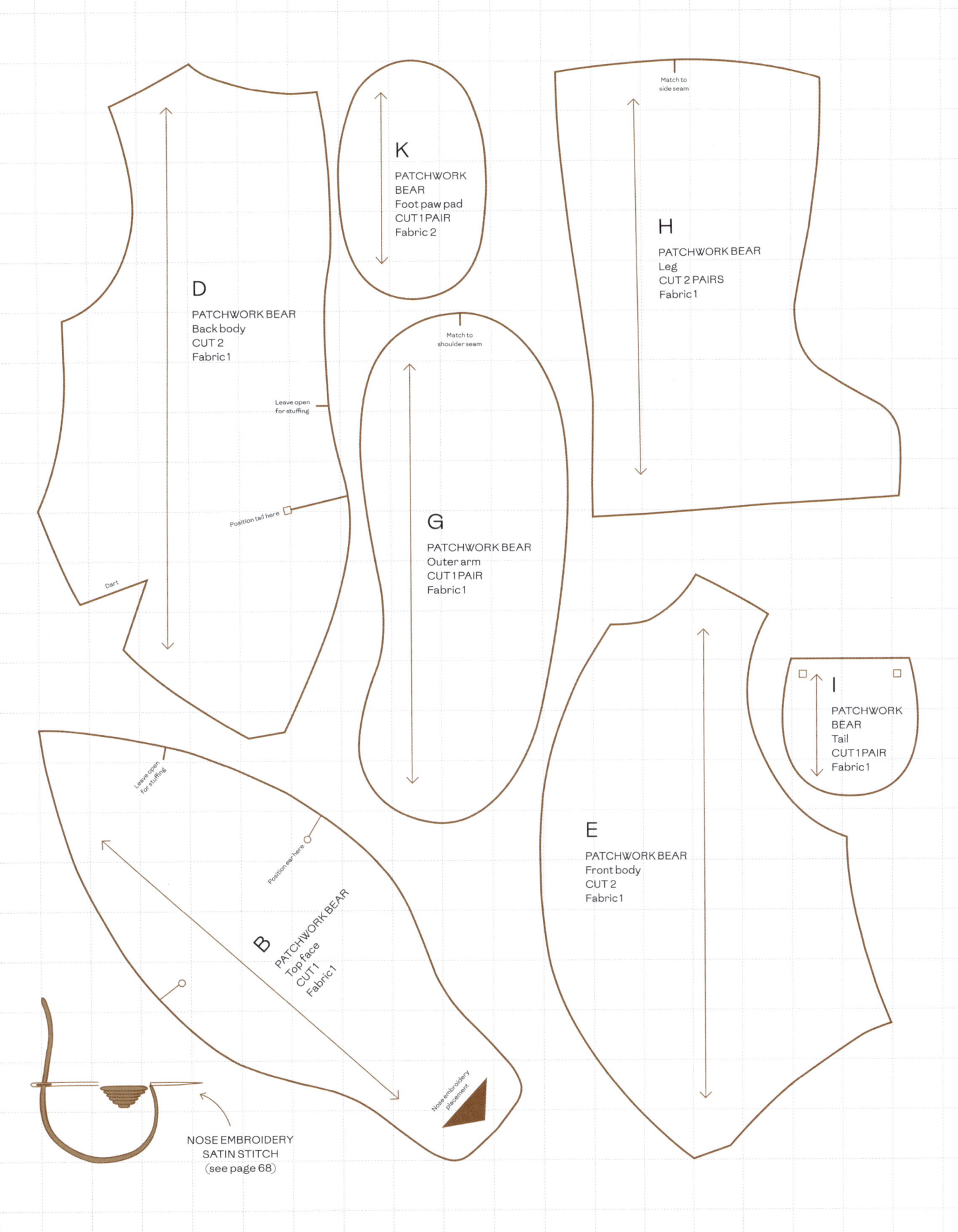

K
PATCHWORK
BEAR
Foot paw pad
CUT 1 PAIR
Fabric 2

Match to
side seam

H
PATCHWORK BEAR
Leg
CUT 2 PAIRS
Fabric 1

D
PATCHWORK BEAR
Back body
CUT 2
Fabric 1

Leave open
for stuffing

Position tail here

Dart

Match to
shoulder seam

G
PATCHWORK BEAR
Outer arm
CUT 1 PAIR
Fabric 1

I
PATCHWORK
BEAR
Tail
CUT 1 PAIR
Fabric 1

Leave open
for stuffing

Position ear here

B
PATCHWORK BEAR
Top face
CUT 1
Fabric 1

E
PATCHWORK BEAR
Front body
CUT 2
Fabric 1

Nose embroidery
placement

NOSE EMBROIDERY
SATIN STITCH
(see page 68)

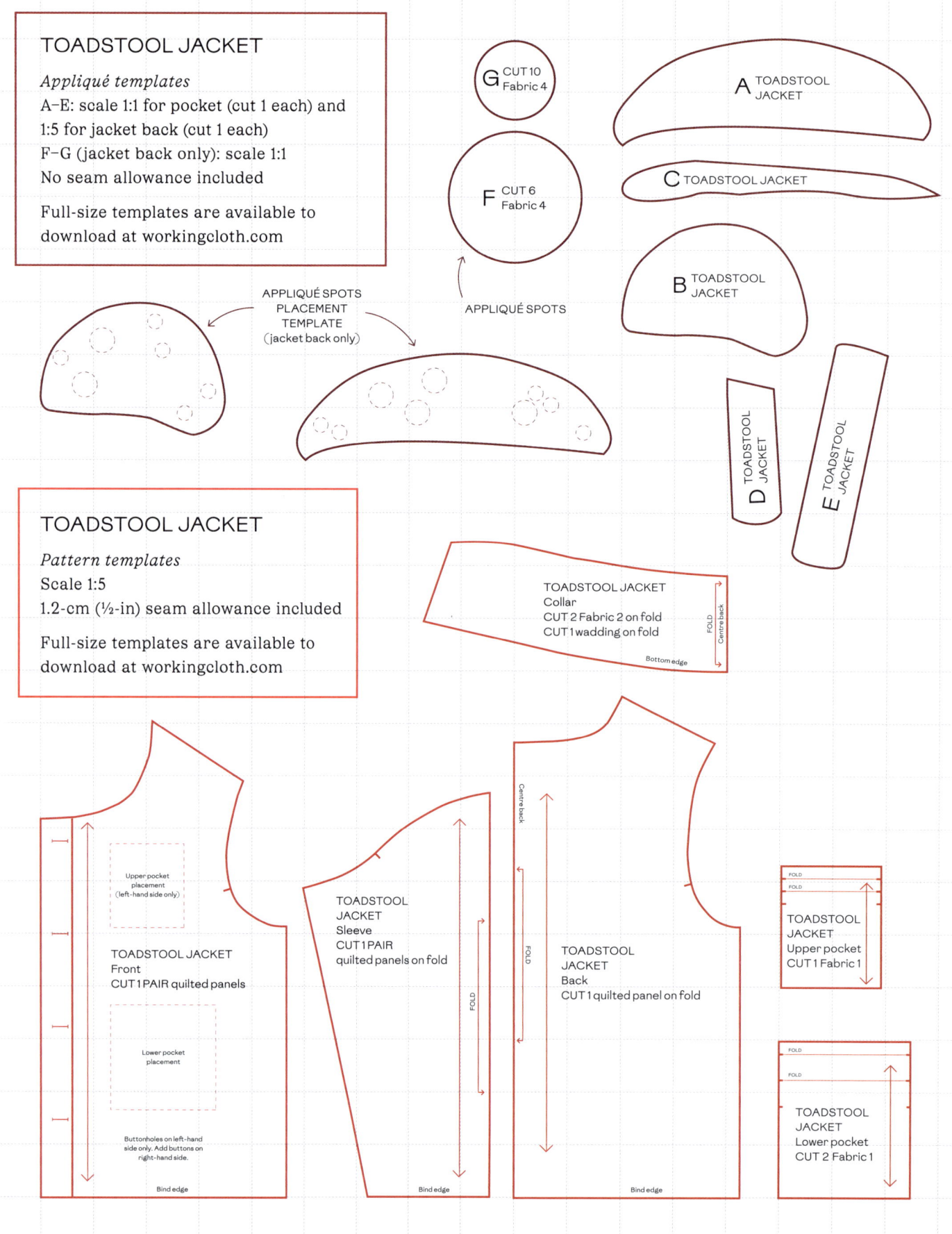

TOADSTOOL JACKET

Appliqué templates
A–E: scale 1:1 for pocket (cut 1 each) and
1:5 for jacket back (cut 1 each)
F–G (jacket back only): scale 1:1
No seam allowance included

Full-size templates are available to
download at workingcloth.com

G CUT 10 Fabric 4

F CUT 6 Fabric 4

A TOADSTOOL JACKET

C TOADSTOOL JACKET

B TOADSTOOL JACKET

D TOADSTOOL JACKET

E TOADSTOOL JACKET

APPLIQUÉ SPOTS
PLACEMENT
TEMPLATE
(jacket back only)

APPLIQUÉ SPOTS

TOADSTOOL JACKET

Pattern templates
Scale 1:5
1.2-cm (½-in) seam allowance included

Full-size templates are available to
download at workingcloth.com

TOADSTOOL JACKET
Collar
CUT 2 Fabric 2 on fold
CUT 1 wadding on fold
FOLD
Centre back
Bottom edge

Upper pocket
placement
(left-hand side only)

TOADSTOOL JACKET
Front
CUT 1 PAIR quilted panels

Lower pocket
placement

Buttonholes on left-hand
side only. Add buttons on
right-hand side.

Bind edge

TOADSTOOL
JACKET
Sleeve
CUT 1 PAIR
quilted panels on fold

FOLD

Bind edge

Centre back

FOLD

TOADSTOOL
JACKET
Back
CUT 1 quilted panel on fold

Bind edge

FOLD
FOLD

TOADSTOOL
JACKET
Upper pocket
CUT 1 Fabric 1

FOLD
FOLD

TOADSTOOL
JACKET
Lower pocket
CUT 2 Fabric 1

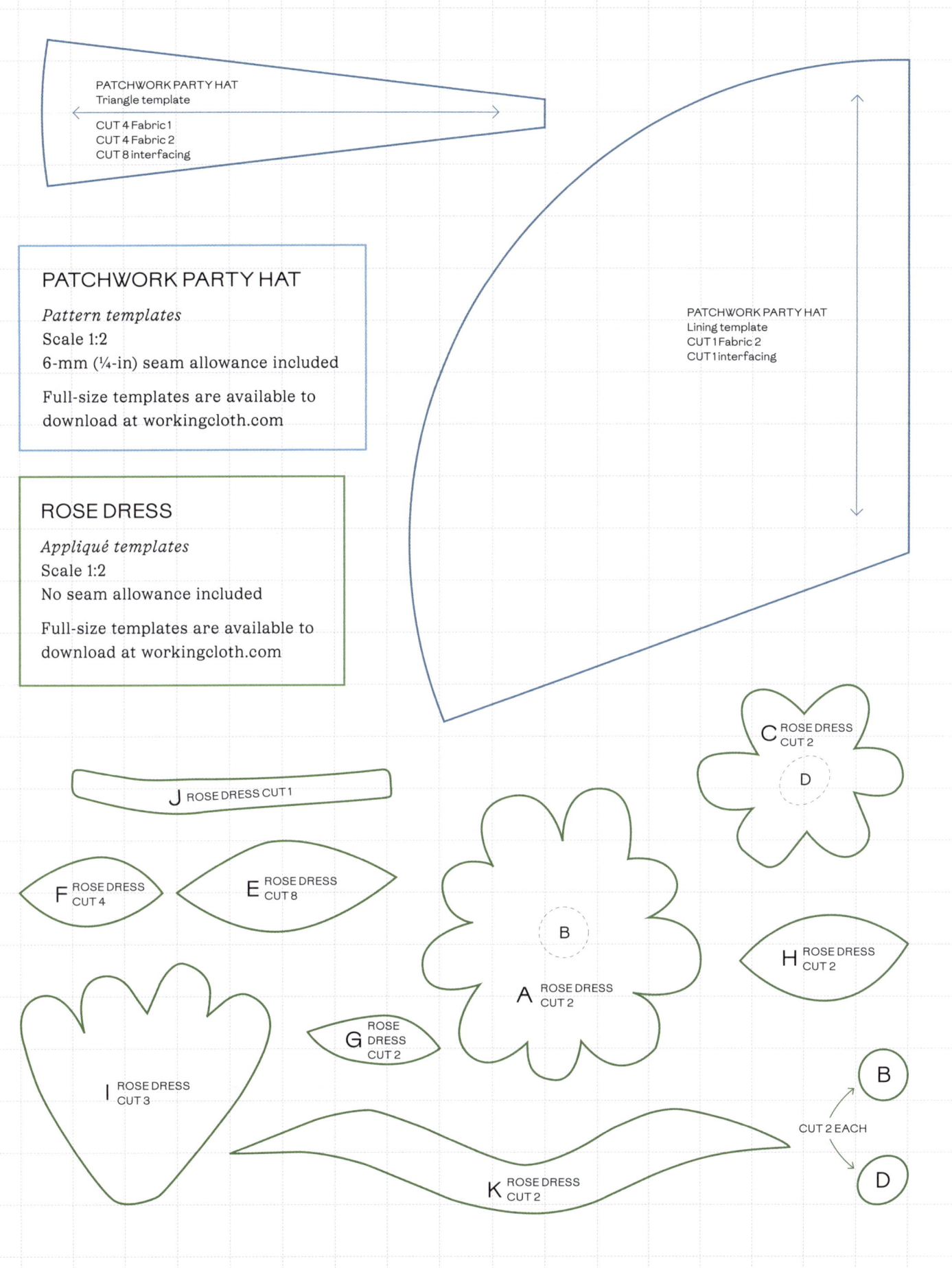

PATCHWORK PARTY HAT
Triangle template

CUT 4 Fabric 1
CUT 4 Fabric 2
CUT 8 interfacing

PATCHWORK PARTY HAT
Lining template
CUT 1 Fabric 2
CUT 1 interfacing

PATCHWORK PARTY HAT

Pattern templates
Scale 1:2
6-mm (¼-in) seam allowance included

Full-size templates are available to
download at workingcloth.com

ROSE DRESS

Appliqué templates
Scale 1:2
No seam allowance included

Full-size templates are available to
download at workingcloth.com

C ROSE DRESS CUT 2

D

J ROSE DRESS CUT 1

F ROSE DRESS CUT 4

E ROSE DRESS CUT 8

B

A ROSE DRESS CUT 2

H ROSE DRESS CUT 2

I ROSE DRESS CUT 3

G ROSE DRESS CUT 2

B

K ROSE DRESS CUT 2

CUT 2 EACH

D

ACKNOWLEDGEMENTS

First off, the people who helped me with the practical bits. All the materials I used in this book are second-hand. Some were generously donated by friends and members of my community, so a metaphorical round of applause goes out to them. Big thanks especially to Elfrida Nilsdotter Ahlby, who gave me an incredible collection of crisp white bed sheets. And to Ellen Price for being my fabric-sourcing wingwoman. Thank you to Lily Tham, Zoë MacCormack and Elliot Keen for your help in making the samples. To Charlie McKay, for taking (what I am sure you'll agree) are beautiful photos, and to his wife, Jess Murphy, for use of her prop and furniture collections. An enormous scoop of gratitude goes out to the indefatigable and immensely talented Tegan Hendel, who designed this book. Lastly, thank you to TOAST for gifting me a dress to wear for the photo shoot.

Thank you to the models in the book: my best friend, Alice Costelloe, her mum, Isobel, sister Frances, and niece Edie. And for the suggestion I rope in their family friend, Emile, and his mum, Rebecca Perry. Thank you all for being beautiful, willing and fun to work with, and especially to Edie and Emile for upping the cuteness factor of the kids' section by at least 1000%.

Next, the emotional-support people. Thank you to my parents for their ongoing encouragement, and to my siblings for theirs. Alice gets a second mention here, not just as a talented faceless model, but as an excellent idea-bouncer, phone-caller and general good friend. Thank you as well to Rose Darkins, skilled both at crafts and calming down friends (me) whose personalities lean towards overexcitement.

The writing of this book came during a tricky period in my personal life: that sticky bit of your early thirties when you are sandwiched between generations and really in the thick of it all (for some this comes earlier and some later). I'd like to say a very big thank you to my editors, Sarah Hoggett and Claire Davis, and to my publishers, Tahlia Anderson and Alice Hardie-Grant, for their patience and kindness while I worked through a parent's illness and a miscarriage. They certainly handled it more gracefully than I did.

Published in 2025 by Hardie Grant Books, an imprint of Hardie Grant Publishing

Hardie Grant Books (Melbourne)
Wurundjeri Country
Level 11, 36 Wellington Street
Collingwood, Victoria 3066

Hardie Grant North America
2912 Telegraph Ave
Berkeley, California 94705

hardiegrant.com/books

Hardie Grant acknowledges the Traditional Owners of the Country on which we work, the Wurundjeri People of the Kulin Nation and the Gadigal People of the Eora Nation, and recognises their continuing connection to the land, waters and culture. We pay our respects to their Elders past and present.

A catalogue record for this book is available from the National Library of Australia

Piece by Piece
ISBN 978 1 76145 034 1
ISBN 978 1 76144 337 4 (ebook)

10 9 8 7 6 5 4 3 2 1

Publishers: Alice Hardie-Grant, Tahlia Anderson
Head of Editorial: Jasmin Chua
Project Editor: Claire Davis
Editor: Sarah Hoggett
Creative Director: Kristin Thomas
Designer: Tegan Ella Hendel
Photographer: Charlie McKay
Head of Production: Todd Rechner
Production Controller: Jessica Harvie

Colour reproduction by Splitting Image Colour Studio

Printed in China by Leo Paper Products LTD.

FSC
www.fsc.org
MIX
Paper | Supporting
responsible forestry
FSC® C020056

The paper this book is printed on is from FSC®-certified forests and other sources. FSC® promotes environmentally responsible, socially beneficial and economically viable management of the world's forests.